RELIGIOUS PLATONISM

JAMES K. FEIBLEMAN

Tulane University

RELIGIOUS PLATONISM

The Influence of Religion on Plato
and the
Influence of Plato on Religion

GREENWOOD PRESS, PUBLISHERS
WESTPORT, CONNECTICUT

Copyright 1959 under the Berne Convention

Originally published in 1959
by George Allen & Unwin Ltd., London

Reprinted with the permission
of the author, James K. Feibleman

First Greenwood Reprinting 1971

Library of Congress Catalogue Card Number 78-161628

SBN 8371-6184-3

Printed in the United States of America

INTRODUCTION
Parrhesia

Scholarship has earned the reputation for being more of a preservative than an instigator. We think of the scholar popularly as one who turns over old ground for the sake of its mustiness, not as one who is concerned with the possible influence exciting ideas may have upon the future. He prefers to look back, just as the artist looks forward and the man of action sees only the present. However, it need not be altogether that way. For there are to be found in the past neglected ideas which could influence the future if they were restored to contemporary interest; the scholar can also exercise imagination if he be possessed of it and many are.

The work of Plato is not unknown to the general public; inexpensive editions are to be found periodically in the market place, and there are few indeed who do not at least know his name and something of what he stood for. The scholars have found Platonism continually absorbing. It is a fair statement that there is nothing that can be said about Plato's philosophy that has not been and does not continue to be a subject of violent controversy. Thus the scholars share with the general public an uncertainty as to what exactly Plato's position was on any topic he undertook to discuss.

The present book if it is noticed at all is not likely to solve the problems that have confronted scholars in the examination of Plato's writings. Nor is it intended to do so. The aim is a far more modest one; and it is to set forth the thesis that Plato had two philosophies and subscribed to two sets of religious ideas consistent with those philosophies. Later thinkers who have followed Plato have seen only one philosophy and one set of religious ideas, which they accordingly adopted and modified. But the other philosophy and its religion have not enjoyed the same success. If, however, they were to be rediscovered and revived, much might be gained both in philosophy and religion.

The present work, however, is chiefly concerned with the religious side. In order to develop this thesis, the history of the furtherance of one of Plato's two religions is traced and the accidents which occasioned the neglect of the other are examined.

The study was suggested by the exceedingly wide divergence which exists between the writings of Plato and Aristotle on the one hand and the use which has been made of them by the western religions and the consequent reputation which they have gained among religious adherents on the other. From the tentative explorers in the realm of speculation which they were, they have been transformed by religious zeal into dogmatic absolutists. The enormous discrepancy suggested that an examination of what Plato and Aristotle said, including also the way in which they said it, might reveal the possibilities of a theology which has never been even stated. And so the necessity of stating it began to seem like an urgency which could not in all honesty be denied. With what success it has been executed remains for the judgment of others. It is difficult not to wonder, however, how many there are who will judge it in a non-partisan spirit. Religious controversy is not a place famous for its dispassionate research into the truth; yet one can always hope, and hope is what we live by.

Chapter VI appeared as a separate article in *The Hibbert Journal*, to whose Editor my thanks are due for permission to reprint.

J. K. F.

New Orleans
Martha's Vineyard
1955–1958

CONTENTS

PART ONE

PLATO'S RELIGIOUS PHILOSOPHY

ARGUMENT

Although Platonism is credited with having exercised a considerable influence upon the western religions, religious Platonism has not often been seriously studied.

It is still possible, evidently, to write a history of philosophy which discusses the influence of Plato on Christianity without showing Plato's own religion.[1]

There is reason to suspect that in religious connections what is often called Platonism is actually Neoplatonism, a religious philosophy which is only partly derived from Plato and which contains important elements not accepted by Plato at all. The reading of Neoplatonism back into Plato is hardly a new mistake but it is one which is doggedly persistent. A recent study asserts, for example, that 'the present tendency is towards bridging rather than widening the gap separating Platonism from Neoplatonism', and this is accomplished by comparing 'Neoplatonism to the system of Plato's first generation pupils . . . rather than to Plato himself'.[2] The misleading assumption that Neoplatonism correctly represents the influence of Plato has had an amazingly long history. It permeated the Middle Ages and survived them, and was so successful that when in the Renaissance Plato was revived scholars succeeded inadvertently in understanding Neoplatonism while reading the actual *Dialogues* of Plato! Professor Merlan performs the trick for himself, more or less deliberately, by reconciling the Plato who is represented by his followers and critics, despite the open and obvious fact that

---

[1] And this in a work running into a number of volumes in which, despite the secular title, considerable space is devoted to the religious ideas of other philosophers, Scotus and Aquinas for instance. See Frederick Copleston, *A History of Philosophy* (London 1951, Burns, Oates and Washbourne), Vol. I.

[2] Philip Merlan, *From Platonism to Neoplatonism* (The Hague 1953, Nijhoff), p. 2.

such Platonism differs sharply from the writings of Plato which have survived. In order to accept his thesis, in other words, we shall have to reject what Plato wrote and substitute in its place what his immediate followers thought that he had written and what Aristotle criticized him for, and we shall have to do this despite the well-known reasons for which abject followers and adverse critics tend to misrepresent the master.

It will be useful, therefore, if we can determine just what Plato's philosophy with respect to religion actually was, and then note how it differs sharply from Neoplatonism. We shall find that Plato wavered between two philosophies, and consequently also between two sets of religious ideas, since with him philosophy came first intellectually and religion second, his method being primarily one of reason. The first of the philosophies of Plato (and the one for which he is chiefly known) is that of idealism. According to idealism, the ideas are more real than the actualities (though both are objective to and independent of the human mind). The second and more neglected philosophy of Plato is that of realism. According to realism, the ideas are as real as, but no more real than, the actualities (though once again both are objective to and independent of the human mind). The Orphic and Dionysiac cults are more consistent with idealism, the native Greek religion more consistent with realism. We shall further find that it was one of these religious philosophies—the idealistic version—which Philo and Plotinus exaggerated and which has come to be called Neoplatonism. The realistic religious philosophy has hardly been noticed even though Aristotle's own religious ideas are consistent with it.[1]

Our aim in general will be to show how the two strands of religious philosophy which are to be found in the Platonic writings first arose and had their influence upon Plato, and then how later men chose the one strand and developed it in a

[1] Despite the freely acknowledged adoption of much of Aristotle by Aquinas, Copleston neglects also Aristotle's religious ideas completely.

particular direction, and what the effect of such a choice has been on subsequent religions.

The argument of the following pages, then, will run as follows. After some preliminary remarks devoted to a consideration of the difficulties brought about by Plato's method of presenting his ideas, it will be contended that (apart from the nominalism of the Sophists) Plato himself had two philosophies. He is well known for his objective idealism, but what is not so well known is that he also maintained a metaphysical realism. The two philosophies are quite distinct. The distinction is perhaps due to the inconsistencies inherent in his influences: he had the philosophical abstractions of the Pre-Socratics and their religious scepticism to go by; he had also the religions of the Greeks. We could perhaps begin to understand Plato's own religious views somewhat better if we first unravelled the religions which he inherited.

The Greeks before Plato had two sets of indigenous gods: the Olympic gods whom they tended with ritual sacrifices, and the earth gods whom they tended with ritual avoidance. Both sets were finite, orderly, separate from men yet held in the proper relationship to men, well established in their reign over the world of the present. But then two foreign religions were introduced into Greece, the Orphic and Dionysiac cults. The Orphic cult featured monotheistic sun-worship, gentleness, vegetarianism, pacifism, spiritualism and the immortality of the soul. The Dionysiac cult featured orgiastic rites, raw flesh-eating ceremonies, and sensualism. Both cults invited the celebrant to aspire to the condition of deity himself, to become a god and an immortal. The Orphic cult came from Crete and bearing strong Egyptian elements but arrived via Thrace. Also from Thrace came the Dionysiac cult. At first they disrupted the orderliness and finitude of the Greek religion. But the Dionysiac cult was shunted into secular channels and ended in the rural and City Dionysia of Athens, and so gave rise to the theatre. The Orphic cult made a deep impression on Plato, and its beliefs were partly adopted by him. In the *Dialogues* they appear joined by abstractions from the more native Greek religions. Thus Plato had two religions, and we will call one his Orphic version and the other his Greek version.

In the second part of this book we shall endeavour to trace the religious influence of Plato, and in particular to show how the choice of the first religion by his successors stifled the development of the second and what the consequences have been.

The argument of Part II runs somewhat as follows. To the extent to which Aristotle touches upon religion and religious beliefs at all, he does so in support of the Greek side of Plato's religion. But it was the Orphic side of Plato which was both elevated into the place of importance in Plato and adopted— or adapted—by the Neoplatonists. Philo and Plotinus worked out Orphic versions of religion, the Jewish and Greek versions respectively; and it was this kind of interpretation which was taken over into Christianity by Augustine and others. Thus Orphism ended as an influence in Christianity, while the Greek side of the Platonic version of religion was never taken up institution-wise at all. When Aquinas, for the Roman Catholic Church, in the thirteenth century, finally got around to incorporating Aristotle, after the model set by Averroes and Maimonides, it was a Neoplatonized Aristotle that was incorporated. Thus part, at least, of the true Plato and of the true Aristotle never reached the position from which they could influence the western group of religions, while the Neoplatonic version of Aristotle reigned and reigns still in Islam, Judaism and Christianity.

The rise of experimental science was felt as a challenge to all organized and institutionalized religions. The leadership in Christianity shifted over accordingly into the movement of Protestantism. While it is true that some modified versions of Protestantism brought Christianity closer to the Greek version of religious realism, that Greek philosophy of religion still waits its proper formulation in modern terms.

The first aim, then, will be to examine the influence of Plato on the western religions in general and on Christianity in particular, both with respect to what it has been and to what it could be. There are three subordinate aims and these are to show that Neoplatonism is both a selection and a distortion of Plato; that Neoplatonism originated with Philo rather than with Plotinus; and, finally, that there are important aspects of Plato's philosophy which have not been and which yet could be applied in an important way to religion and especially to western religious problems.

CHAPTER I

PLATO'S METHOD

To set forth with any order or completeness Plato's ideas on religion would require a whole book or perhaps several. And this is to suppose that it could even be done. For it is never a simple matter to be sure that what you have learned from Plato on a topic is what he believed. It is more often than not the case that a proposition which is held to represent a position can be balanced with another proposition in some other dialogue which is either its opposite or its contradictory. Then again, did Plato say it, or Socrates; and if someone else, such as Parmenides or the Athenian Stranger, then is it what Plato himself believed or not, and how are we to know? And if it is what Plato believed, then did he believe it throughout, and how can we be sure?

Can the religion of the *Laws* be squared with the attitude towards religion in the *Euthyphro?* The general picture of the preoccupations of man in his youth is that of thought oriented towards the understanding of the feelings through action. In his old age, little opportunity for action remains, and the feelings, too, have abated; then the orientation of thought shifts to the speculation concerning conditions which are to prevail after death. Youth is concerned with this world, age with the next. Are we to suppose that so vigorous a man of thought, feeling and action as Plato was any exception?

It is quite possible, of course, that he changed his position, say for instance as from the *Euthyphro* in his youth to the *Laws* in his old age; but there is another and better reason for the difficulty about committing him to one view or another. He is so tentative and suggestive about his most fundamental ideas that he does not wish to assert flatly what must sound, when stated absolutely, less subtle and profound. After explaining how the world as we have it arrived at its present state due to the efforts of the *demiourgos*, Plato said, 'This is how the world came into being, according to the likely account'.[1] After the somewhat large effort of detailing the cave allegory in Book VII of the *Republic*, Socrates added, 'God knows whether it is true'.[2] And in the *Meno* Socrates said, 'Most of the points I have made in support of my argument are not such as I can confidently assert.'[3] Shorey remarks that, 'Plato was much less prodigal of affirmation about metaphysical ultimates than interpreters who take his myths literally have supposed'.[4] However, the Athenian Stranger of the *Laws* seems in little doubt, and is at times extremely dogmatic.

Whatever position one comes to concerning Plato's opinions, there is usually a good reason to defend the opposite to some extent. We shall not, then, undertake to commit him to one didactic account but only to mention such aspects of it as will bear on the early history of its influence. We are handicapped further by the fact that the whole of philosophy is applicable to the whole of theology and from thence can be conveyed to religion. Each of the various subdivisions of philosophy: metaphysics, epistemology, logic, ethics, aesthetics, has its own special bearing on theology. These would have to be worked out separately in the case of Plato, and then applied to religion as well as examined in the light of his own philosophy of religion. All that we can hope to do within the proportions of this essay is to indicate some of the neglected elements of a religious character in the *Dialogues*, and to point out a few of their implications.

The first and most important point, perhaps, is that which is contained in the relevance in Plato's method. The well-known

[1] *Timaeus*, 30b. Three translators agree on the wording of this phrase: R. G. Bury, A. E. Taylor and F. M. Crawford.   [2] *Republic*, 517b.
[3] *Meno*, 86b. See also P. Shorey, *What Plato Said*, p. 515.
[4] Paul Shorey in the Loeb *Republic*, ii, p. 130.

form of the Socratic elenchus, in which opponents state their position and are logically brought to self-refutation, leaves the topic open or with a suggested answer. The method itself, then, imparts a tentativeness to the question, and this is intended to be stimulating rather than satisfactory. The significance of inquiry on the given topic plus the tentativeness of any answer which might be made, stands out clearly in the dialectic employed by Plato.

Plato did not try to do much with the dialogue form. It is of course a dramatic vehicle, yet he passed over most of its dramatic possibilities, setting the stage in each dialogue only sketchily at the beginning, and using the many voices chiefly to obtain multiplicity of viewpoints and an uncertainty of proposed solutions. He spoke of the serious loss of 'our helpless bewilderment by the problem' (i.e. in this instance of the nature and origin of desire),[1] and he said that 'we are not now contending for a mere victory, whether for my cause or yours; the duty of both is to champion the truth'.[2] Of another point he asserted that 'God knows whether it is true';[3] as for us, we are never absolutely sure,[4] and 'we know practically nothing'.[5]

Those who deal with Plato nowadays are partisan in one spirit or another, much like those who were the contemporaries of Socrates. The Marxists and logical positivists would hang him in effigy: while for others he can never be wrong about anything. The solid approval or mass condemnation of the doctrines Socrates supported with Plato's aid overlooks completely the tentative nature in which they were put forward, and the fact that most of the arguments in the *Dialogues* end indecisively. There is a tentativeness to the dialectical method and a probation for its conclusions which have been overlooked as forces in the argument. They set problems without absolutely resolving them.

---

[1] *Philebus*, 34D. See also 36E.   [2] *Ibid.*, 14P, A. E. Taylor trans.
[3] *Republic*, 517B, Shorey trans. Cf. Shorey, *What Plato Said*, p. 515, on the *Meno*, 86B.   [4] *Republic, ibid.*   [5] *Laws*, 732A, R. G. Bury trans.

What has happened to this method in the history of Platonism? Many studies have been devoted to the analysis of the method, far fewer to its effect upon the content of the arguments in which it is employed. Plato's was not the method of certainty; and so those who have since become his absolute adversaries or absolute advocates, far from raising a sort of unplanned and unacknowledged giant dialectic, are actually living betrayals of their want of understanding. Plato's work was probative, tentative and above all inquisitive; it has been used as though it were finalistic, absolute and assertory. We are learning in other areas every day how much more profound are the ideas which can be suggested by the method of uncertainty, and those who call themselves Platonists have assisted us in forgetting that the method is very old. Thus if Plato does have any religious ideas, he is not firmly fixed on them and does not intend to bind anyone else to them with absolute belief. Advocates of religions are much given to the practice of being sure of the truth of what they advocate, whereas Plato was not. Thus his ideas on religion must have a different meaning.

Again, theology is either speculative or justificatory—in the case of established religions, usually the latter. Plato's theology is purely speculative. In short—and this is perhaps the most important note it is possible to strike here—Plato's philosophy is *not* primarily a religious philosophy. A complete philosophy must take into account, and endeavour to give an explanation of, the activities in every aspect of society; it must probe behind every institution and leave nothing unexamined. Hence religion must be treated as well as every other type of interest. It does not follow that in Plato's philosophy religion is central or paramount. Plato, like all the Greeks, had no word for religion; they used instead 'piety' (*eusebés*) and 'holiness' (*hósion*),[1] and we shall note later what holiness meant to Plato.[2]

---

[1] Jane Harrison, *Prolegomena to the Study of Greek Religion* (New York 1955, Meridian Books), p. 2.   [2] *Ibid.*, pp. 2–3.

CHAPTER II

PLATO'S TWO
PHILOSOPHIES

In the Platonic *Dialogues* it is possible to discern the outline of four distinct philosophies. There is, to begin with, the nominalism of the Sophists, subdivided in turn into subjective idealism and materialism. We might take Protagoras as the type of the first subdivision (Man is the measure of all things),[1] and Thrasymachus as the type of the second (justice is the interest of the stronger).[2] Whether we take the subject or the object to be the real makes no difference from one point of view, for in both cases we have chosen one end of the knowledge relation, and attempted to meet the metaphysical requirements with epistemological criteria. There is, in addition to the nominalisms, the philosophy of objective idealism and the philosophy of realism.

It is not pertinent to our purpose here to set forth in detail the four philosophies contained in the *Dialogues*. Such an undertaking would be out of proportion to our theses; in addition, the distinction between Plato and his mouthpiece, Socrates, on the one hand and their opponents, the Sophists, on the other, is already well recognized. What is perhaps not so well recognized is that Plato wavered between two philosophies of his own: an objective idealism and a realism. The distinction is generically founded on the difference between the two degrees of the reality of universals. For the objective idealist, which Plato himself was most of the time, the Ideas or Forms (the intelligible things) are more real than the particulars of sense (the sensible things);

---

[1] *Cratylus*, 386A.　　　　[2] *Republic*, 338C.

whereas for the realist, which Plato was some of the time, the sensible things are as real as intelligible things; both are fully real. The confusion of the two philosophies can be seen most clearly in the *Republic*, with its realistic picture of the perfect state to be established in this world and its idealistic allegory of the cave, in which this world is a mere appearance. To anticipate somewhat a conclusion we shall need to examine further, the life that is lived in this world as the result of a belief in the reality of this world, is sure to prove better for more people than the life that is to be lived in this world as a result of a belief in the next; although both, of course, can be equally religious lives. Yet the immortality of the soul is hardly to be deduced from the social order of the *Republic*. It is idealism which is usually intended when reference to Platonism is made, and so a brief exposition of it is all that is needed here. We could not hope to do justice to the metaphysical realism of Plato in so short a space; we can only indicate it and defer its representation to another, and a later, work.

First, then, Plato's metaphysical idealism.

A. PLATO'S IDEALISM

It is generally agreed that Plato speaks through Socrates and not through his controversial opponents, though as in every case of interpretation in the *Dialogues* there are exceptions even to this, for it may be otherwise in the *Parmenides*. And it is agreed further that what Socrates is advocating is a variety of objective idealism, based on the independent being of the Ideas or Forms and on their superior reality. The actual world, on this view, is an appearance, sensible things being inherently ephemeral. For Plato, the dark region was not the earth, which has some sort of being however tenuous, but non-being itself.[1] Being is like the sun, and the earth is closer to non-being but occupies an intermediate realm. In the allegory of the cave,[2]

---

[1] *Republic*, 514A ff.   [2] *Ibid.*, 479c–d.

for instance, the concrete objects of existence are mere shadows of the real. Only the Ideas are truly real, and the particulars are not so.[1] The existing universe of sensible things is a world of becoming, a mixture of being and non-being. It was created by the demiourgos, reducing a chaos to a cosmos by using the eternal Ideas as models,[2] thus assuming that the Ideas (or intelligible things) had their being before God, as the demiourgos employed them in order to create the actual world by means of imitation. The mathematical objects, the universal ideas (except those represented by worthless objects, such as hair, mud and dirt), these are the only reals; considered as the Ideas, or Forms, they are absolute, separate, simple, eternal, immutable, intelligible objects independent both of the mind which knows them and of the actualities which are their copies. Together, they form a system, with the mathematical objects as the lowest of the Ideas and The Good or The One as the highest.[3] Nothing can be learned from sense experience;[4] hunger, thirst and sex as desires are irrational.[5] He who believes in beautiful things but not in beauty lives in a dream and mistakes the resemblance for the reality.[6] Thought is closer to truth than action.[7] Plato scorned those who 'preferred their ears to their intelligence'[8] refusing to discuss material things which can be seen and touched when in fact the mind could be led upwards to reason about pure numbers.[9] It is possible to have direct knowledge of the Ideas;[10] indeed, the ideas abide in a super-celestial place[11] and are visible only to the intelligence.[12] The intelligible objects are the source of all true knowledge which is gained by way of reason and recollection. Innate ideas, acquired in a previous state, exist in the mind, and by reminiscence can be evoked (anamnesis).[13] The sensible world of becoming cannot possibly be an object

[1] *Republic*, 479B–E. [2] *Timaeus*, 28A–38B. [3] *Republic*, 509D ff.
[4] *Phaedo*, 65A–G; *Republic*, 529B. [5] *Republic*, 439d.
[6] *Ibid.*, 476c–d. [7] *Ibid.*, 473a. [8] *Ibid.*, 531a–b.
[9] *Ibid.*, 525d. [10] *Phaedrus*, 250C ff.; *Symposium*, 209E ff.
[11] *Phaedrus*, 246E. [12] *Ibid.*, 247C.
[13] *Meno*, 81A–86; *Phaedo*, 72E–76B; etc.

of knowledge, it can produce only opinion. The true objects of knowledge are the intelligible things, the Ideas. Reality is rational and is available only to the mind. The Ideas fit together and as ideals form together the Idea of the Good, which stands to the other Ideas as the sun to the sensible world. Knowledge of the Forms is the only good. The soul is immortal, the body perishes; the most important knowledge is to know oneself. The ethical ideal is the well-ordered soul in which reason rules the spirited and appetitive faculties (will and desire respectively). The good life is not a life of pleasure but rather one of reason. The truly strong work for justice, which is due proportionality; the ideal of action is that of harmony.

The soul exists and acts as an intermediary between the intelligible and sensible worlds. Its immortality is proved by the nature of opposites,[1] it is unlike the body which perishes[2] because it is in and of the sensible world, and like the Forms it contemplates[3] the thoughts it recollects from a previous life.[4] It is simple and indivisible,[5] like other eternal things,[6] and it is self-moving, like the stars.[7] Were it mortal, its vices would have destroyed it; yet they do not, thus proving its immortality.

God is the supreme soul, the Mind which knows the intelligible objects but whose function is to create the sensible world in terms of the intelligible model furnished to it by the Ideas.

Such in barest outline is the philosophy of Plato as it is generally understood, and as indeed it is definitely to be found in the *Dialogues*. Platonism would be a precise enough affair, and its religious interpretation easy to effect, were that all.

B. PLATO'S REALISM

There is another philosophy occasionally advocated by Plato which is partly inconsistent with the one we have given and seldom completely recognized. This is the philosophy which for

[1] *Phaedo*, 71, 103 ff.   [2] *Ibid.*, 80, 94.   [3] *Ibid.*, 76.
[4] *Ibid.*, 73–6.   [5] *Ibid.*, 93.   [6] *Ibid.*, 79 ff.   [7] *Timaeus*, 41.

want of a better name has been called realism. Plato could have learned from Parmenides the independent reality of the Ideas or Forms apprehended by the mind; he could have learned from Heraclitus the reality of the world of change disclosed to the senses, for the Heraclitean fire is an essential ingredient of existence.[1] Realism gives to both realities an equal importance. Briefly, it shares with the idealism just described the reality of the Ideas or Forms but adds to them a greater measure of the reality of the actual world. Instead of the allegory of the cave in the *Republic*, with its shadow version of actuality, we have the analogy of the sunlight in the *Parmenides*[2] with its fragment version of actuality. But even the allegory of the cave is not to be adduced altogether to the defence of idealism over realism. The allegory of the cave and the divided line is, after all, an allegory, not a literal description. There it is made clear that the Ideas are to the mind as the sun is to sight. The sun *as such*— and in this allegory—is an appearance, and so not to be taken seriously. We have here an interpretation of actuality according to which actual concrete objects are as real as the Ideas or Forms though not as complete or perfect, much in the same way in which a slice of cake is just as 'cakey' as a whole cake, without being as much cake. The appearances now are real appearances; the receptacle is as eternal as the Forms,[3] and it is the receptacle which receives the Forms to compose sensible things, which therefore have in them a measure of reality. The limited void is that which receives the Ideas;[4] all attempts to limit the Ideas or Forms to the condition of the four elements (i.e. the infinite, the finite, the mixed and the cause of the mixed) have failed,[5] and the reason for the failure is that the four elements belong to existence only, whereas the Ideas have their being apart from existence. Plato introduced the reality of actuality as the

---

[1] *Philebus*, 29B–C.   [2] *Parmenides*, 131A.   [3] *Timaeus*, 49B ff.
[4] *Ibid.*, 50D, 51A.
[5] E.g. H. A. Wolfson, *Philo* (Cambridge, Mass. 1947, Harvard University Press), I, p. 304 *fin*. But see David Ross, *Plato's Theory of Ideas* (Oxford 1951, Clarendon Press), pp. 132–6.

'receptacle' in the Timaeus.[1] The 'errant cause',[2] the 'nurse of all becoming',[3] the 'fosteress'[4]—the role is indicated plainly enough. Whether substance or merely space has been debated, but the receptacle in either case is the irrational factor which receives the Forms. The 'errant cause', the receptacle, conjecture and the mixed, carry with them the reality of the actual world of existence. The 'mixed' (a mixture of the finite and the infinite, or of quality and quantity) and 'the cause of the mixed' (creation), are also ingredients of existence.[5] Conjecture (*eikasia*) is the apprehension of reality by means of images.[6] Sense experience can now be added to reason and recollection as a source of true knowledge. Knowledge comes from reasoning about sensations, and not directly from thoughts about being.[7] For instance, Timaeus affirms that sight is of the greatest help to us; without it, we would know nothing of the stars or the sun, and we would not have the notions of number and of time.[8] Consider, for example, the painstaking observation of bees, in which the unproductive man, the mere 'consumer of goods' is compared to the stingless drones.[9] The senses are as necessary as reason to the salvation of every animal.[10] Has not someone's keen observation of the life of the bee been taken pretty seriously here? And is not sense perception 'sometimes' a 'pure pleasure of the soul itself'?[11] We are able to learn from experience much in the way we can learn about the sun by looking at its reflection in water.[12] The creator of the senses has lavished much on seeing and being seen.[13] Socrates thought it wise to seek for what 'is good in man and the universe',[14] and conceded the argument

[1] See Raphael Demos, *The Philosophy of Plato* (New York 1939, Scribner), Ch. II.

[2] *Timaeus*, 48A. Literally, 'the errant cause, and how it is its nature to set in motion'.   [3] *Ibid.*, 49A, 49E, 52D.

[4] *Ibid.*, 88D.   [5] *Philebus*, 27B. Quantity is infinite and quality finite.

[6] *Republic*, 511D. See Richard Robinson, *Plato's Earlier Dialectic* (Oxford 1953, Clarendon Press), pp. 190 ff.   [7] *Theaetetus*, 186B–C.

[8] *Timaeus*, 47a.   [9] *Republic*, 552C; *Laws*, 901A.   [10] *Laws*, 961d.

[11] *Philebus*, 66C.   [12] *Phaedo*, 99E–100A.

[13] *Republic*, 507C.   [14] *Philebus*, 64A.

of Protarchus that to be 'concerned only with divine knowledge' is 'a ridiculous state of intellect in man'.[1] For the sensible things; change, life, soul, understanding, are also fully real.[2] We can learn from sensation, in the sense that thought is provoked by it, especially when perception yields a contradictory impression;[3] and the memory elicited from the slave in the *Meno* occurred in some terrestrial experience, for memory is the retention of sensation.[4] The origins of thought lie in sense perception; more specifically, it is at that point where we receive the contradictory impression of two opposite qualities that reflection is provoked.[5] Thus even the contradictions evident in the conflicts of actuality are not excluded from being known, for 'that which wholly is, is wholly knowable'.[6] Indeed, every Platonic analogy and myth furnishes evidence that it is possible to learn from experience.

Philosophers can become kings only by concerning themselves with the affairs of this world.[7] The *Republic* as a model is an ideal which is to be approximated in fact.[8] It is a social order in which there is justice, and it contains harmonic relations between its elements. Corresponding to the well-ordered soul, there is a well-ordered society in which the philosopher-king rules the soldiers and the producers. It would be difficult to reconcile the entire conception of the *Republic* with objective idealism. The idealists do not found republics in *this* world, only in the next, for in this world there are only appearances which are not to be taken seriously. 'Fortune and opportunity co-operate with God in the government of human affairs.'[9] The search for the natural society is what lies behind the Socratic dialectic, in this dialogue, at least. The conception is that men differ in their natural aptitudes and that everyone should do that for which nature has fitted him,[10] and it is further argued,

[1] *Philebus*, 62B–D.
[2] *Sophist*, 248E–249B.
[3] *Republic*, 523B, 524D.
[4] *Philebus*, 34A–B.
[5] *Republic*, 523C.
[6] *Ibid.*, 477A, Rouse trans.
[7] *Ibid.*, 473D; 520A–C.
[8] *Ibid.*, 472E.
[9] *Laws*, IV, 709B, R. G. Bury trans.
[10] *Republic*, 453D–454D.

in favour, that assigning music and gymnastics to the wives of guardians 'is not contrary to nature'.[1] The harmony expected of the proper co-ordination of the three parts of the soul[2] is a realistic rather than an idealistic notion since it has regard for the natural functioning of the whole man, on the assumption that what a man ought to be ideally is what he can be actually.

The idealist in ethics is an ascetic, the nominalist a libertine; and so in cautioning against both and arguing in favour of a middle way, Plato sets up a realistic ethics. We must satisfy the lower cravings to get to the higher pleasures.[3] The path to wisdom lies through the senses by means of moderation. We must 'neither starve nor surfeit the appetites',[4] for the soul as well as the body is moved by sensation.[5] The good life is not the intellectual life merely but the mixed life of thought and sensation.[6] Plato quoted Homer with approval, that it is better to be alive than dead,[7] and he never argued that the good things of this world were to be altogether denied; he said only that we had to get beyond and above them—yes, but only by going through them, not by denying them. This is the theme of the ladder of love in the *Symposium*. Hence for Plato matter is not evil, it is simply by itself not enough.

As to the mortality of the soul, Plato is sure that the soul survives the body, but wonders what its fate will be. No harm after death can in any case come to a good man,[8] but a good man is one who leads the proper social life, for there is a good life for society, as we have already noted. In the realistic version of Plato's philosophy, we shall have to go to Socrates' speech to the jury, in which he expresses his ignorance of what is to happen to him after his death.[9] Here at least, where there are two alternatives and no final decision between them, it is instructive to find one of the alternatives consistent with the contentions

[1] *Republic*, 456C *et passim*.   [2] *Ibid.*, 441C–442B.
[3] *Ibid.*, 587A.   [4] *Ibid.*, 571E.   [5] *Philebus*, 34A.
[6] *Ibid.*, *passim*.   [7] *Republic*, 516D, quoting *Odyssey*, xi. 489.
[8] *Apology*, 41C.   [9] *Ibid.*, 40C–D.

in another dialogue of Simmias and Cebes, the dialectical opponents of Socrates, that the soul is inseparable from the body and dies with it.[1]

We have decided to call the second philosophy of Plato, and the neglected version, realism; but we must hasten to distinguish it from Aristotelian realism and the realism of Thomas Aquinas. It differs from Aristotelian realism in that Aristotle did not admit the independent reality of the Ideas or Forms, and also in that he did have a positive doctrine of substance, of a substratum which goes far beyond the 'receptacle', the 'errant cause' and 'conjecture', as Plato had them. For the sake of ease of reference we had better refer to the conventional objective idealism of Plato as Platonic idealism and to his second philosophy as Platonic realism, employing both in the technical sense only, in which they have been employed above. For we shall need these when we come to discuss the Neoplatonic and subsequent religious interpretations of Plato. Platonic realism differs from the realism of Thomas Aquinas in that Aquinas is a rigid Aristotelian (which Aristotle of course was not) and one who adopted a Neoplatonic interpretation of Aristotle, at that. To say more here on this topic would be to get somewhat ahead of our story.

[1] *Phaedo*, 85D–88B.

CHAPTER III

THE GREEK RELIGIOUS
INHERITANCE

A. ORTHODOX RELIGIONS

In order to understand what Plato did with religion, it might be helpful to know what religions were prevalent in the Greece of his day. For there were many religious currents flowing, and all of them were by no means consistent.

Plato's religious inheritance may be divided into a theory and a practice.

The theory he inherited from previous philosophers, notably the Ionians and the Eleatics. What did they bequeath him? A primary interest in nature, an abstract method of doing philosophy, and a certain measure of scepticism towards the gods. In the triad, god (or the gods), nature and man, the Greek concern was chiefly with nature,[1] *physis* precedes *nous*. The interest in nature came from the effort of the cosmological philosophers to find an essential world-stuff, as for instance the 'water' of Thales, the 'infinite' of Anaximander, the 'air' of Anaximenes. The abstract method of doing philosophy came from the work of Heraclitus and Parmenides, who endeavoured to interpret the world within the framework of a system, Heraclitus by dealing with the world of flux and change, Parmenides by working with the permanence of the logic of discourse. The scepticism towards the gods came from men like Xenophanes; in the few dozen fragments remaining of

[1] Werner Jaeger, *Paideia* (Oxford 1939, Blackwell), trans. G. Highet, Vol. I, p. 150.

his work, it is clear that he put the investigation of nature ahead of theological explanations and had his doubts about the super-natural.[1]

The philosophy of nature eventually resolves into the question of truth: what is there? The philosophy of man eventually resolves into the question of practicality: what is best for us? And the search for the one involves an outlook which conflicts with or precludes the search for the other. For the Greeks generally, the way from man to the gods lay through nature;[2] in the world of the western religions, Judaism, Christianity or Islam, the direction has been changed, and the way to God for man lies in a direct path which excludes nature (hence the difficulty of harmonizing natural science with religion). We shall have to reorient ourselves if we are to understand Greek religious ideas, for the Greeks supposed man to be imbedded in nature as a part of it, and they held the whole of nature to be actively related to the gods.

Plato's practical religious inheritance consisted in the current Greek religious beliefs and practices. There was no uniformly established priesthood and no sacerdotal literature; all our knowledge of Greek religious beliefs and practices comes from lay sources, since there were no other written records, but we know something of them. They were primarily of two kinds: the Olympic pantheon and the Chthonic deities, and their respective observances of ritual tendance and ritual avoidance. Neither set of gods was final or absolute in power, for destiny (*moira*) or necessity ruled the Olympic gods, and chance (*tyche*) ruled the Chthonic gods. Did the Olympic gods come down with the Greeks from the north, and the Chthonic deities invade Greece from the Asiatic mainland by way of the Aegean, as some current thinking would lead us to suppose? We shall

[1] See Kathleen Freeman's translation of H. Diels, *Ancilla to the Pre-Socratic Philosophers* (Oxford 1948, Blackwell), especially Fragments 11, 12, 14, 15, 18, 27, 34 and 38.

[2] In the Greek cosmogony, heaven and earth existed before the gods. See H. J. Rose, in *La notion du divin* (Geneva 1952, Vandoeuvres), p. 21.

probably never know with certainty. If we take into consideration both the Olympic pantheon and the Chthonic deities, then we are dealing with a very considerable number of gods, and even these were not all. It has been supposed until mid-century that the Chthonic gods were the older, being of Asiatic origin. Certainly they are very old; but there is new evidence for the ancient age of the Olympic gods as well. Of the recent finds at Pylos, one authority says, 'Here beyond all possible doubt is evidence that the Olympic gods were worshipped in fifteenth century Knossos',[1] or, in other words, a thousand years before Plato.

In Homer we find the Olympic gods only. In Hesiod we find also the heroes and the good spirits of the dead (*daimones*) as well. For the Greeks certainly there was a plethora of gods. In the culture to which Plato was born there were gods in the heavens, such as those who moved each of the stars; and there were gods on Olympus, chiefly the divine family of Zeus, 'The Twelve': Zeus, Hera, Poseidon, Demeter, Apollo, Artemis, Ares, Aphrodite, Hermes, Athena, Hephaestus, and Hestia.[2] And there were gods in the earth; Kore, Themis (or Gaia), Dionysus, Chthon, to name but a few; and there were divine heroes, such as Herakles and Asklepios;[3] and there were ghosts, the *daimones* and the Keres: the Erinyes, gorgon, siren and sphinx. It was a world filled with gods of every sort, and all in a sense were nature gods; there were gods on the mountain, gods in the earth and sea, gods only half separated from nature, gods of the here and now, of common experience and of the present. They had in common that each knew his domain and was confined to it, and so shared the properties of order and limit.

---

[1] 'The Revelations of Pylos', by L. R. Palmer, in *The Listener*, Vol. LIV (1955), p. 892.

[2] W. K. C. Guthrie, *The Greeks and Their Gods* (London 1950, Methuen), pp. 110–13.

[3] Seven types of cult-heroes and hero-gods have been distinguished. See Lewis Richard Farnell, *Greek Hero Cults and Ideas of Immortality* (Oxford 1921, Clarendon Press), p. 19.

Plato inherited a set of religious beliefs and practices which were concentrated in the main on this world and the present. There was little transcendental emphasis. In Homer's account, Odysseus is told that it is better to be a living slave in the house of a cruel master than lord of all the dead, and Plato agrees early in the *Republic* as we have already noted; while at the end of the *Republic* Plato has him preferring to return to this world in the next life as an ordinary man who has no cares.[1] For the Greeks life was not a preparation for death and otherwise to be renounced. It was instead a day in the sun, a reprieve for the enjoyment of reason. This at least is the Olympic religion; our own western religions are more like the Chthonic deities or the Orphic cults.

However, the Olympic gods were different from the Chthonic gods both in tone and in their human relevance as well as probably also in point of origin. In the generations immediately preceding Plato, there was an attempt to make the gods into the advocates of morality in place of the amoral forces they had been. That Plato's arguments in this direction in the *Republic* had the example in the plays of Aeschylus of the transformation of the gods into moral personalities, is evident.[2] The epitome of activity is violence; only, to the harmony of the Greek ethos, violence is always harmful. Hence the Erinyes, the Furies, are able to be counted among the Chthonic deities. There was no want of violence in Greek culture generally, nor of harmony in its stipulated ideals. Is it not fair to argue that the Olympic gods in general represent *necessity* and the Chthonic deities *chance*, and that the essence of the Greek genius was its endeavour to reconcile chance and necessity?

But religious syncretism seems ever ready at hand to those who would save conflicting or even divergent faiths by means of reason. The two sets of gods were combined despite their

---

[1] *Republic*, 620C.
[2] C. J. Herrington, *Athena Parthenos and Athena Polias:* A Study in the Religion of Periclean Athens (Manchester 1955, University Press), p. 54.

differences when it came to deciding about the human soul. The fate of the dead in the Greek account is difficult to define precisely.[1] That there was an after-life was believed, but guesses as to its character varied widely. There are, first off, the Islands of the Blest, to which souls may go which are not condemned to the Hades of the underworld. Those of noble birth have the privilege of translation to Elysium without death, according to Homer; and the souls of heroes may remain behind to influence mortal events in favour of the living, according to Hesiod. The Eleusinian mysteries was typical of Greek city religions; imported from Crete and built around the worship of Demeter, goddess of fertility, it promised a better life in the next world. The shrine at Eleusis with its branch at the Acropolis, was in charge of fertility but could also with appropriate rites bestow immortality.[2]

On the whole the Greek religious observance seems to have been more a matter of attraction than compulsion. The Greek society was not a closed affair, despite the legal execution of Socrates and the picture of the closed society given by Plato in the *Republic* and the *Laws*. Socrates himself was born of no such society as that which his pupil pictured in these two dialogues, and, as is well known, ostracism unofficially was to be his fate; his escape was arranged, and it was he himself who insisted upon his martyrdom. The Greeks were singularly happy in one respect, that 'owing to the character of Greek religion they were free from any priestly class that might have strong traditions and unreasoned doctrines of their own, tenaciously held and imparted only to a few, which might hamper the development of free science'.[3] It is possible to say that there was no organized religion in the modern meaning of that phrase. The oracles and shrines and temples and mysteries existed, and there were the limits to disbelief that were set by the boundaries of the culture

---

[1] See, e.g., Guthrie, *The Greeks and Their Gods*, pp. 300 ff.
[2] *Ibid.*, pp. 282 ff.
[3] Frederick Copleston, S.J., *A History of Philosophy* (London 1951, Burns, Oates and Washbourne, 3 vols., Vol. I, p. 16.

in which all were immersed. But there is no record of any punitive action against atheists despite Plato's recommendation in the *Laws*. Xenophanes does not seem to have been punished for his utterances. It would be wrong not to include in the Greek religious inheritance the powerful and authentic strain of scepticism which runs through Greek thought. The names are many, from Pyrrho of Elis to Xeniades of Corinth, but Xenophanes will concern us chiefly, since his doubts are levelled specifically at religion.

Xenophanes made strenuous efforts to purge the beliefs about the gods of all wrong-doing and indeed of all anthropomorphism.[1] We are earth-born and to earth return,[2] and we know no certain truths,[3] especially not about the gods.[4] There is, however, one supreme god,[5] and it is proper to praise him 'with decent stories and pure words'.[6] No absolute knowledge is possible but so far as we can know God is abstract and One, unmoving and governing by means of time.[7] That Euripides had followed Xenophanes in reforming the moral conceptions of religion has been recognized. Miss Freeman cites particularly the *Heracles* and the *Autolycus*[8] and *Iphegenia in Aulis*.[9] The tradition of Xenophanes runs through the *Euthyphro* of Plato and persists into Hellenistic times, when it flourished again in Alexandria under Aenesidemus, Agrippa and Sextus Empiricus.

Not all scepticism is devoted to religion, of course; it touches upon all the provinces of philosophy; and not all religion is a matter of belief; there are also the observances.

Religious observances in Greece put more emphasis on the performance of the rites than on the degree of belief. Mercifully for those everywhere who have in charge the enforcement of

---

[1] Fragments 11 and 15. In the edition of Kathleen Freeman, *Ancilla to the Pre-Socratic Philosophers* (Oxford 1948, Blackwell). All references to the Fragments of Xenophanes are to this edition.　　　　　　　　　　　　　[2] Fr. 27.
[3] *Ibid.*, 18, 34, 35.　　　[4] *Ibid.*, 15.　　　[5] *Ibid.*, 23.　　　[6] *Ibid.*, 1.
[7] Kathleen Freeman, *The Pre-Socratic Philosophers* (Oxford 1946, Blackwell), pp. 95–99.　　　　　　　　　　　[8] 21 (Xen.) C. See Freeman, *Ibid.*, p. 94.
[9] *Iph. Aul.*, 386 sqq. Freeman, *Ibid.*, p. 94.

official religions, it is possible to see the ritual observed, but thus far quite impossible to measure the intensity of belief. If a man says that he has the faith, who shall know of his sincerity; and if he be sincere, by what means are we to tell how strong it is in him? It is not even clear in the case of the fifth and fourth-century Greeks just what sort of conformity was expected. There were, for instance, temples to some gods at whose festivals the law permitted even ribaldry.[1] The rural regions fostered the Chthonic rites, while those in the cities were on the whole more concerned with devotion to the Olympic gods. When we come to the question of how a man was expected to behave towards the gods, we receive two different answers. For broadly speaking, the Chthonic religion emphasized the kinship between the divine and the human, while the same attitude towards the Olympic gods was regarded as a kind of hubris. So obligation was confused.

There are two points not yet covered; ghosts and the Orphic cult. Since both importantly concern our theme, we shall have to say a brief word about them.

Religion in its lower reaches is never clear-cut. It shades off gradually from belief to superstition. Now, what we have come to praise as belief amounts to a positive and affirmative adherence to what we desire ultimately, while what we condemn as superstition is more a negative avoidance of what we abhor. The Olympic deities were admired for their charmed life, but only after the appropriate propitiation of the Chthonic deities had made this possible; and so we return to our starting point and note how ritual avoidance served as a kind of preliminary stage of ritual tendance, though not always, of course, nor necessarily, in that chronological order. Ritual avoidance, moreover, was an endless affair; there were evil demons, too, and ghosts which were the Keres, and the spirits of the dead hovering about, all of whom had to be propitiated constantly in common-place ways as well as in formal rites.

[1] Aristotle, *Politicus*, 1336b16.

The Orphic and Dionysiac cults were late-comers to Greece. What was the 'inherited conglomerate', to use Gilbert Murray's phrase, against which the pre-Socratics were inveighing? Xenophanes and Heraclitus, for instance, were attacking some sort of religious irrationalism; but what sort? There were in the Greece of the fifth and fourth centuries religious cults and secular philosophies—the followers of Orpheus and those of Socrates, say—but there was no theology and no institutional and hieratic religion, in the modern western sense. Monotheism, too, was certainly not Greek,[1] and there was no politically powerful priestly class. The Greeks and their gods had been this-worldly, sensible and rational; then there entered the foreign gods; Orpheus and Dionysus. Orpheus was other-worldly, Dionysus was irrational and orgiastic. To the extent to which Greek thinkers succumbed to either of these gods, they became ungreek. For the Greeks held their religions in stride until they encountered the Asiatic gods, who threatened to take the whole culture over. Not everyone agreed, of course. A typical rejection is that exemplified in the story of Antisthenes, who when he was being initiated into the Orphic mysteries was told by the priest that as a result of admittance to the rites he would enjoy many good things in Hades. 'Why then,' asked Antisthenes, 'do you not die?'[2]

The Orphic religion exercised so great an influence upon Plato that we shall have to deal with it in a chapter of its own.

When we speak, then, of the Greek religious inheritance, as we have been doing, and say that a man does or does not accept it, what can we mean except the immersion in the culture of which religion is only one institution, and one, moreover, with its borders very imperceptibly altered? In so far as we are able to speak of the flourishing of the Greek culture at all, we know it to have been more preoccupied with its own present than it was with either its past or its future. It conceived of the present

[1] Cf. H. J. Rose, in *La notion du divin*, p. 21.
[2] Diogenes Laertius, *Lives of Eminent Philosophers*, VI. 4.

in terms of ideals as well as actualities, but of ideals closely tied to the actualities—a culture too absorbed in what it was achieving and in what its achievements could mean than in how it had got where it was or what the future could hold as a result of what it had accomplished.

In short, the present was for the sake of the meaning of the present, and was not a mere extension of the past or a springboard for extrapolation into the future. If we are to be correct, then, in our interpretation of Plato's religious inheritance, we shall see that it was an intensification of experience and an enrichment of existence rather than something lurking in wait with reward or punishment when the life's work was done. The gods were simply the first level of abstraction, that is all. To 'believe' in Zeus was only to say that there is order in the world.[1] Greek religion was an example of transparent facilitation in institutional life; the institution working for the individuals who were its members and not imposing itself upon them by force. It exercised its effects through attraction, not through compulsion. In general, the Greek religion inspired proportion and correction, a feeling for the fitness of things, rather than love or fear, and an awareness of the natural order. We have only to contrast it backwards with the religion of the Babylonians and Assyrians, neither of which were too far off from the Greeks in space or time, for whom life was 'stifled beneath the dogmas of what was surely one of the harshest religions ever practised by man'[2] or with the Jews, who emphasized man rather than nature in relation to God. Every great culture has in its religions all these elements, and the Greeks were no exception. We are speaking, therefore, of a matter of emphasis, of shifting arrangements and of crucial differences in evaluation. The atmosphere of the Greek religious inheritance benefited from the high noon of reason, which logic bestowed upon experience, and from its vivid contemporaneity.

[1] Bruno Snell, *The Discovery of the Mind* (Oxford 1953, Blackwell), p. 25.
[2] Georges Contenau, *Everyday Life in Babylon and Assyria* (London 1954, Arnold), pp. 301–2.

B. THE EXAMPLE OF EURIPIDEAN SCEPTICISM

Plato was twenty-seven years old when Euripides died at the advanced age of eighty. It may be helpful to see what a sophisticated man and an intellectual artist believed about religion, and was able to display in the theatre of that period. It may tell us something about the prevailing atmosphere of ideas among the more intelligent men.

The conclusion to which we shall be led is that the religion of Euripides was the same as the Greek religion of realism in Plato, a religious outlook accepted by Aristotle but neglected by the followers of both philosophers. There is a consistent religious view expressed in the plays of Euripides, though it is voiced by a number of very different characters. Perhaps after all it was not Euripides' own view; we cannot know, still, it was a consistent view and a Greek view and we shall have to account for it. The following is a brief summary of Euripides on religion. Many and strange are the works of the gods; often what we expect to happen, does not happen; and what we do not know to be there, we suddenly see.[1] But there is some confusion about the gods, whether they themselves stand for chance and necessity or are subordinate to chance and necessity. But in either case, these two categories are those of divinity, for either they are the gods or they are superior to gods. God, we are assured, needs nothing.[2] God is law,[3] and we are the gods' slaves—whoever the gods be.[4] But then, it seems, the gods too are ruled by law.[5] The gods have compassion for human misery, but both gods and men are ruled by necessity.[6] Gods and the law are not the same;[7] it is necessity which orders events (*anangke*):[8] where there is necessity, there the strongest of men has found a master.[9] It is

[1] *Alcestis*, 1158–61.
[3] *Iphegenia in Aulis*, 1096–8.
[5] *Hecuba*, 799–800.
[7] *Hecuba*, 1029–30.
[9] *Hecuba*, 397.

[2] *Madness of Hercules*, 1345.
[4] *Orestes*, 418.
[6] *Electra*, 1329–30.
[8] *Electra*, 1301.

foolish to struggle against necessity,[1] for necessity knows no pity.[2]

The relation between chance (*tyche*) and necessity is not made clear. In any case, they are very close. Chance has two subdivisions: there is a chance that precipitates the operation of necessity, and a chance that allows for the conflict between necessities. Necessity, of course, is of only one sort: the rule of natural law. The chance that prevails as though it were law is of the first sort;[3] the chance that reverses fortunes is of the second.[4]

When authorities differ as to whether Euripides was a rationalist or an anti-rationalist,[5] they are choosing different Euripidean gods; the rationalist preferring necessity and the anti-rationalist, chance. But in both cases they are inadvertently agreeing that Euripides was a naturalist in rejecting the stock theology of his day and in leaning heavily on a combination of agnosticism and the inclination to suspect that there are designing divinities of some sort.

Man's virtue is to discern the right, and from inborn law and order, to serve the state.[6] If wrong ever triumphs over right, we are to believe no more in gods.[7] Wrong in man is evidenced by arrogance, and our presumptions are that we wish to be gods.[8] But we were redeemed by reason from chaos and mere animality;[9] justice is greater than all human efforts, the very purpose of life.[10]

Man's fate is always mixed.[11] Earth, the life-fosterer, must take its own back again.[12] Do not grieve for the dead, for all must die.[13] The hope is that death brings—nothing.[14] Death is nothing-

---

[1] *Madness of Hercules*, 282–3.
[2] *Hecuba*, 1295.
[3] *Suppliants*, 550–7.
[4] *Children of Hercules*, 612–13.
[5] Cf. R. P. Winnington-Ingram, *Euripides and Dionysus* (Cambridge 1948, University Press), p. 5.
[6] *Iphegenia in Aulis*, 560–70.
[7] *Electra*, 584–4.
[8] *Suppliants*, 214–19.
[9] *Ibid.*, 202–3.
[10] *Electra*, 954.
[11] *Iphegenia in Aulis*, 160.
[12] *Suppliants*, 531–6.
[13] *Andromache*, 1270–2.
[14] *Children of Hercules*, 591–6.

ness,[1] the end of all things,[2] at least for those who are properly buried. The souls of the unburied dead leave their bodies and hover about those who could mourn them.[3]

The threat to Greek rationalism from the invasion of the transcendental gods of the Orient was met in different ways. Euripides was a rationalist who exposed the irrationalism of the religion of Dionysus in the *Bacchae*.[4] Euripides himself made a distinction between the Orphic-like religion of Dionysus and the ordinary rational Greek religion of the Olympic gods. In the *Bacchae* Dionysus has struck the women of Thebes with madness, old men dance in his honour like young men, and everyone has parted with reason. Finally, Pentheus, the king who has opposed Dionysus loses his reason, too, and becomes subservient to the god.[5] Aeschylus, earlier, evidently had a play, now lost, the *Pentheus*, which was part of a trilogy on the same topic as the *Bacchae*. Plato met and endeavoured to incorporate the threat of the Oriental religion by rationalizing it, an attempt which failed and which left him with disparate sets of religious ideas. Euripides was opposed to irrationalism in all its forms and was moreover always able to recognize it. He condemned the whole tribe of seers and said it was all one curse—abominable and useless.[6] A seer tells mostly lies.[7]

Euripides was not an atheist, surely, but a cautious believer who wished to hold his faith within the bounds permitted to it by the rules of logic and by the factual evidence. A rationalist of the broader sort has to find a place in his scheme of things for irrationalisms, and so reason is never final but only the good. The Olympic gods are to be rendered their measured due, but always within the limits of moral right, and always with the understanding that the earth gods have a certain negative set of requirements of their own: we came from the earth and we ◖

---

[1] *Iphegenia in Aulis*, 1251–2.   [2] *Medea*, 153.   [3] *Hecuba*, 30–2.
[4] Dionysus-Orpheus-Bacchus, the entire company of Eastern mystery-gods. See *Bacchae*, 561 *et passim*.   [5] *Bacchae*, 615 ff.
[6] *Iphegenia in Aulis*, 520.   [7] *Ibid.*, 958.

return to the earth, and for a little while in between we are privileged to look upon the sun. But the ghosts are banished from credence and the Dionysiac excesses of transcendental madness laughed out of court. Religion is for the intensification of existence and not for its denial. As with Plato, justice furnishes a consideration weightier than either religion or the more prosaic individual affairs.

CHAPTER IV

THE INFLUENCE OF ORPHISM

A. ORPHIC DOCTRINE AND RITUAL

We have noted that there were two well-defined Greek religions: the Olympic pantheon and the Chthonic gods, and that these in a way exhibited some common properties, notably limit and order. It must not be supposed, however, that these properties were dominant in a way which excluded their opposites. It is true that at one end of the spectrum of belief we have a set of precise doctrines, but at the other there was 'a floating mass of popular belief which was the inheritance of every Greek.[1]' Besides the Olympic and Chthonic gods, which are inherently Greek in their characteristics, there were mystic importations: the rites of Dionysus, the Orphic cult, the Pythagorean mysteries. We shall be concerned here primarily with one of these: Orphism. However, the members of this last group are not as easily separable as all that; each influenced and was influenced by the others, and Pythagoras, Dionysus, Apollo and the Hesiodic theogony all made their mark on Orphism.

What was Orphism in ancient Greece? A set of books containing poems devoted to religious beliefs? Adherence to a school of philosophy? Participation in common rites and doctrines?[2] Orphism meant in all probability a number of books bearing his name and written over many centuries by a number

---

[1] Guthrie, *The Greeks and Their Gods*, p. 310.

[2] Ivan M. Linforth, *The Arts of Orpheus* (Berkeley and Los Angeles 1941, University of California Press), p. 288.

of hands, containing doctrines of a theological and cosmological nature, and a number of rites and mysteries supposed to have been instituted by him.[1]

But all of the ways in which his tradition survived 'represent him as personally active'.[2]

First of all, in the case of Orpheus we do not know whether we are dealing with a man or a myth. The authorities differ as much as the traditions. Harrison supposed that he was an historical person,[3] and Guthrie thinks he is able to detect strong evidence of a genuine personality whose characteristics are, among others, those of the musician and magician, as well as certain gentleness and peace and inclination towards civilization.[4] Modern scholarship sees a personification of the river cult, Orpheus being *ephruceis* (= on the river bank), traceable to Phoroneus and so to Cronus.[5] Orpheus has been called a philosopher though perhaps for odd enough reasons[6] and it is alleged that Pythagoras claimed him in ascribing poems to him.[7] Diogenes Laertius spoke about the Thracian Orpheus whose antiquity could not be questioned but whose claim to be called philosopher was in doubt because he had charged the gods with responsibility for human suffering.[8] He must have been considered an authentic person for Pythagoras to have ascribed some of his own poems to him, as one authority claimed he did.[9] Certainly as late as Plato's own day, Antisthenes was initiated into the Orphic mysteries.[10] Aristotle, on the other hand, thought that Orpheus had never existed.[11] Nevertheless,

[1] Ivan M. Linforth, *The Arts of Orpheus* (Berkeley and Los Angeles 1941, University of California Press), p. 289.

[2] *Ibid.*, p. 272.   [3] *Prolegomena to the Study of Greek Religion*, p. 469.

[4] W. K. C. Guthrie, *Orpheus and Greek Religion* (London 1952, Methuen), III, iii.

[5] Robert Graves, *The Greek Myths* (Baltimore 1955, Penguin Books), i, p. 114.   [6] Diogenes Laertius, *Lives of Eminent Philosophers*, I. 5.

[7] *Ibid.*, VIII. 8.   [8] *Ibid.*, I. 5.

[9] *Op. cit.*, VIII. 8.   [10] *Op. cit.*, VI. 4.

[11] *The Works of Aristotle*, ed. Ross, vol. xii, *Select Fragments* (Oxford 1952, Clarendon Press), p. 80.

the name of Orpheus was included in the list of ancient and wise men by Celsus,[1] 'Orpheus, a man who, as all agree, possessed a pious spirit and also died a violent death'.[2] He was believed to have been an actual person, therefore, as late as the third century of the Christian Era. We would do well to heed the late Professor Cornford's warning and not 'allow the cloud of legendary marvels surrounding Orpheus, Epimenides, or Pythagoras to detract from their serious significance for the history of religion and philosophy'.[3] Orpheus has some of the characteristics of the Olympic gods, but he was not clearly one; and whether he was[4] or was not[5] a Chthonic vegetation god, the truth probably is that we are dealing with a myth built on a hard core of truth. The magical and super-natural events ascribed to Orpheus may have been woven about the life of an actual man who lived in Thrace. Be that as it may, the Orphic mysteries seem to have been based on much older material,[6] and may have been introduced into Athens by Onomacritus during the reign of the Pisistratids about the middle of the sixth century, possibly in a forged version.

Certainly, we have much to set straight if we could. Orpheus was a Greek who in Thrace tried to substitute the quietude of the Greek Apollo for the frenzy of the Thracian Dionysus, and met his death at the hands of the Maenads, the followers of Dionysus. (Or he came from Crete and introduced the orgiastic cults into Greece from Asia.[7] There is a tradition that

[1] *Contra Celsum*, I: 16–17: II: 55.

[2] *Ibid.*, VII: 53 (trans. H. Chadwick, Cambridge 1953, University Press), p. 439.

[3] F. M. Cornford, *Principium Sapientiae* (Cambridge 1952, University Press), p. 104.

[4] See Robert Graves, *The Greek Myths*, I, p. 114: J. G. Frazer, *Balder the Beautiful* (London 1923, Macmillan), II, p. 294.

[5] Guthrie, *Orpheus and Greek Religion*, p. 56.

[6] Harrison, *Proleg.*, pp. 622–3; Kathleen Freeman, *The Pre-Socratic Philosophers* (Oxford 1946, Blackwell), p. 11.

[7] See for instance, Harrison, *Proleg.*, pp. 566, 575. In a later work she declared that what distinguished Orphism 'from the rest of the popular religion of Greece' were 'certain imported elements of Oriental and mainly Iranian nature-worship

he visited Egypt, which is interesting. He went down to Hades to recover his wife, Eurydice, and sailed with the Argonauts to Colchis.[1] Who is to separate out the facts from such charming legends? In all events, the Orphic tradition is a confusion—there are at least three versions of the cosmogony, for instance—but one which consists of an intermingling of ordered structures; many themes are interwoven, and the consequent suggestiveness is immense. We have to pick our way delicately, seeking out features which we can discern most clearly, remembering all the while that we are dealing in Orpheus more with the name of a tradition than with a single influence, or rather with a single influence over which has become encrusted an entire tradition.

We shall look, then, at the Orphic doctrine, first at the doctrine of man and then of nature, and next as nearly as we can at the Orphic religious ritual. Guthrie insists that there was no ancient philosophy of man, none in fact until the fifth century; there was a philosophy of nature only. The philosophy of man arose late amid controversy.[2]

The Orphic *teletai* constituted a body of hieratic beliefs, a sacred *logoi*, more dogmatic and more abstract than the religion of the Homeric poems, and as distinct from it as from the Chthonic theology. The Orphic doctrine of man centres upon the belief in immortality. After the Titans caught and ate the infant Dionysus, son of Zeus and Persephone, they were burned

and formal mysticism. The Greek spirit always tended to humanize and indivi-
dualize its daimones into personal gods, Iranian mysticism kept them disinte-
grated and dispersed in the medium of nature from which they sprang.'—
Jane Harrison, *Themis* (Cambridge 1927, University Press) p. 462. Finally, she
asked point-blank, 'Is it rash to suppose that Orphism owed its main impulse
to the infiltration of Persian religious doctrine?'—*Ibid.*, p. 466. The view that
the Greeks 'tended to humanize' their gods can be reconciled with Guthrie's
view that the philosophy of nature prevailed until quite late (see p. 47, n. 1.);
the anthropomorphic account of nature is still an attempt to account for nature
rather than man.

[1] The references are in Robert Graves, *The Greek Myths*, I, p. 113.
[2] *The Greeks and Their Gods*, p. 339.

to ashes by a thunderbolt from Zeus. From the smoke of their remains sprang the human race, which thus inherits chiefly the wickedness and bodies of the Titans but also a little bit of the divine soul-stuff of the god.[1] Thus man has a mortal and an immortal part, and the body is a prison-house of the soul.[2] Cornford affirms that the distinction between the Dionysian and the Orphic view of immortality is that only 'Orphism is focused on the individual soul, its heavenly origin and immutable nature, and its persistence, as an individual, throughout the round of incarnations'.[3] Upon death the soul is freed for the bliss or punishments of the after-life. For this reason it has been argued that Orpheus held 'to a version of the doctrine of original sin. The soul was enclosed in the body as in a tomb or prison, to punish a very early crime committed by the Titans'.[4] In this world in the meanwhile, then, we are obliged to practise the life which will best fit us for the next, and this is a life of asceticism.[5] The transmigration of souls is also a feature. Those who believe in transmigration are always vegetarians for obvious reasons. Beans must also be abstained from on occasion. Peace and quietness[6] are balanced by *ekstasis* and immortal hope, borrowed from Dionysus. The follower of Orpheus was led to hope that he could become a god.[7] The doctrine of nature can be put second here, after the doctrine of man, reversing the usual order, because Orpheus, being chiefly interested in man, God and the relations between them[8] may have borrowed his doctrine of nature.

[1] The references are given in E. R. Dodds, *The Greeks and the Irrational* (Berkeley 1951, University of California Press), p. 155.

[2] Guthrie, *The Greeks and Their Gods*, p. 311, n. 3.

[3] F. M. Cornford, *From Religion to Philosophy* (New York 1957, Harper), p. 179.

[4] Solomon Reinach, *Orpheus* (New York 1930, Liveright), p. 88.

[5] Orphic asceticism is Pythagorean. See Harrison, *Proleg.*, p. 507; also the rites of aversion in Diogenes Laertius, *Lives of the Philosophers, Life of Pythagoras*.

[6] Harrison, *Proleg.*, p. 475.   [7] *Ibid.*, pp. 495, 503, 570.

[8] Cf. Guthrie, *The Greeks and Their Gods*, p. 316.

Accounts of the Orphic theogony vary. It begins with Water and Earth, and then, begotten of these, *Chronos*, or Time, and *Adrasteia*, or Necessity. *Chronos*, Ageless Time, was a primordial monster, inseparable, however, from the law of necessity; while *Adrasteia*, Necessity, is without body and is spread over the whole universe, holding it together. From the body of *Chronos* came Aether, Chaos and Erebus, black night.[1] In these, we are further told, *Chronos* begat The Egg. The Egg is the World Egg, and from it came *Phanes* (*Eros* or love).[2]

The Orphic theogony accounts for the gods, but there is evidence, in other accounts of Orpheus, of monotheism. Also, Orpheus had been to Egypt, before he married Eurydice, and he returned with the monotheistic sun-worship of Ikhnaton.[3] It was said also that Orpheus neglected Dionysus in favour of the sun whom he called Apollo.[4] Eros-Phanes was to knit together the world, which had been rent asunder through destructive hate.[5] Next, strangely, Zeus swallowed Eros-Phanes and the world and recreated the world. The doctrine of man is set beside that of nature, when Orpheus raised justice next to Zeus.[6]

The Orphic eschatology is in conformity with the belief in the immortality of the soul. After death the soul of the Orphic goes to Hades, repeats the formula which identifies him and asks for the cold water from the lake of Memory. He drinks and thereafter enjoys lordship among the other heroes.[7] The soul of the Orphic in this way is saved from the eternal return to the

---

[1] Freeman, *Ancilla*, Orpheus, Fr. 13.

[2] There are inconsistencies in the various versions, as any examination of the Orphic fragments must show. The order in which the first beings occur is often shuffled, though the cast of characters remains more or less the same.

[3] Orphism owed two other ideas to Egypt: the identity of the mortal with the divine—that man can become a god; and the ritual enactment of the death of the god. See Farnell, *Greek Hero Cults*, p. 383. Certainly, it was 'alien to the earlier spirit of Hellenism'—*Ibid.*, p. 402. Harrison has cited evidence from Eratosthenes in *Themis*, p. 465.   [4] Harrison, *Proleg.*, p. 461.

[5] Freeman, *Ancilla*, Orpheus, Fr. 16.   [6] Harrison, *Proleg.*, p. 506.

[7] Cf. Guthrie, *The Greeks and Their Gods*, p. 322.

body, having 'flown out of the sorrowful circle'.[1] Of the ordinary man, ten lives were required but of the Orphic only three.

The Orphic ritual was a preparation for the immortality of the soul and the life after death. The best account is the elaborate one reconstructed by Jane Harrison,[2] but there are dissenters, as for instance Professor Dodds.[3] We might begin by listing the practices claimed for Orphism. There are: rites of purification and oaths of purity;[4] vegetarianism;[5] asceticism;[6] sun-worship;[7] prayers for peace;[8] bliss or punishment for the liberated soul; ritual formularies for escaping the eternal return called for by transmigration by setting the soul free from the prison-house of the body.[9]

Of these Professor Dodds is prepared to accept only the first, the second and the last. He has pointed out, too, that the similarity with the Pythagoreans is striking.[10] Since Orphism is older than Pythagoreanism, it is probably the former that influenced the latter rather than the reverse. Many of the practices of Orphism were common to the Pythagorean brotherhood, although some were not. Pythagoreanism, too, was a religion, one based on a mixture of mysticism and mathematics, a sort of reification of numbers which were in this way prepared for the kind of qualitative treatment that occurs so often when specific abstractions are clothed in the attributes of universal values. Orphism had none of this, of course. Our purposes are not turned aside by this contingency. We have taken our considerations on the basis of Orpheus and the Orphic religion. It cannot be separated from Pythagoreanism because of the similarities; and though it can be separated from the Dionysiac cult, as for instance in the case of the omophagic rites of the tearing and

---

[1] Cf. Guthrie, *The Greeks and Their Gods*, p. 323.   [2] *Proleg.*, Ch. X.
[3] *The Greeks and the Irrational*, p. 147.   [4] *Proleg.*, p. 537.
[5] *Ibid.*, p. 507.   [6] *Ibid.*, p. 507.   [7] *Ibid.*, p. 461.
[8] Cf. the liturgical Homeric *Hymn to Ares*, alleged to be Orphic, in H. G. Evelyn-White trans., *Hesiod and the Homeric Hymns* (London 1936, Heinemann), pp. xxxix and 289.
[9] Harrison, *Proleg.*, pp. 588–9.   [10] *The Greeks and the Irrational*, p. 149.

eating of raw flesh, chiefly of bulls, there is contrast and frequent confusion here. As we have already indicated, Orphism undoubtedly contained Dionysiac and Appolinian elements, even though these were in sharp opposition. 'When our historical information begins the Dionysiac frenzy had already been tamed by the joint activity of the state and the Delphic oracle. Mysticism was not dead, only repressed, and it took refuge in certain religious movements of an almost sectarian character, especially Orphism.'[1] What large religion does not have these paradoxes? If they did not, we could approach the topic of religions without so often having to leave our reason behind.[2] The main point is that through these three religions elements were brought into Greece that were not essentially Greek.

The chief goal of the Orphic mysteries was the survival of death through 'union with the divine'[3] in which the worshipper *became* god by means of a series of rites, beginning with rites of initiation, of purification and cleansing, and ending with rites of marriage and birth.[4] 'From the time that the neophyte enters the first stage of initiation, i.e. becomes a mystic (*mustes*), he leads a life of abstinence (*hagnon*). But abstinence is not the end. Abstinence, the sacramental feast of raw flesh, the holding aloft of the Mother's torches, all these are but preliminary stages to the final climax, the full fruition when, cleansed and consecrated, he is made one with the god.'[5] 'He wears white garments, he flies from death and birth, from all physical contagion, his lips are pure from flesh-food, he fasts as before the Divine Sacrament. He follows in fact all the rules of asceticism familiar to us as Pythagorean'.[6] The Pythagoreans, paradoxically enough, called it the 'Orphic Life'.[7] Union with the god is symbolized in the sacred marriage, with the initiate having real or, later,

[1] Martin P. Nilsson, *Greek Popular Religion* (New York 1940, Columbia University Press), p. 103.

[2] Harrison, *Proleg.*, p. 495: 'On the altar of his Unknown God, through all the ages man pathetically offers the holocaust of his reason'.

[3] *Proleg.*, pp. 473 ff.; esp. pp. 477, 563.   [4] *Ibid.*, p. 564.

[5] *Ibid.*, p. 500.   [6] *Ibid.*, p. 507.   [7] Diogenes Laertius, I. 5.

symbolic, intercourse with the priestess, the fertility ceremony of the *Liknophoria* involving consecration with the *liknon* or cradle-winnowing basket filled with fruits and *phallos*.[1] But the chief ritual perhaps was life itself, the way of philosophy conceived as the continual observation of ritual, the pure life of *Katharsis*.[2]

What does it all add up to for our purposes? It was the urge to escape from the inadequacy of ordinary experience into the serenity of spiritual life that accounted for the religious movement of Orphism.[3] It is necessary at this point to remind ourselves that we are not here interested in Orphism for its own sake but only in its influence through Plato upon the western tradition of Platonism. We shall then turn next to a consideration of the influence of Orphism on Plato. First, however, it is necessary to remind ourselves that Orpheus was not inherently Greek. Compare the Orphic doctrine of man with the general Greek view, and it is easy to detect an interloper. 'The Orphic mystery religion is a complete reversal of the true Greek view of life, according to which the corporeal man is the real man and the soul merely a sort of strengthless shadow image.'[4] For the Greek, with his sense of the finite, there was more emphasis on this world than on the next. The present, its reasons, feelings and actions—in that order—were his main concern. Contrast this with the Orphic view. 'There is no room for an immortal soul in any philosophy of this period.'[5] Zeller makes the point that Orphism had made familiar to the Greeks an asceticism and a concern for personal salvation which was the exact opposite of the Socratic concern for knowledge.[6]

---

[1] *Proleg.*, pp. 517 ff.

[2] J. Burnet, *Early Greek Philosophy* (London 1930, Black), pp. 82–3.

[3] Erwin R. Goodenough, *Jewish Symbols in the Greco-Roman Period* (New York 1954), Vol. IV, p. 59.

[4] Eduard Zeller, *Outlines of the History of Greek Philosophy* (London 1931, Kegan Paul), p. 15.

[5] John Burnet, *op. cit.*, p. 84. That the soul was not a Greek idea but an Orphic one, see also Guthrie, *op. cit.*, p. 346.   [6] Zeller, *op. cit.*, p. 314.

Again, for the Greeks, the gods were gods, however like men they were in their appearance and conduct, and there was a distance between gods and men. The 'immortal hope' of becoming a god, advocated by the Orphic religion, would have been for the Greeks what they had always regarded as *hubris*, or divine insolence.[1] The Orphics held out 'the possibility of attaining divine life'[2] in the next world, but the aspiration of the Greeks was wrapped up in the life of this world.

Orpheus was an imported deity, like Dionysus. He is not usually mentioned among the deities to whom the Greeks sub-scribed when they first came to the Hellenic peninsula, although the Olympics and Chthonians usually are.[3] But the importation was welcome. Orpheus was incorporated into the mysteries,[4] while Dionysus formed the centre of the festivals, the rural and city Dionysia.[5] The Greeks had a way of dealing with any foreign elements which happened to enter their culture. 'Orpheus, the ideal of the Orphic, is a Dionysus tamed and clothed, and in his right mind—in a word, Apollinised.'[6] Orpheus, according to Cornford, is a stage on the way from Dionysus to Apollo, and Orpheus 'more at home with the Muses than with the Maenads' and with 'the more savage parts of his ritual expurgated or toned down to a decent symbolism'.[7]

In the older Greek religious inheritance the lines were clearly drawn. The world was finite, present and well-defined. We have seen that there were gods in the heaven for whom there should be sacrificial tendance, and gods in the earth who demanded ritual avoidance. There was a balance here between the equal importance of earth and sky, between the two sets of gods:

[1] Cf. Harrison, *Proleg.*, p. 476.
[2] *Ibid.*, p. 416.
[3] See, for instance, J. L. Myres, *Who Were the Greeks?* (Berkeley 1930, University of California Press), Ch. IV.   [4] Harrison, *Proleg.*, pp. 539–71.
[5] Sir Arthur Pickard-Cambridge, *The Dramatic Festivals of Athens* (Oxford 1953, Clarendon Press), pp. 40-103.
[6] F. M. Cornford, *From Religion to Philosophy*, p. 195.
[7] *Op. cit.*, p. 196.

those on Olympus and those underground, which had a meaning of its own full of philosophical significance and which could be upset only with peril to its effects.

Across this neat and static pattern there flared dynamically the future-bent figure of Orpheus. 'It was the work of Orpheus to lift these rites[1] from earth to heaven, but spiritualized, uplifted as they are, they remain in their essence primitive.'[2] He took what was good in this world and lifted it towards the next through the higher station of the Olympics: from the earth-present through heaven to the future-immortal. In this way, an infinite intent was added to the finite and ordered rational Greek cosmos by irrational and non-Greek influences. But at the same time, it is only fair to add, he distorted the Greek balance, took the emphasis off the present, replaced finite satisfactions with infinite yearnings, and gave Greek culture, in general, a different turn, a turn to something non-Greek.

The lines will not be easy to sort out, yet it should be possible to show these two, and in a way quite separate and distinct, influences at work in the *Dialogues* of Plato. To this task we next direct our efforts.

Authorities ancient and modern differ as to the degree to which Plato was influenced by the Orphic tradition and writings. It was thought early that Plato was 'full of echoes of the writings of Orpheus'.[3] Plato was 'deep-dyed in Orphism', according to Harrison.[4] Some authorities would go so far as to credit most of Plato's philosophy to Orphism, e.g. Macchiro.[5] Here we shall endeavour to divide some of the evidence into the Orphism which is explicit in the *Dialogues* of Plato and the Orphism which is implicit.

B. ORPHISM EXPLICIT IN PLATO

We cannot gather much from the explicit references to Orpheus

[1] I.e. the burial rites of the underworld.   [2] Harrison, *Proleg.*, p. 505.
[3] Olympiordorus, quoted in Guthrie, *op. cit.*, p. 312.   [4] *Proleg.*, p. 472.
[5] See Werner Jaeger, *Paideia*, II, p. 394.

in the *Dialogues*. These are not many—some fifteen, but they do tell us something. We learn, for instance, that 'one or two thousands of years ago some of them (i.e. the arts) were revealed to Orpheus'.[1] Music was in fact 'the art of Orpheus'.[2] He was perhaps not the greatest of poets, a position reserved for Homer; for some poets are inspired by Orpheus, but the most by Homer.[3] Protagoras, the Sophist, claimed that Orpheus was a practitioner of the ancient art of sophistry but fearing the odium it involved in those days disguised it in a decent dress, sometimes in mystic rites and soothsayings.[4] Protagoras, Plato readily admitted, impressed his listeners, 'enchanting them with his voice like Orpheus'.[5] Orpheus was a genuine historical person to Plato, as real, evidently, as Hesiod and Homer.[6] He was 'the son of Oeagrus'[7] the Thracian King, whether or not he was also the son of the muse, Calliope. There is at least one direct quotation from Orphic writings. The first five choices of possessions are: moderation, beauty, wisdom, sciences and arts, pure pleasures of perception and knowledge. Then

> But with the sixth generation (says Orpheus)
> Cease the rhythmic song.[8]

Plato evidently knew about the Orphic religion and its practices, for he mentions the 'Orphic life', this is, 'keeping wholly to inanimate food and, contrariwise, abstaining wholly from things animate'.[9]

In the *Laws* there are many restrictions recited. Among them, no one 'shall venture to sing an unauthorized song—not even should it be sweeter than the hymns of Orpheus'.[10] For the incongruity and senselessness of some music would, in Plato's opinion, 'furnish a theme for laughter to all the men who, in Orpheus' phrase, "have attained the full flower of joyousness".'[11]

[1] *Laws*, 677D.   [2] *Ion*, 533C.   [3] *Ibid.*, 536B.
[4] *Protagoras*, 316D.   [5] *Ibid.*, 315A.   [6] *Apology*, 41A.
[7] *Symposium*, 179D.   [8] *Philebus*, 66C.   [9] *Laws*, 782C.
[10] *Ibid.*, 829E.   [11] *Ibid.*, 669D.

Plato knew about the Orphic theogony also, for he mentioned Orpheus in connection with the marriage of Ocean and his sister Tethys.[1] And he quoted in evident agreement the sayings of the Orphic poets that the body is the tomb of the soul.[2] Some of the Orphic ideas meet with favour and are accepted by Plato, but not all of the Orphics are so well received. 'They produce a bushel of books of Musaeus and Orpheus, the offspring of the Moon and of the Muses, as they affirm, and these books they use in their ritual, and make not only ordinary men but states believe that there really are remissions of sins and purifications for deeds of injustice, by means of sacrifice and pleasant sport for the living, and that there are also special rites for the defunct, which they call functions, that deliver us from evils in that other world, where terrible things await those who have neglected to sacrifice'.[3] It was that same Orpheus whose soul was seen 'selecting the life of a swan, because from hatred of the tribe of women, owing to his death at their hands, he was unwilling to be conceived and born of a woman'.[4]

There are samples of references here to the story of Orpheus' birth, his excellence at his profession, his beliefs about the soul, the manner of his death, and of his choice of rebirth. And there are many references to his writings and their profusion, including two direct quotations from them. There is an allusion to the Orphic theogony, and a good description of the Orphic ritual religion. The evidence, in short, though scanty is sufficient to convince us that Plato was familiar with the figure of Orpheus as a man and as the centre of a religious cult which was complete with a theogony, a liturgy and an eschatology.

The explicit references to Orpheus do not exhaust the evidence for Orphism in Plato. Before endeavouring to complete our following of the trail of Orpheus across the *Dialogues* we shall have to take account also of the implicit evidence.

[1] *Cratylus*, 402B.   [2] *Ibid.*, 400C.
[3] *Republic*, 364E–365A.   [4] *Ibid.*, 620A.

C. ORPHISM IMPLICIT IN PLATO

The question of where to begin, and, more importantly, where to end in tracing the influence of Orphism in Plato in those passages in which he makes no explicit reference, is difficult to answer. To what extent did Orphism affect the very ground of his work? There is sufficient explicit and implicit evidence to lead most authorities to answer that the influence was a strong one and the respect held by Plato for the Orphic writings and tradition considerable.[1] We shall never learn the facts. Perhaps there are no well-defined facts to learn; the influence of ideas has a way of shading off imperceptibly. All that we can hope to do is to indicate where there seems to be clear evidence, and to offer some strong heuristic guesses at the rest. One extreme guess is that of Proclus, that 'being' for Plato was the Orphic World-Egg.[2] Certainly Plato, speaking through Aristophanes, said that if the might of Eros were understood, men would have provided him with great temples and altars, and solemn sacrifices.[3]

It is not always clear when Plato is talking about the Orphics and when about the Pythagoreans, or other mystic cults. But he makes many references to the mystics without further specification. Taylor thought that Socrates might have been initiated into the Orphic religion early in life and that it might have made a deep impression.[4] Certainly he gave lip service to some mystic cults and must have meant more than that, as when he says, for example, that 'the greatest of blessings come to us through madness, when it is sent as a gift of the gods. For the prophetess at Delphi and the priestesses at Dodona when they have been mad have conferred many splendid benefits upon Greece',[5] a statement which is at the very least favourable.

[1] E. G. Guthrie, *Orpheus and Greek Religion*, pp. 238–44.
[2] Quoted in Harrison, *Proleg.*, pp. 647–8.
[3] *Symposium*, 189C.
[4] A. E. Taylor, *Socrates* (Garden City, New York 1953, Doubleday), p. 51.
[5] *Phaedrus*, 244A.

At the very end of his life Socrates confessed to having recently composed a Hymn to Apollo.[1] But then on the other side we encounter criticism equally, as when the Athenian Stranger, Plato's spokesman, is shocked by the doings of the gods in the ancient and inherited theogonies of the Orphic variety, though preferring them to the account of the materialists (probably Democritus).[2] Despite his criticism we may take it that he was more influenced than not.

Plato seems to have accepted the Orphic myth of the origin of man from the smoke of the thunderbolt that burned up the Titans, when he speaks of the people who 'display and reproduce the character of the Titans of story'.[3]

The body is a prison.[4] Socrates declared that he 'once heard one of our sages say that we are now dead, and the body is our tomb'.[5] The Orphic rites of purification prepared the initiate for the next life in which the soul is free of the body. Professor Kitto points out that Plato 'distinguished sharply between body and soul; but for all that, it is not a typical Greek idea'.[6] In the *Dialogues* the purification ritual of the Orphic cult becomes transformed somewhat. It is the mind which is to be purified and made ready for its journey, apart from the body and after the death of the body, for 'the mind', he said, 'is the pilot of the soul'.[7] Purification will consist 'in separating so far as possible, the soul from the body'.[8] The true philosophers, we are told 'are in every way hostile to the body and they desire to have the soul apart by itself alone'.[9] The analogy of the acquisition of wisdom as a kind of purification is often employed. For, as Socrates observed, 'restraint and justice and courage and wisdom itself are a kind of purification', and 'as they say in the mysteries,

---

[1] *Phaedo*, 60D, 61B. [2] *Laws*, 886C.
[3] *Ibid.*, 701C., R. G. Bury trans.; E. R. Dodds, *The Greeks and the Irrational*, pp. 156, 176–7, n. 132.
[4] *Phaedo*, 62B. [5] *Gorgias*, 493A, W. R. M. Lamb trans.
[6] H. D. F. Kitto, *The Greeks* (Harmondsworth 1956, Penguin), p. 173.
[7] *Phaedrus*, 247C. [8] *Phaedo*, 67B, H. N. Fowler trans.
[9] *Ibid.*, 67E, H. N. Fowler trans.

"the thyrsus-bearers are many, but the mystics few"; and these mystics are, I believe, the true philosophers'.[1] From the nominalism of the Sophists to the realism and idealism of the Platonic metaphysics amounted to an 'initiation'. For, as Socrates said, 'The uninitiated are those who think nothing is except what they can grasp firmly with their hands, and who deny the existence of actions and generation and all that is invisible'.[2] Plato knew that there had been an Orphic religion whose devotees practised vegetarianism.[3]

Perhaps the most obvious effect of Orphism on Plato occurs in the allegory of the cave[4] in the use made there of sunlight, in the sun as the giver of light[5] and also in the *Parmenides*.[6] The influence of the sun image is strongest when light is equated with being and darkness with non-being.[7] The idea of the good, we are told, gives 'light' to the world.[8] It was the sun, in fact, to which Socrates offered a prayer in the morning before he went about his business.[9] Orpheus is alleged to have made a journey to Egypt where he must have learned the sun-worship which he brought to Thrace and introduced in Greece.[10] There are many references to Egypt in Plato.[11] The favourite oath of Socrates was to swear 'by the Dog',[12] a reference, evidently, to Anubis, the Egyptian dog-god. Greece's debt to Egypt has been under-estimated; according to Pausanias, the worship of Helios had been established at Corinth.[13] Sun-worship may not have taken hold, but the abstraction from sun-worship in the

---

[1] *Phaedo*, 69C, H. N. Fowler trans.
[2] *Theaetetus*, 155E, H. N. Fowler trans.
[3] *Laws*, 782C-D, R. G. Bury trans.
[4] *Republic*, Book VII.   [5] *Ibid.*, 507D–508C.   [6] 131B.
[7] *Republic*, 479C.   [8] *Ibid.*, 517B-C.
[9] *Symposium*, 220D. Burnet was sure that the Allegory of the Cave was of Orphic origin. See John Burnet, *Early Greek Philosophy*, p. 83, n. 3. Also J. A. Stewart, *The Myths of Plato* (London 1905), p. 252, n. 2.
[10] The references are given in Robert Graves, *op. cit.*, p. 112.
[11] See for instance in the Index to the Jowett edition.
[12] *Apology* 22A; *Lysis*, 211E: *Gorgias*, 461A.
[13] Quoted in Harrison, *Proleg.*, p. 609.

Dialogues shows that it made a profound impression on Plato and, as we shall later see, on his successors.

The most familiar Socratic discussion is that of the immortality of the soul. Here perhaps we are confronted with the clearest evidence of Orphic influence. The flat statement that the soul is immortal is made just so by Socrates in the *Phaedrus*[1] and its alleged proof as well as illustrative myth is given in terms of self-motion in the pages following this passage. The Socrates of the *Phaedo* believed in the immortality of the soul and the Socrates of the *Meno* believed in its pre-existence. In the *Gorgias* he seemed convinced of an after-life, that leading the good life in this world will prove 'evidently advantageous also in the other world',[2] and in the *Republic* 'that our soul is immortal and never perishes'.[3] In the *Phaedrus*[4] he predicted that the gods will release us when they choose from the prison-house of life. On the other hand, however, the Socrates of the *Euthyphro* and of the *Apology* either did not think so or at the very least was in some doubt. In the *Republic*[5] Plato castigated the 'begging priests' who 'go to rich men's doors' promising indulgences. 'Plato is thoroughly Orphic when he says in the *Phaedrus*[6] that the soul sinks to earth "full of forgetfulness and vice." '[7] The sacrosanct burial rites of the Orphics are implied by the passage in the *Phaedo*.[8]

There seems to be little doubt that when the soul survived the body it went on for Plato to a last judgment and a future life. Most authorities agree that such ideas of a last judgment and a future life either came from the Orphic tradition or were strongly influenced by it. It is to the Orphics and not to the Achaeans that Plato owed what Harrison called 'the dark disgrace of a doctrine of eternal punishment':[9] that every soul must be judged naked and dead, separated from the body but retaining

---

[1] 245C.   [2] 527B, W. R. M. Lamb trans.
[3] 608D, Paul Shorey trans.   [4] 62D.
[5] 364B.   [6] 248C.   [7] Harrison, *Proleg.*, p. 581.
[8] 70C. The point is Harrison's, *Proleg.*, p. 599.   [9] *Proleg.*, p. 612.

from the body all its natural gifts, and the experiences added to that soul as a result of the man's various pursuits[1] by judges also naked and dead, then to be assigned to journey either to the Islands of the Blest or to Tartarus.[2] In the *Republic*[3] there is the myth of Er, the warrior who died and, having witnessed the last judgment, returned to give an account of it.

The doctrine of rebirth is clear in the *Phaedrus*.[4] It is clear also in the *Phaedo*.[5] Anamnesis in the *Meno*[6] and in the *Republic*[7] is consistent with it: both the River of Lethe and the Plain of Oblivion.

Like everything else in Plato, the issue is confused when we endeavour to draw hard and fast lines. On the whole, Plato (or Socrates) believed in the immortality of the soul, after the Orphics, but then in at least one place he condemned them for their notion of immortality in terms of a future reward and punishment[8] and he repeated many times with approval, as we have noted, the story of the fate of the soul in the last judgment and subsequent dispatch to the Islands of the Blest or to Tartarus. Socrates' insistence on the immortality of the soul must have been an uncomfortable idea in his day when most concern was oriented around the present. It was Orphic, and difficult to spread among finite rationalists. He was heavily influenced by the Orphics, and knew it for he often spoke of them with favour, as we have shown in the last section; yet in the *Phaedrus*[9] is that curious passage in which one who 'will lead the life of a prophet or someone who conducts mystic rites' is only counted fifth in the importance in which souls fall to earth, after philosophers or lovers of beauty, musical or loving natures, lawful kings or warlike rulers, politicians or men of business or financiers, and hard-working gymnasts, and only just above poets or other imitative artists, craftsmen, sophists or demagogues or tyrants! Plato's own religion was civic; the religion of Orpheus

[1] *Gorgias*, 524D, W. R. M. Lamb trans.   [2] *Ibid.*, 523A–524A.
[3] 614B ff.   [4] 248C–E.   [5] 70C–D.   [6] 81A.
[7] 621A.   [8] *Republic*, 363D–E.   [9] 248D–E.

was individual and personal.[1] Orpheus may have been monotheistic; Plato believed in many gods.[2]

These are striking resemblances between many of the Platonic
myths and those in the Orphic tradition, notably those in the
Gorgias,[3] the *Republic*[4] and the *Statesman*.[5] Plato's idealistic
epistemology, in which the actual world is an appearance, and
all knowledge respecting it an opinion, so that sense perception
is a poor and unreliable source of true knowledge, may have
its source in the Orphic religion.[6] Contempt for the world of
sense perception would logically go along with contempt for
the body. The other-worldliness of Orpheus is not Greek, and
neither is the derogation of the body in favour of the soul.
Both the frenzy of the Dionysiac religion and the asceticism
of the Orphic religion were un-Greek. Reason working together
with the proportional recognition and celebration of things as
they are, is equally opposed to the life of pure sensual pleasure
and to the abstention from all sensual pleasure.

The cultural orbit of Orpheus cut across the nature gods of
the present world, both those of earth and of Mt. Olympus,
bringing with it immortal longings for another world, longings
for immortality foreign to the Greek cosmology, the unnatural
practices of asceticism and of the denial of this world, and
transcendental gods from Thrace or Crete, Egypt or Asia.
The chances are, then, that the Orphic writings pulled Plato
(or Socrates) out of his true path a little, and in the effort to
abstract the philosophy from the theology and the mythology,
he gave more emphasis to the Ideas than to the receptacle, an
error which Aristotle tried to correct, with his own consequent

[1] A. J. Festugiere, *Epicurus and His Gods* (Oxford 1955, Blackwell), trans.
C. W. Chilton, p. 4.   [2] E.g. *Philebus*, 25B.
[3] Werner Jaeger hints that the myth of *Gorgias* may be an Orphic myth.
See his *Paideia*, II, pp. 151–2.
[4] See also the last judgment of the *Republic, ibid.*, p. 368.
[5] 268E–273E.
[6] See Kathleen Freeman, *The Pre-Socratic Philosophers* (Oxford 1946,
Blackwell), p. 18.

over-emphasis on the other side. Plato was bowled over by Orpheus and never recovered his equilibrium. Metaphysical realism and this-worldliness was what he had wanted to advocate; whereas metaphysical idealism and other-worldliness was the theology to which Orphism brought him.

CHAPTER V

PLATO'S TWO
RELIGIONS

We have seen something of what the Greek religions were like when Plato came upon the scene, and we have traced the influence of Orphism upon his work. We began with a thesis to the effect that Plato had two philosophies, in addition to those of the Sophists to which he was opposed. It is now our plan to show that Plato had also two religions. One is a kind of super-naturalism, consistent with his idealistic philosophy and with the Orphic religion, the other is a kind of naturalism consistent with his realistic philosophy and with the traditional Greek religion.[1] We could not hope to show this, of course, if all the references and allusions and relevancies to religious topics in the *Dialogues* could be reconciled to a single point of view. They cannot.

A vivid instance is afforded by the effort to come to some conclusion concerning Plato's belief about God. A fertile source of confusion is the repeated indifference to whether he is talking about God or about the gods. Any case for monotheism in Plato would have hard going. But let us consider God now as in the singular only, in order to illustrate another difficulty. For one authority, at least, God in Plato is 'the supreme organizing

[1] A similar distinction was observed by Professor Arthur O. Lovejoy in his *The Great Chain of Being* (Cambridge 1936, Harvard University Press), p. 24 and pp. 49 f. He draws there the distinction between Plato's religious 'other-worldliness' and religious 'this-worldliness'. See also in this connection Cornford's distinction between the scientific and the mystical, which he derives from Diogenes Laertius' grouping of the Greek philosophers into an Ionian and an Italiote succession, *From Religion to Philosophy*, p. vi.

mind behind the universe',[1] while for another he is limited to the demiurgic function of filling the receptacle with the Forms, a sort of principle of individuation connecting the two worlds.[2] The truth seems to be that for Plato God was both: one version belonged to Plato the idealist, the other to Plato the realist. Plato had two philosophies, as we have noted; he had also two religions. It is impossible to reconcile certain passages in the *Apology*, the *Symposium*, the *Euthyphro* and the *Republic*, with others in the *Phaedo*, say, and the *Laws*. We shall, then, endeavour to separate the two religions.

A. THE ORPHIC VERSION OF IDEALISM

It may be assumed that we have stated much of what is contained in Plato's idealistic version of religion in that chapter where we traced the influence of Orphism (chapter IV), and we shall adopt this assumption. The additional references in this section, then, will be considered to be an extension. In this section and the next, the proportions will be the same as they were in chapter II, above: as much more space will be devoted to Plato's realistic religion as was there devoted to his realistic philosophy; and the reason is, again, that he has generally been credited with having advocated an idealistic philosophy and religion, so that the case for them has only to be mentioned and does not need to be proved; whereas the case for his realistic philosophy and religion has to be made considerably stronger, for it is by no means a familiar one.

According to Plato, God 'holds the beginning, the end, and the centre of all things that exist';[3] God, not man, is the measure of all things.[4] Atheists are to be punished.[5] God is the author of good only, He never deceives or changes.[6] There is God, then

---

[1] Guthrie, *The Greeks and Their Gods*, p. 338.
[2] Demos, *The Philosophy of Plato*, Ch. V.
[3] *Laws*, 715E.   [4] *Ibid.*, 716C.
[5] *Ibid.*, 767C–E, 855C ff., 907D ff.   [6] *Republic*, 379B.

and there are gods, and there is the good. And God is good and the good is ordered by God but God is not the same as the good but the author of good, and the author of good only,[1] and the good cannot be defined.[2] Evil is the opposite of good. It does not belong to the gods but to mortals. To escape from evil means to become like a god.[3] Evil is due to human defects.[4] It has its source in the material constituent inherited from the original chaos.[5] 'Human affairs are unworthy of earnest effort'[6] yet the righteous life is the most pleasurable in the end.[7]

We cannot know the soul as it was in its first and purest state because of the material body.[8] But as it existed before the body, so it will exist after, for the soul is immortal.[9] When men die, it is only their bodies which perish. Death is the disconnection of the soul and the body.[10] But the soul is not the same for having been in the body; it is marked by its material experiences.[11] Presumably, the soul has had many such experiences in previous lives, as the doctrine of *anamnesis* would indicate. Harrison professed to have traced this specific doctrine in Plato to primitive initiation ceremonies, specifically to the *rite de passage*.[12] The soul is likened to reason, the attendant *daimon*,[13] 'the god within the mind'.[14] The soul is the only source of motion.[15] The soul is reason, like the charioteer driving the two steeds, one the disciplined emotions and the other the undisciplined appetites.[16]

[1] *Politicus*, 379b.   [2] *Republic*, 507B *et passim*.
[3] *Theaetetus*, 176A–B.   [4] *Epinomis*, 976A.
[5] *Politicus*, 273B; *Timaeus*, 53A; *Symposium*, 195C.
[6] *Laws*, 803B.   [7] *Ibid.*, 733 ff.
[8] *Phaedrus*, 245C–D. Plato's debt to Orpheus for his theory of the soul appears to have been considerable. Farnell has observed of him on this point that 'his debt seems to have been great, his gratitude small'.—*Greek Hero Cults*, p. 380.   [9] *Republic*, 611A.
[10] *Gorgias*, 524B.   [11] *Ibid.*, 524D–525A.
[12] *Themis*, p. 513.   [13] *Timaeus*, 90A; *Symposium*, 202E.
[14] *Phaedo*, 107D, 113D; *Republic*, 617D–E. The phrase is Pope's, quoted in Paul Shorey, *What Plato Said* (Chicago 1934, University Press), p. 536.
[15] *Phaedrus*, 245C–D; *Laws*, 895B–896B.
[16] *Ibid.*, 245B; cf. *Republic*, 506E.

The mind 'always rules the universe', an old doctrine but one with which Socrates agreed.[1] *Nous*, then, is the origin of *logos*, and the world-mind is the origin of the world. The life of the human mind and of wisdom is the most divine of lives, the nearest the human can come to the divine.[2] It would be folly to argue from this point of view that Athena delights in the dance, though Plato does so later.[3]

As with the Jews, there was a great distinction in what the fates meted out to the good and the evil man. The soul of the man who when living indulged too much in sensual pleasure and lived a life of the body is 'weighed down by this and dragged back into the visible world . . . and flits about the monuments and the tombs . . . as shadowy shapes'.[4] It is otherwise with the good man.

'When a good man dies, he has a great portion and honour among the dead, and becomes a spirit . . . Every good man, living or dead, is of spiritual nature and is rightly called a spirit.'[5] There is much emphasis on the immortality of the soul, and many pictures of the last judgment and the other world and its rewards and punishments. And so we are told that the truth of the last judgment in the description of the after-life[6] is a conjecture concerning immortality: something like it, however, must be true. And we learn of a heaven of bright space above this marshy earth and of a subterranean hell beneath it, of four rivers in layers connected by a central core called Tartarus. Briefly, the dead are judged when they are led to the place of judgment, each by his own daimon, and then sent to fare accordingly, the good to heaven and their reward in the Island of the Blest,[7] and the bad in varying degrees across the various rivers to their respective punishment.

---

[1] *Philebus*, 30D, H. N. Fowler trans.   [2] *Ibid.*, 33B.
[3] *Laws*, 653.   [4] *Phaedo*, 81C–D, H. N. Fowler trans.
[5] *Cratylus*, 398B–C, H. N. Fowler trans.
[6] *Gorgias*, 523A ff.; *Phaedo*, 109B–114D.
[7] *Republic*, 614D ff.; *Gorgias* 523B–524A, 526C; *Phaedo*, 111A.

How are we to account for the fact that Plato accepted such a supposititious version of eschatology? Salvation, like sin, was introduced into the Western world by the Orphic religion. 'Opposed as it is to what we are accustomed to regard as the Hellenic spirit, Orphism, through its influence on Plato, became an important factor in later religious thought'.[1] That Plato did so accept such a version is evident from the numerous versions of it which he repeated. Aside from the clear hand of Orpheus, one other explanation is possible. It would not have been difficult, after all, to take the perfection of the logical order as contained in the pure being of the Ideas or Forms, and to slip it over, as it were, from a second natural world to a super-natural and hypothetical next world, as though, being timeless, it covers like a carapace all possible worlds. And well it might, and still be poor evidence for the existence of another world into which we are born when we have perished in this one; for where a contrast is to be made of what our conduct was with respect to morals, and what it could have been had it been better, the consequent effect, the entire purpose, of the next world, perfect though it may be and more glorious in many ways than this, is to make the necessary adjustments, in terms of rewards and punishments, of the injustices perpetrated and practised in this world.

B. THE GREEK VERSION OF REALISM

We turn now to a religion of Plato which stands in some contrast to the one we have just examined. No one seems to have studied his realism for its religion or to have searched the *Dialogues* for religious statements consistent with his realism.

Our first consideration must be the attitude which Plato maintained towards the religion which he inherited as an Athenian. The Greeks, we noted earlier,[2] had no word for religion, only

[1] A. Seth Pringle-Pattison, *Studies in the Philosophy of Religion* (Oxford 1930, Clarendon Press), p. 211.   [2] Ch. III.

for piety and holiness. In Plato's opinion 'it is not without reason that tragedy is reputed a wise thing and Euripides a great tragedian',[1] and it was his habit to quote Euripides favourably.[2] But the measure of scepticism which we have seen that there was in Euripides is either rejected by Plato or embodied implicitly in his point of view as it is sometimes expressed, as for instance in the *Euthyphro* and the *Apology*. Only in one place in the *Dialogues* does Euripidean scepticism succeed in raising doubt, and that is where Plato declared that 'Euripides may have been right in saying.

"Who know if life be not death and death life?" '[3]

There is little doubt that Plato accepted the traditional religious beliefs and practices of his land and people. He declared that he would leave all religious matters; the founding of temples, the performance of sacrifices, and other forms of worship of the gods, to the Apollo of Delphi.[4] We owe due service, he declared, to all gods and minor divinities.[5] His instructions were, first to honour the Olympians and next the Chthonian deities, then the daemones and finally the heroes.[6] This, he said, is 'aiming most straight at the mark of piety'.[7] Socrates' last words were concerning the cock he said that he owed to Asklepios.[8] He said elsewhere that if people were to hear about the sufferings and revenges of the gods they should be told only to a few and then after sacrificing not a pig but some huge and unprocurable victim.[9] As for the Keres, they pollute and corrupt all the fair things in human life.[10] The passages in praise of Dionysus are many.[11] There is reason to suspect that the daemons are genuine, since the gods and heroes who surround them in this passage assuredly are.[12] Socrates said, in effect, that he did not believe in

[1] *Republic*, 568a.
[2] E.g. *Republic*, 568b; *Gorgias*, 484e, 485e; *Symposium*, 199a.
[3] *Gorgias*, 492e.   [4] *Republic*, 427B–C; *Laws*, 759C.
[5] *Laws*, 717B.   [6] *Ibid.*, 717A–B.   [7] *Ibid.*, 717A–B.
[8] *Phaedo*, 118A.   [9] *Republic*, 378A.   [10] *Laws*, 937D.
[11] E.g. *Gorgias*, 472A; and, surprisingly enough, *Laws*, 665A, especially 672A, 672B and 844E.   [12] But see Paul Shorey, *What Plato Said*, pp. 546–7.

religious myths but that he had no time to investigate them. He did not know himself yet, so why should he investigate 'irrelevant things' when he could accept the customary belief about them?[1] Socrates did not usually feel that he could 'confidently assert' his conclusions but he was sure that the 'belief in the duty of inquiring after what we do not know will make us better and braver and less helpless'.[2]

There are reasons to suppose that Plato wished to restore the state religion[3] and this is the strongest kind of evidence for acceptance, for surely no one would wish to restore that in which he did not have faith. The attempt to clean up the account of the Olympic gods, so that they would not appear to commit the foolishnesses of mortal men, is a case in point.[4] Those who do not believe that the gods exist, that they care for man, and that they cannot be turned aside by sacrifices and prayers, are to be imprisoned.[5] Priests should not be disturbed in their duties, and others who are needed should be established.[6]

That Plato believed in many gods can hardly be doubted, because of his repeated references to them,[7] especially the statement, 'All things are full of gods',[8] which would seem to commit him to pantheism. More evidence of pantheism is contained in the belief that the sun has a soul and that this soul is the soul of a god, and similarly with all the other stars.[9] There were at least two gods, one for good and one for evil,[10] but let us continue to consider that Plato was speaking of God in the singular, on the assumption that the term could be read generically also. There is abundant enough evidence that Socrates believed in the existence of more than one god.[11]

---

[1] *Phaedrus*, 229C–230.   [2] *Meno*, 86B.

[3] Cf. Ronald B. Levinson, *In Defence of Plato* (Cambridge 1953, Harvard Press), p. 189. But see also *op. cit.*, p. 357, n. 265 (4).

[4] *Republic*, 377A; *Euthyphro*, 6A.   [5] *Laws*, 885B, and Book X *passim*.

[6] *Ibid.*, 759.   [7] See e.g. *Laws*, 759; *Republic*, 508a.

[8] *Laws*, 899B.   [9] *Ibid.*, 899B.   [10] *Ibid.*, 896E.

[11] E.g. *Phaedrus*, 273E, 279B; *Philebus*, 25B, 61C.

'Now as for the maker and father of this universe, to find him out is hard, and to speak of him, when one has found him, before all mankind impossible.'[1] Again, 'a word of prayer to the gods, Dionysus or Hephaestus, or whatever power has the prerogative',[2] contains a certain measure of agnosticism. Socrates urged elsewhere that explanation must come 'from a god, if there is any god to listen to my prayers'.[3] Those who pretend to be children of the god speak without proofs either probable or exact.[4] How can we accept the idea of a god who is 'an immortal animal having soul and body conjoined in one and grown together for all time?'[5] There are occasions when the whole Olympic pantheon fares no better.[6] The element of scepticism necessary to attack the self-seeking of so much religious adherence has been under-estimated in the criticism of the *Euthyphro*, a work of realism in religion. But the tempering of super-naturalism is not by any means confined to this dialogue. There is, for instance, the *Philebus*, and there are others. Parmenides asserted in the dialogue named after him that God could not know the particulars of our world nor have any knowledge of human affairs, and Socrates seemed to agree.[7] There is clear evidence that the Ideas or Forms were not thoughts in the mind of God for Plato; to the contrary, if he could not know particulars he could and did know universals, and he is said to contemplate the Ideas.[8] God knows the Ideas, but they are independent of Him and not subordinated to Him.[9] God finds the Ideas or Forms and the receptacle or space both eternal and uncreated, ready-made, so to speak, and He mixes them.[10] The Ideas contain the Idea also of necessity, whereas chance

---

[1] *Timaeus*, 28C, A. E. Taylor trans.
[2] *Philebus*, 61C, A. E. Taylor trans.   [3] *Ibid.*, 25B.
[4] *Timaeus*, 40E ff.   [5] *Phaedrus*, 246C–D, H. N. Fowler trans.
[6] *Euthyphro*, 5D–E.   [7] *Parmenides*, 134C–E.
[8] *Phaedrus*, 247D. See R. Demos, *op. cit.*, pp. 119, 123–4.
[9] Sir David Ross, *Plato's Theory of Ideas* (Oxford 1951, Clarendon Press), pp. 43–4; 78–9.
[10] See R. Demos, *op. cit.*, p. 106.

belongs to existence. But the proverb is right: God Himself cannot compel necessity.[1] There is a strong role of chance in human affairs, but chance does co-operate with God.[2] Thus Plato clearly believed in the reality of both worlds and considered God an intermediary with control over the actualization of the Ideas. He strengthened being at the cost of creation, and confined God's efforts to persuading the receptacle to receive the Forms, and so enters the picture after the facts, with His power greatly diminished as a result of encountering two intractable levels. God is hard to find and when found He is found to be neither all-knowing nor all-powerful. Furthermore, the worst impiety is that God can be wooed by prayer;[3] to suppose that the gods do not exist, that they are careless, or that they could be bribed, are crimes.[4] God, in fact, does not have need of man or of anything.[5] It is improbable that the gods should feel either pleasure or its opposite.[6] God is simply the cause or the intelligence behind the universe.[7]

Plato sought the divine in things which were both concrete and eternal, which the Ideas assuredly were not. Indeed the only concrete things which were also eternal, so far as he could discover, were the stars, which he thought to be fixed.[8] In this way he escaped from the narrow confines of the civic religion and moved towards the cosmic without being limited to a personal conception of it. In this he was followed by Aristotle.[9]

God leads us towards the good life[10] but the Good is not God.[11] The Ideas constitute a second natural order, not a super-natural order. The Ideas are not personalities and the highest Idea is therefore not God.

[1] *Laws*, 741A. [2] *Ibid.*, 709B. [3] *Ibid.*, 906D.
[4] *Ibid.*, 885B. [5] *Euthyphro*, 15A. [6] *Philebus*, 33B.
[7] *Ibid.*, 30C. [8] *Timaeus*, 47C; *Laws*, 818D.
[9] *De Caelo*, I, 10–12, and II, 1. [10] *Crito*, 54E.
[11] See Paul Shorey, *What Plato Said*, p. 231: 'But the statement that the idea of good *is* God is meaningless.' On the other side, is Constantin Ritter, *The Essence of Plato's Philosophy* (London 1933, Allen and Unwin), p. 374: 'the highest Idea, the Idea of the good, is nothing else but God'. The view taken here is Shorey's.

The good is a pattern[1] and so a god. Evil is disorganization and so not merely human.[2] Both good and evil are abstract, and neither confined to God nor man, although anything which is divine cannot be evil,[3] and what is evil can also be funny.[4] Reason is the guide of the good life,[5] truth the leader of all goods.[6] Intelligence is closer to the good than pleasure: the good has beauty, symmetry and truth.[7] The right use of the good depends on knowledge of the good.[8] That moral considerations dominate is as plain as that Crete is an island;[9] men desire the good[10] and in working towards the good life, example is better than admonition.[11]

Immortality is an unknown. To say that no harm can come to a good man is not to say that an after-life is assured.[12] To the contrary, the soul as well as the body fades.[13] A sleep or a departure to a better world: both sound good.[14] Plato was not sure.[15] After all, there is no absolute distinction to be drawn between man and nature; there is a *nomos* for material objects, too.[16] This is not, of course, to degrade man by bringing him down to the natural world: beautiful things partake of absolute beauty.[17] The natural sort of immortality lies through one's children and their children.[18] Heroes, as Hesiod tells us, return to earth as hallowed spirits who become guardians of the good and averters of evil.[19]

The notion of justice is closer than the good to God, though both are close, for justice is the minister of God.[20] In at least two dialogues we learn that holiness is a subdivision of justice: all that is holy is just, but not all that is just is holy;[21] and, again,

---

[1] *Republic*, 540A. [2] *Laws*, 906B–C. [3] *Phaedrus*, 242E.
[4] *Ibid.*, 242E. [5] *Gorgias*, 527E. [6] *Laws*, 730C. [7] *Philebus*, 65A.
[8] *Republic*, 505B–C. Cf. also *Euthydemus*, 291B; *Politicus* 305E; *Cratylus*, 398B. [9] *Laws*, 662B. [10] *Gorgias*, 466E. ff. [11] *Laws*, 729B.
[12] *Apology*, 30C–D; *Gorgias*, 527D. [13] *Symposium*, 196A.
[14] *Apology*, 40–1. [15] *Phaedo*, 95B ff. [16] *Ibid.*, 97C–D.
[17] *Ibid.*, 100C. [18] *Laws*, 721C. [19] *Republic*, 469A.
[20] *Laws*, 715D–E.
[21] *Euthyphro*, 12A. Religion is a matter of justice, but justice is not simply a matter of logic. See for instance in Aristophanes, *The Clouds*, for the distinction between the just and the unjust *logos*.

the possession of wealth is of most value to the good man, for it helps a man not to cheat and 'not to remain in debt to a god'.[1] On the other hand, however, it is better to suffer wrong than to do wrong.[2] The *Republic* is an essay on justice, justice in this world—and the next. In the course of the attempt to discover the meaning of justice in this world, an ideal state is pictured in the abstract, a paradigm laid up in heaven[3] by which we govern ourselves on earth. Justice is the best thing for the soul itself.[4] The just man has his reward equally from gods and men, and in this world, as well as in the next,[5] the balance between the divine and the human, the heaven and the earthly, is maintained as neatly as possible. He must seek 'the life that is seated in the mean and shun the excess in either direction, both in this world so far as may be and in all the life to come; for this is the greatest happiness for man'.[6]

One of the strongest arguments for the Greek version of realism in Plato's religion is the emphasis he gave to the attempt to establish a good life on this earth. The two longest dialogues, the *Republic* and the *Laws*, though both containing evidence for the belief in the immortality of the soul, are chiefly efforts to draw up the blue-prints for a successful commonwealth in this world.

The concern with the next world seems always to be personal, while the concern with this world is social. This distinction, as we shall note very much later, has had disastrous consequences. However, Plato evidently appreciated the need for compromise, and for living in the world in terms of the conditions imposed by the world. It is a ridiculous thing to have only divine knowledge, and Socrates agrees with Protarchus that man must have knowledge also of the human sphere if he is to find his way.[7] The world has its autonomy and when God lets it go it revolves away from the way in which He turns it.[8] Everywhere, then, there is the mixture of the divine and the mundane, the human

---

[1] *Republic*, 331B.　　　　　　　　　[2] *Gorgias*, 469C. See also *Crito*, 49C.
[3] *Republic*, 592B.　　　[4] *Ibid.*, 612B.　　　[5] *Ibid.*, 612C–613E.
[6] *Ibid.*, 619A.　　　[7] *Philebus*, 62A–B.　　　[8] *Statesman*, 269C–D.

body and soul, for example.[1] Knowledge is of the divine,[2] yes, but it is not of the divine only:[3] it is knowledge also of transitory things.[4] And the mixture of the immutable and the transitory is capable of giving us the most adorable life.[5]

Evidently, we can succeed in the next world entirely in selfish terms for there it is every man for himself; whereas success in this world compels more social co-operation and consists in the main in some sort of social order whereby we may get along best with our fellow-men. We are led to assume that there is in the next world no society of immortal souls. Putting aside the pointed observation that this would seem to call for the death of ethical considerations along with our bodies, it is clear that Plato meant to include among his most important concerns the establishment of the good life in this world for religious reasons, not by the raising of a church (there was evidently to be no such institution in the *Republic*, at least) but rather by the observance of such holiness as the rendering of justice could accomplish. Justice, of course, requires the exercise of reason. Religious realism places reason over emotion[6] 'prayer is a perilous practice for him who is devoid of reason'.[7] The good life was a social life for the Greek citizen of Athens, and for the other city-states, too, for that matter. The holy life in no sense indicated a withdrawal from the affairs of this world, but rather an ethical mandate in regard to the mode of social participation.

C. SOCRATES AND RELIGIOUS NATURALISM

The final distillation of the Greek version of realism in the religious philosophy of Plato consists in the example of the life of Socrates and the teaching which can be elicited from his life. To some extent it must be possible to say that Plato had his own religious ideas which he expressed in two ways: through

[1] *Philebus*, 30A–B.   [2] *Laws*, 875C–D.   [3] *Philebus*, 62B–E.
[4] *Ibid.*, 61D.   [5] *Ibid.*, 61E.   [6] *Laws*, 713E–714A.
[7] *Ibid.*, 688B, R. G. Bury trans.

Socrates as his spokesman, and through the example of the life and martyrdom of Socrates. These do not always mean the same thing, and we shall try to maintain the distinction by turning now to examine the way of life of Socrates and its possible import. In short, we propose to look at Socrates in the role of saviour, with Plato as one of his disciples.

The idea is not a new one, though it has not always been looked upon with favour. Greek scholars who are also committed Christians find the analogy between the ministry of Socrates and that of Jesus odious, while conceding the remarkable parallel.[1] The true religious life for the Greek realist, judging by the behaviour of Socrates, is how to conduct oneself in this world, not how to escape from it. The materialist would have to be acquisitive of wealth in order to be consistent, the idealist would renounce it altogether; but the realist would admit neither alternative, for he would wish to show how he could deal with materials in terms of ideals, how he could treat the things of substance in terms of those of logic. Socrates lived as a realist; his life was devoted to inquiry of a detached kind. It was Socrates' life which led to Aristotle's kind of holiness, the holiness of rational inquiry.

Human beings are and perhaps always have been predominantly interested in survival. The selfish concern to continue in existence takes priority over all others; it is the prerogative passion. The practical interest in survival long antedates the theory of evolution. Indeed, all religions are based on the effort to cater to the personal desire for survival, and the theory of the immortality of the soul also rests on it. But there is a religion, and a philosophy, which are not based on it, and these have regard for the discovery of the truth *whatever it may be*. 'The unexamined life is not worth living', Socrates said.[2] But the search for the truth undertaken by Socrates and recommended by him was without motive of personal survival, and was for the sake

[1] E.g. Lane Cooper, *Plato: On the Trial and Death of Socrates* (Ithaca 1941, Cornell University Press), Preface, pp. vii-viii. [2] *Apology*, 38A.

of the truth rather than for the sake of the seeker after the truth. Socrates said, 'But you, if you do as I ask, will give little thought to Socrates and much more to the truth'.[1]

Socrates refused to undertake political action. He was not a politician,[2] not a public man;[3] he was reported to have been capable of prolonged meditation, once having remained in a trance for twenty-four hours.[4] The still small voice of conscience, the divine sign or monitor[5] which he so often said always spoke to him at critical times had a mystical flavour; yet it was the voice of a rationalist, for it never told him what to do but only what not to do. His conscience, in short, was a logical conscience and he promised to obey reason only.[6] He was martyred for it in the event of 399 B.C. when on orders of a state jury he was required to drink the fatal cup of hemlock.

Professor Cooper chose the death of Socrates and of Jesus to make the unfavourable comparison for Socrates, and he quoted Luke to clinch the argument: 'Father, into thy hands I commend my spirit'.[7] Professor Cooper added, 'No pagan could say it'.[8] This is true; Socrates' view was somewhat different. We detect it in his address to the jury which condemned him to death. 'To fear death, gentlemen, is nothing else than to think one is wise when one is not; for it is thinking one knows what one does not know.'[9] No Christian could have said it. There are of course other passages in the *Dialogues* in which opinions are credited to Socrates that a Christian could have said, though even here we should remember that 'All the remarkable traits in Socrates' teaching which seem to have the charm of Christian feeling are actually Hellenic in origin'.[10]

Some members of the band of disciples are well known. They included, besides Plato, Euclid of Megara, Antisthenes the Cynic, Diogenes of Corinth, Aristippus the Cyrenaic,

---

[1] *Phaedo*, 91C, H. N. Fowler trans.   [2] *Apology*, 31C.
[3] *Gorgias*, 473E.   [4] *Symposium*, 220C–D.
[5] *Apology*, 31C; *Euthyphro*, 3B; *Republic*, 496C; *Theaetetus*, 151A; *Euthydemus*, 273A; *Phaedrus*, 242C.   [6] *Crito*, 46B.   [7] *Luke* xxiii., 46.
[8] *Plato*, p. viii.   [9] *Apology*, 29A.   [10] Werner Jaeger, *Paideia*, Vol. II, p. 42.

Xenophon, and others. It was a rich fare that Socrates and Plato spread before their contemporaries, abundant and alive but full of contradictions and hence suggestive of many positions which while irreconcilable still stemmed from the same source. The religious import of the moral teaching and behaviour of the Cynics and Cyrenaics had a Socratic flavour. The later heads of the Middle Academy and of the New Academy had beliefs which could without difficulty be traced to Plato, although their subsequent reputation has been to mark a departure. Both Arcesilaus and Carneades, for instance, could have rightfully claimed that their religious scepticism came right out of the *Euthyphro.* And so could the religious scepticism of Euripides, who is quoted so often by Plato.

So much for the life itself. What lessons can we learn religion-wise by contemplating it as an exemplar? A Gospel According to Socrates was first suggested by Erasmus. 'As Christianity is gradually reduced to a natural religion, and Jesus to a teacher, Socrates along with Jesus becomes another great teacher of natural religion to whom we can pray', such was the Erasmian interpretation of the Platonic Socrates.[1] Socrates taught that knowledge is distinct from the knower, and that it is divine. He taught that the only evil is ignorance. He taught that knowledge begins with the limitations of the self, and that the moral law is to be found in nature. The 'Platonic tolerance' of which Yeats wrote issues from Plato's willingness to let the adversary be heard, whether that adversary be motivated by the opportunism of the Sophist or the muscle of a bully. 'Thrasymachus and Protagoras are . . . there in the dialogues to be destroyed, yet they represent something in human nature—the bully or the Sophist in all of us—that is indestructible.'[2]

What Plato was attacking always was the certainty of other

[1] Philip Merlan, in the *Journal of the History of Ideas,* Vol. VIII (1947), p. 416, n. 33.

[2] *The Resurrection,* a play, quoted in 'Platonic Tolerance' by G. S. Fraser, a review of *Autobiographies* by W. B. Yeats (London 1955, Macmillan), in *The New Statesman and Nation* for May 21, 1955.

men's beliefs, not their right to have beliefs but the absoluteness of their beliefs. As we shall later see, none of Plato's successors will be capable of a piece of writing so inconclusive in its entirety as the *Laches*, for instance. For Plato some measure of uncertainty as to what there is was always present in the atmosphere of his beliefs, sufficient at least to protect him from absolutes. He was engaged primarily in the search for truth, and the emphasis is kept on the search. The search for the truth would not be undertaken by a man who thought that he knew it or by one who held that it did not exist. And so the curiosity of Socrates who regarded detached inquiry as holy was based on a belief both in his own ignorance and in the objective existence of a knowledge which he sought. He taught the limits of ignorance, and that the beginning of wisdom is the fear of false knowledge, upon which no true happiness, no ultimate satisfaction, can be founded. He knew the enemy of true knowledge as absolutism; the only absolute that the true seeker after truth can accept is reason itself; and the only method, man's ability to reason. The goal is the knowledge of positive reason.

There is nothing inherently irrational about religious questions, only about some of the answers. The questions themselves ask about being—and for directions. In Plato's approach to religion made from the standpoint of metaphysical realism, with its two-storeyed natural world of fact and of logic, examined by sense experience and by reason, there is an interest and a search, and a minimum of the emotionalism which usually accompanies all super-natural explanations.

Plato's religious ideas have to do with the background assumptions of the public religion of the Greeks in the absence of an official creed. He tried to set down, as did Aristotle after him, what he thought the practice of the religion meant. We have other reasons for interpreting it, for we are faced with creeds. And Philo and Augustine had their different reasons as well, for, as we shall see later, their work was to reconcile Plato's philosophy with alien creeds.

PART TWO

THE RELIGIOUS INFLUENCE
OF PLATO

CHAPTER VI

ARISTOTLE'S RELIGION

The question of whether Aristotle's philosophy was that of Platonism or that of a position opposed to Platonism has been greatly debated ever since Porphyry wrote his Introduction to Aristotle's *Categories* in the third century. It is still being debated today. The assumptions underlying the present work include the proposition that Aristotle is the leading Platonist. There is very little in Aristotle's metaphysics and ethics and psychology that was not first in Plato. On some points they differed. But Aristotle did two things: he arranged the ideas of Plato in orderly fashion, and he opposed the early Neo-Pythagorean interpretation of Plato made by the nephew who inherited the Academy in Aristotle's day: Speusippus.

There are, however, very many ideas in the discussions of religion in Plato that are not to be found in Aristotle, or, if found, are not given anything like the same emphasis. Chief among these, perhaps, is the idea of immortality, second only, perhaps, to the upholding of the conventional religion. The difference between Plato and Aristotle is the prevailing note of scepticism in Aristotle which exists also in Plato but which is more consistently maintained in Aristotle. Scepticism in religion is the healthy principle that the evidence ought not to be exceeded. In the *Phaedo* it is exceeded, and it is exceeded in the *Laws*, although not so in the *Euthyphro* or the *Apology*. In Aristotle the principle is always present; and if he is misled, it is the facts that have misled him in most cases. For temperamentally, Aristotle is a partial sceptic.

Be that as it may, however, the similarity of Aristotle's religious ideas to one of the two religions we profess to have distinguished in the Platonic *Dialogues* is clear. The Greek religion of realism, its realistic philosophy and its naturalism, as these are found in Plato[1] are, as we shall see, in accord with the theology advanced by Aristotle.

A supporting piece of evidence is Aristotle's fondness for Euripides. Aristotle quotes him more than the other poets, more than Aeschylus for instance. That Aristotle was familiar with the plays of Euripides, the number of references to him in the extant works of Aristotle attests: there are some twenty-nine direct references and some seven indirect. Moreover, although Aristotle was not above endorsing the ridiculing of a side of Euripides that he did not like,[2] he also quoted him often with approval.[3] Euripides is frequently made to speak for the poets,[4] though, it is true, not on specific points of religion. No doubt the influence is there. But Aristotle formulated his own religious ideas under the naturalistic side of Plato; and although they are often in agreement with the Euripidean outlook, the influence would be difficult now to show. But the point is that scepticism, like faith, is never dead; only, where the object of faith changes from religion to religion, the object of scepticism is always the same, namely, religion. And the caution to believe about religion no more than reason and fact would allow, was learned by Euripides, possibly from Xenophanes, and passed on, possibly to Aristotle.

Admittedly, Plato was more concerned with religion than was Aristotle, if the number of pages devoted to religious questions are any indication of interest. Aristotle's theology is a topic which does not seem to have troubled him overmuch. 'Aristotle says excellently that we should nowhere be more modest than in matters of religion. If we compose ourselves

---

[1] See above, Ch. V(B).   [2] *De Sensu*, 443b30.
[3] E.g. *Ethica Nicomachea*, 1142a2; *Magna Moralia*, 1209b36; *Ethica Eudemia*, 1244a10; *Politica* 1277a18.
[4] E.g. *Magna Moralia*, 1212b27; *Politica*, 1252b8.

before we enter temples. . . . how much more should we do this
when we discuss the constellations, the stars, and the nature of
the Gods, to guard against saying anything rashly and impru-
dently, either not knowing it to be true or knowing it to be
false!' The words are Philo's but they do sound like Aristotle's.[1]
Aristotle's own words are, however, no less emphatic. The
common sense based on reason and fact which he maintained
in the face of other topics did not desert him in religion. 'Our
forefathers in the most remote ages have handed down to their
posterity a tradition, in the form of a myth, that these bodies,
i.e. the heavenly bodies, are gods and that the divine encloses
the whole of nature.'[2] This Aristotle accepted, but he could not
accept much more, for he goes on to add, 'The rest of the tradition
has been added later in mythical form with a view to the persuasion
of the multitude and to its legal and utilitarian expediency',[3]
such as that the gods have human form. Aristotle has left us
a fragmentary account only; but in those of his works which
have survived we can detect the outlines of a set of beliefs
concerning nature, God and man, and the relations between
them, which is at least not inconsistent with his general position.
Aristotle's chief concern seems to have been with nature and
with man, in that order, and to a far lesser extent with God.
He has left us books, for instance, devoted to nature, such as the
Physics, and others devoted to man, such as the *De Anima*,
but none which is altogether devoted to God. We have to
reconstruct his views on God from comments scattered throughout the other books.

First, then, as to nature. Nature is 'the immediate material
substratum of things which have in themselves a principle of
motion or change'.[4] Aristotle's metaphysics begins with the
categories, and his categories are those of *physical* nature:

[1] *Sen.* Q.N.7.30. See *Select Fragments* in the *Works of Aristotle* ed. by
Sir David Ross (Oxford 1952, Clarendon Press), p. 87. Philo quoted Aristotle
with approval but he did not follow him in this.
[2] *Metaphysics*, 1074b1, Ross trans.
[3] *Ibid.*, 1074b5.　　　　　　　　　　　　　[4] *Physics*, 193a28–30.

substance first and then the modifications of substance: quantity, relation, quality and the opposites, and motion. Matter (*hulé*)[1] is that aspect of substance which is capable of taking on form. Form (*eîdos*) is the shape specified in the definition of the thing.[2] Form for Aristotle is always immanent form. The formal and the material are causes of change, and so are the efficient cause, which sets things in motion, and the final cause, or that towards which things move. Every actual thing comes-to-be and passes-away, and in these processes of becoming makes the potential actual and the actual potential again.

The universe is eternal. 'The same things have always existed', in the sense that 'actuality is prior to potency'.[3] The change from potency to actuality could come about through art, nature, luck or spontaneity.[4] There is a first movement that is not moved by anything else,[5] and it occupies the circumference of the world.[6] The final cause is a last term, so that the process is not infinite.[7]

The next category in the order of the understanding of nature is that of human nature. The transition from the inorganic to the organic in nature takes place by way of the soul. 'The knowledge of the soul ... contributes above ... all, to our understanding of Nature.'[8] The soul is 'the first grade of actuality of a natural body having life potentially in it', i.e. 'of a naturally organized body'.[9] It is 'the essence of the whole living body'.[10] There could be no separate existence of the soul unless it could act;[11] but instead it is the cause and movement.[12] 'The soul is inseparable from its body';[13] 'it is not a body but is something relative to a body'.[14] It is part of nature[15] and itself has many parts:[16] sensation and knowledge are within the soul;[17] while the mind, 'that

---

[1] *Physics*, 190b24.　　[2] *Ibid.*, 193a30.　　[3] *Metaphysics*, 1072a5–10.
[4] *Ibid.*, 1070a5.　　[5] *Physics*, 242a19.　　[6] *Ibid.*, 267b8.
[7] *Metaphysics*, 994b9.　　　　　　　　　　[8] *De Anima*, 402a5.
[9] *Ibid.*, 412a 28–b5.　　[10] *Ibid.*, 415b11.　　[11] *Ibid.*, 402b10.
[12] *Ibid.*, 432a17.　　[13] *Ibid.*, 413a4.　　[14] *Ibid.*, 414a20.
[15] *Ibid.*, 403a28.　　[16] *Ibid.*, 433b1–4.　　[17] *Ibid.*, 417b23.

whereby the soul thinks and judges',[1] 'is in its essential nature activity',[2] and 'seems to be an independent substance implanted within the soul and to be incapable of being destroyed'.[3] The soul, then, does not survive the body, but the mind does, but still the mind is not the person. As Guthrie says, 'The description of the thinking part of us in *De Anima*, iii, 4 and 5, makes it clear that there can be no survival of individual personality and no room therefore for an Orphic or Platonic eschatology of rewards and punishments, nor ... for a cycle of reincarnations'.[4]

We have next to consider nature and God together. The world of nature is a world of physical and biological existence. It is uncreated and eternal; it was not created by God but has always existed and will always exist. 'God and nature create nothing that has not its use.'[5] Philo insisted that 'Aristotle was surely speaking piously and devoutly when he insisted that the world is ungenerated and imperishable, and convicted of grave ungodliness those who maintain the opposite'.[6] Sextus Empiricus reminded us that 'Aristotle used to say that men's thoughts of gods sprang from two sources—the experience of the soul, and the phenomena of the heavens'.[7] The world of nature is the work of the gods.[8] He was quoted as having insisted that 'the world itself is divine, a reasonable immortal animal',[9] that 'the world itself is a god'.[10] Nature consists of an actuality of separate individual objects together with their potentialities of matter possessed by forms, continually changing in terms of opposite qualities. The world of nature is one of substance and becoming, of concrete individuals together with their modifications, engaged in continual motion. However, 'The world refuses to be governed badly'.[11] Nature depends on God[12] who introduces order into the unlimited. God arranged that coming-to-be should itself come-to-be perpetually, the closest approximation to eternal

[1] *De Anima*, 429a21.   [2] *Ibid.*, 430a17.   [3] *Ibid.*, 408b18.
[4] Guthrie, *The Greeks and Their Gods*, p. 370.   [5] *De Caelo*, 271a33.
[6] *Select Fragments*, ed. by Ross, p. 88.   [7] *Ibid.*, p. 84.
[8] *Ibid.*, p. 86.   [9] *Ibid.*, p. 94.   [10] *Ibid.*, p. 97.
[11] *Metaphysics*, 1076a4.   [12] *Ibid.*, 1072b14.

being under the condition that not all things can possess being at the same time,[1] the opposites, for instance. God holds the universe together;[2] and He does so, moreover, by being loved.[3] The relation between God and the world of nature in-sofar as it is active is one prompted by the world. God is the supreme object of desire; He moves the world by His active intellect. He is passive towards the world but the world is prompted to be active towards Him by moving, and this means by seeking His perfection. God, then, is the Unmoved Mover.

We have sketched briefly Aristotle's conceptions of nature, the soul and the relations of nature to God. We have now to look at his conception of God (or of the gods).

Men imagine gods and their way of life to be human, he said.[4] Some people say that there are gods but in human form, but they are 'positing nothing but eternal men'.[5] Xenophanes said that the One is God but this can be neglected entirely as being a little too naïve.[6] There is one prime mover and so there is only one heaven,[7] according to Aristotle; but since he spoke, like Plato, indifferently of 'God' or of 'the gods' and posited a different god for each of the fixed stars, it is difficult to tell whether he ever decided how many gods there are— one or forty-seven or fifty-five.[8] The God-like property of the heavenly bodies rests on their immutability, which is evident to the senses. 'For all men have some conception of the nature of the gods, and all who believe in the existence of gods at all, whether barbarian or Greek, agree in allotting the highest place to the deity, surely because they suppose that immortal is linked with immortal and regard any other supposition as inconceivable.'[9] 'God is thought to be among the causes of all things and

---

[1] *De Gen. et Cor.*, 336b30–35. [2] *Politics*, 1326a32.
[3] *Metaphysics*, 1072b14. [4] *Politics*, 1252b24.
[5] *Metaphysics*, 997b10. [6] *Ibid.*, 986b25–28.
[7] *Ibid.*, 1074a32. [8] *Ibid.*, 1074a12. But see also *Physics*, 259a.
[9] *De Caelo*: 270b5–12. Cf. *passim* for the evidence of the senses concerning the existence of the star-god as 'primary bodily substance'.

to be a first principle.[1] God is removed to a great distance,[2] and, 'as a brute has no vice or virtue, neither has a god';[3] his state is higher than virtue. That God even now possesses the good, does not mean that anyone gains.[4]

Homer appropriately called Zeus king, for he is the king of the gods.[5] Like the good, God is better than the things that are praised.[6] 'The gods surpass us most decisively in all good things'.[7] God is 'a living being that partakes of knowledge'[8] yet ' "intelligible living being" could not be a property of God'.[9] Aristotle is very clear in rejecting the personal anthropomorphic gods. The gods 'do not make contracts or return deposits', they do not perform 'liberal acts', they have no money.[10] 'God has but does not use the capacity to do bad things any more than a good man.[11] The activity of God is immortality (i.e. eternal life)'.[12] God is eternal, self-dependent, a living being, most good.[13] It would be silly to suppose the gods active or productive, for what would they do or produce? But they are alive, and there is only one thing left for living beings who are neither active nor productive; they are contemplative.[14] God has no external actions over and above His own energies, but this does not take away from His perfection.[15] 'The activity of God, which surpasses all others in blessedness, must be contemplative',[16] since He is neither productive nor active. 'Thought is held to be the most divine of things observed by us.'[17] God thinks about His own thoughts;[18] God's thinking is a thinking on thinking,[19] and He thinks eternally.[20] We assume the gods to be above all other beings blessed and happy.[21] God

---

[1] *Metaphysics*, 983a8, Ross trans. [2] *Nicomachean Ethics*, 1159a5.
[3] *Ibid.*, 1145a25, Ross trans. [4] *Ibid.*, 1166a22.
[5] *Politics*, 1259b13. [6] *Nicomachean Ethics*, 1101b30.
[7] *Ibid.*, 1158b35. [8] *Topica*, 132b11.
[9] *Ibid.*, 136b6–7. [10] *Nicomachean Ethics*, 1178b10–15.
[11] *Topica*, 126a34–36. [12] *De Caelo*, 286a9.
[13] *Metaphysics*, 1072b28. [14] *Nicomachean Ethics*, 1178b8.
[15] *Politics*, 1325b28. [16] *Nicomachean Ethics*, 1178b21.
[17] *Metaphysics*, 1074b16. [18] *Ibid.*, 1072b19.
[19] *Ibid.*, 1074b34. [20] *Ibid.*, 1075a10. [21] *Nicomachean Ethics*, 1178b8.

enjoys a single and simple pleasure: for He does not move, and pleasure is found more in rest than in movement.[1] God is happy by reason of His own nature.[2] God's actuality is pleasure.[3]

Such activity is ceaseless and eternal, nevertheless is drawn towards a goal and the goal is its God. All that is not God is form and matter; no matter, then no form; but God is the only form existing without matter. Since God has no matter He cannot change; He is perfect and so has no reason to change. He is instead the eternal cause of all the change in the world, the unmoved mover, the pure actuality. But though He does not change He is continually active, and His activity consists entirely in the thought of what is highest and best: He thinks about Himself and so about His own thoughts, and this is pure enjoyment. As we are sometimes, so He is always.[4]

About the role of man in relation to God in theological terms, Aristotle is clear. To praise the gods is to refer them to our standards, which seems absurd.[5] Praise involves a reference to something else; and to what else would you refer the gods? Instead, it is better to call them blessed and happy.[6] God cannot be injured and therefore cannot be wronged;[7] yet one should honour the gods[8] for they are absolutely honourable.[9] The religious life is the rational life, the holy life is the life of reason. 'If reason is divine, then, in comparison with man, life according to it is divine in comparison with human life.'[10] Expenditures connected with the gods are called honourable—votive offerings, buildings, and sacrifices—and similarly with any form of religious worship.[11] 'It is enough with the gods, as with one's parents, to give them what one can.'[12] The philosopher is dearest to the gods. For if they have any care for human affairs, as they are thought to have, it must be for what is best and most like

---

[1] *Nicomachean Ethics*, 1154b26.   [2] *Politics*, 1323b23.
[3] *Metaphysics*, 1072b16.   [4] *Ibid.*, 1072b14–15.
[5] *Nicomachean Ethics*, 1101b19.   [6] *Ibid.*, 122b19.
[7] *Topica*, 109b33.   [8] *Ibid.*, 105a5.   [9] *Ibid.*, 115b32.
[10] *Nicomachean Ethics*, 1177b30.   [11] *Ibid.*, 1122b19.   [12] *Ibid.*, 1164b5.

them, i.e. reason.[1] 'Now if there is any gift of gods to men, it is reasonable that happiness should be god-given because it is the best.'[2] Since God is pure form and we grasp pure form only in the mind, we approach closest to the condition of God when we reason. Faith for Aristotle meant degree of belief, and degree of belief was determined by the force of demonstrative reasoning.[3] Faith as opposed to or divorced from reason was a later and non-Greek conception. Reason is the divine part of the human being. To be 'immortal as far as we can'[4] means to think the most abstract thoughts, for 'the faculty of active thought' alone seems 'capable of separate existence'.[5] In short, there may be a survival of the disembodied reason, which may mean simply the reunion of human reason with the divine reason.

The moral order is a social order; man is an animal as well as rational, and so for practical ends he needs to have an ordered society. The family is necessary for sexual reasons and the state for economic ones. The state is served if there is the widest diversity of interests, but strict justice must be administered, and for this constitutional law must be held supreme. But all this means a concession to natural conditions and does not represent man at his highest and best. Moral virtue demands the good life of practical conduct, but the best life is the intellectual life which searches for knowledge for its own sake.

As the Greeks saw it, the religious problems are centred about nature: nature, God and man, and the relations between them. God is remote from nature, whereas man is imbedded in nature; but neither God nor man can be understood apart from nature. The very remoteness of God is measured in terms of nature, although it is of concern chiefly to man and neither to nature nor, for that matter, to God. God, for Aristotle, is

[1] *Nicomachean Ethics*, 1179a25–30. [2] *Ibid.*, 1099b11.
[3] For an excellent discussion of 'faith' in Plato and Aristotle, see H. A. Wolfson, *The Philosophy of the Church Fathers* (Cambridge 1956, Harvard University Press), Vol. I, Ch. VI.
[4] *Nicomachean Ethics*, 1177b30. [5] *De Anima*, 413b24 ff.

remote and draws us towards Him because of what He is, not what He does, though we can and should imitate in a small way what He does. God is remote, contemplative and quiet, utterly charming, and unconcerned with practical human affairs, a sort of immortal prototype of what Aristotle must have wanted himself to be. The philosopher is most like the gods in that he reasons most of mortal men, and he is therefore dearest to the gods as well.[1] Thus we are left of the religious problems chiefly nature and man, which are entirely naturalistic concerns. Aristotle did not devote many pages of his extant works to the topic of God or the gods. But what he has to say on the topic is in accord with the indigenous Greek religion and with the religion of Plato's realism. It is not in accord with the Orphic idealistic tradition and therefore had little if any influence on the Neo-platonists.

It was in fact to be many centuries before Aristotle was to have any influence on the western religions. His effect was first felt in any force in the thirteenth century—some seventeen hundred years after his death. His philosophy was incorporated into the Jewish religion by Maimonides, into the Moslem religion by Averroes, and, slightly later, into Christianity by Aquinas, and we shall pause to examine these events in chapter X. Suffice to say here that when the western religions did incorporate the works of Aristotle, it was his metaphysics and his ethics rather than his specifically religious ideas which were found the most congenial. A Neoplatonic idealism was combined with a kind of nominalism: these have more in common than either has with realism. Aristotle's own religious ideas are too thoroughly Greek, too metaphysically realistic, too naturalistic, too anti-Orphic,[2] too rational, to be anything but incompatible with a transcendental, super-natural and revealed religion, which all three of the western group are. This antagonism, which is inherent in Aristotle's religion, has usually been passed over; and the inconsistency of adopting his metaphysics, which is

[1] *Ethica Nicomachea*, 1179a25–30.   [2] *De Anima*, 410b28.

ARISTOTLE'S RELIGION 95

consistent with his religious ideas, while at the same time rejecting those religious ideas, is simply ignored.

Aristotle's religion, in short, is one of naturalism, whereas the three western religions, which in the thirteenth century adopted his metaphysics in combination with Neoplatonism, were committed to super-naturalism. It is no small wonder that they omitted and overlooked Aristotle's own religion; the wonder is that granting its existence they were able to reconcile their beliefs with his metaphysics without it.

CHAPTER VII

PHILO'S PHILOSOPHY OF RELIGION

A. THE BIRTH OF NEOPLATONISM

With Aristotle, our account of the greatest name in religious Platonism comes to an end: there was only one. The Stoics we shall consider later, but they were not in this class. The greatest Platonist was born and died with Aristotle. The story of religious Platonism is taken up in a serious way in another form and its development occurred in another city. The Greek philosophy the Jews, Christians and Moslems took over was not Hellenic but Hellenistic: it issued from Alexandria, not from Athens. Alexandrian philosophy derived from Athenian but it took a different direction; it operated from a different set of presuppositions, and it was qualitatively different.

As a matter of fact, the pivotal figures in a field are rarely the earliest. For our purposes, the first great name in the Platonic tradition so far as ideas on religion are concerned is Aristotle; the second, Philo. The effect of Aristotle on the western religions was not felt until much later, almost not until the end of the Middle Ages, in fact; whereas the effect of Philo began much earlier. It was Philo and not Aristotle who first carried the effect of Plato into the western religions. Although Philo's name is not so well known in this connection, the term, Neoplatonism, is; and Philo was the chief founder of Neoplatonism. Aristotle, however, as we shall see when we come to the successors of Plotinus: Porphyry, Iamblichus and Proclus, played no small role. 'The name, Neo-Platonism, which may be retained, since its use is so firmly established is really too narrow, and it has been rightly remarked that its representatives might as well be called Neo-Aristotelians.'[1] If the arguments in this book be accepted, Aristotle himself was, after all, only the leading Platonist, and so the inclusion of his influence on religion could still be justified in terms of the broader term, Neoplatonism.

Neoplatonism as a philosophy may be distinguished from the philosophy of Plato in many ways. We may choose six.

First and perhaps foremost of these is the predominance in Neoplatonism of an interest in religion, with its subordination of philosophy to religion. The Neoplatonists either failed to distinguish between philosophy and religion while according the emphasis to religion, as Plotinus, or they made a clear distinction between philosophy and religion and, with equal clarity, subordinated philosophy to religion. In revealed religions, such as Judaism was at first and Christianity later, there could be no question of an appeal to reason superior to revelation. Plato was a rationalist, and there was no authority above that of reason. For the Neoplatonists, reason served religion without distinction or was placed in a position inferior to the revelations it was intended to support.

In Philo, as we shall presently note, the triumph of revelation over reason is accomplished by the allegorical method: revelation is made to reveal that it includes, albeit cryptically, the philosophical reasons.

The second way in which the Neoplatonists differ from Plato is in their use of allegory. The method was employed by Porphyry for the textual interpretation of Homer's poems. It was employed widely by the Stoics as a way of accepting the popular religion without having to accept also the superstition and anthropological literalness which was involved in it. Now, in Plato there had been no such method; the *Dialogues* of Plato are of course not works in textual criticism, and Plato

---

[1] Johann Eduard Erdmann, *A History of Philosophy*, trans. by W. S. Hough, 3 vols. (London 1922, Allen and Unwin), Vol. I, p. 236.

was not constrained to make his own ideas out of other writers' words. Whatever Plato was, he was no Platonist. The Neoplatonists often found themselves in this predicament with respect to Plato.

The third important way in which Neoplatonism is distinguished from the philosophy of Plato is in the absoluteness of belief. Plato's method, as we have seen, is one which includes a certain amount of uncertainty; whereas the Neoplatonist is always certain. The method of reason is speculation, and where there is certainty of belief there can be no speculation. The method of revelation is faith, and by faith is meant complete and total surrender to belief regardless of the reasons. The dialectic of Socrates as set forth in the Platonic dialogues was an instrument for probing meanings and for raising questions. The truth was allegedly hard to determine. But not so for Philo. He had the truth already given to him in the Jewish Scriptures, and they left no room for doubts. 'Moses sets no value on probabilities and plausibilities, but follows after truth in its purity.'[1] All of the Neoplatonists were sure that they knew what the truth was. And so they introduced a dogmatism of answers to those very questions about which the Greeks were so significantly doubtful.

The fourth important way in which Neoplatonism differs from Platonism consists in the shift from the finite to the infinite. Plato and the Greeks generally did not have to emphasize the finite—they assumed it. Their ideal conceptions had limits and were no less ideal for that. The Greeks and Plato with them were very much concerned with due proportionality, with order and measure and limits; whereas for the Neoplatonists the excesses of transcendentalism were very much to the fore. The Neoplatonists insisted upon the infinite for their conceptions and indeed made infinity itself a central doctrine.

The fifth way in which Neoplatonism differs from Platonism

---

[1] *Sacr.*, 12. When translations of Philo are used in direct quotations, they are those of the Loeb edition.

was the omission of an interest in nature. Nature for the Greeks was the arena in which was played out the human drama of the struggles from man to God. Nature for the Neoplatonists was a relatively unimportant affair, and moreover one more than slightly derogated, being tied up as it was with the human body rather than the human soul and a source of evil temptation and weaknesses only. From the divine drama, nature was excluded or omitted, and in its place there was substituted the super-natural. For the Greeks, nature lay between God and man; for Neoplatonism, God and man were directly connected, without the intermediation of nature.

The sixth and last way in which we shall claim a distinction between Plato and Neoplatonism is in the matter of the social relations of the individual. Plato believed that the individual could be fully himself only in a good society; the purpose of the individual was the service of society. The Neoplatonists by contrast thought that the individual could be fully himself only if he served God.[1] Paradoxically, however, Plato held this truth to be, like all the truths which he advocated, only for the Greeks and not for the barbarians. The Neoplatonists by contrast held their truths to be of universal import. It is possible to see in later Greek thought, in the ideas of Alexander and the Stoics for instance, the increasingly general notion that universal truths and perfect ethics and politics should be for the whole world and not merely for the Greeks. Later Greece endeavoured to distribute the Greek achievement to the entire world. The Neoplatonists inherited and adopted this later tendency. The *polis* was, as Philo said, to become the *megalopolis;*[2] and he saw the *logos* as a universal law.

The character of Neoplatonism is therefore quite different from that of Plato's own philosophy. Only too often the two are confused, and Plato is made responsible for views and for emphases to which he was in no wise committed. For Plato,

[1] Cf. Eduard Zeller, *Outlines of the History of Greek Philosophy* (London 1931, Kegan Paul), p. 291. [2] *De Josepho*, VI, 28–31.

philosophy was primary, and although he had tremendous religious interests, and a large part of his writings so far as we have them are concerned with religious questions, they were by no means his only interests, and the method of inquiry into them was tentative and speculative, and its conclusions always arrived at by reason. Neoplatonism has by contrast an altogether different flavour. Long before the advent of Christianity, Neoplatonism was concerned primarily and almost exclusively with religious questions. The pre-occupation with God is paramount; God is the beginning and the end of everything, and all conceptions are permeated with His participation. Beginning in its strongest vein with Philo's work on the reconciliation of Greek philosophy with Judaism, and with Plotinus' reconciliation of Greek philosophy with Greek religion, it was absolute in its beliefs and subordinated reason to faith, with the resultant accent on religious values rather than on logic and fact. Thus when religious Platonism passed into Neoplatonism it had already assumed a form in which it could become the established charter of institutions of religion or of churches. What it lost in flexibility, it gained in amenability to imposition; it could now be adopted as an absolute, and obedience to it compelled.

A transitional work between the view of Plato and that of Hellenistic Neoplatonism is the *Epinomis*, a doubtful dialogue of Plato, which is either a work of Plato's old age or—what is more likely—a spurious, early Hellenistic work. In either case, it belongs in topic and tone with the Hellenistic period. It deplores the world and this life, and seeks wisdom rather than knowledge. It tends to obliterate the distinction between Greek and non-Greek which was so precious to every Greek. It is more interested in the sum of the Ideas and in their unity than in their separate status. It marks the departure from Plato's rationalism and love of life, and begins the preoccupations of the Hellenists. Plato for instance almost certainly never wrote that we 'learn from our Father above how to count',[1] or that

[1] *Epinomis*, 978C.

we should 'lead the life of higher piety',[1] probably not even in his old age. These passages mark a Hellenistic mixture of the traditions of Pythagoras and Plotinus, though the work may have been earlier than Plotinus.

The man chiefly responsible for the change from Platonism conceived as the philosophy of Plato, including his religious ideas, to those of Neoplatonism, is Philo. In 1953 it was still possible to write a book on Neoplatonism which mentions Plotinus many times but not Philo once.[2] Nevertheless, Philo was responsible, almost single-handed, for the tradition of Neoplatonism, for which Plotinus has received most of the credit. Those who are sceptical as to this claim are referred to the writings of Philo in the Loeb edition, and to Wolfson's masterly study.[3] The repeated burden of Wolfson's work is the revision of Plato by Philo, and the acceptance of Philo's version by all subsequent religious philosophy. Philo, in short, invented 'Neoplatonism'.

Historically, Neoplatonism began when the Jews encountered Greek rationalism. The Bible was translated into Greek by Jewish scholars in Alexandria. The Greek language and literature were thus opened up to the Jews, and the Jewish revelations to the later Greeks. The Septuagint had a deep effect upon all subsequent philosophical and religious thought. The Jews had

[1] *Epinomis*, 980B.

[2] Philip Merlan, *From Platonism to Neoplatonism* (The Hague 1953, Nijhoff). Since Plato is also excluded in a work devoted to Platonism and Neoplatonism, the absence of Philo ought not to be too much of a shock: 'We prefer to compare Neoplatonism to the system of Plato's first-generation pupils . . . rather than to Plato himself' (p. 2. See also pp. 3, 195). Merlan is after all only following a long tradition. For instance, in introducing Plotinus in translation, Thomas Taylor wrote in 1817 that 'the philosophy of Plato is deeply indebted to two men, Plotinus and Proclus'. (*Select Works of Plotinus*) [London 1818, Black and Son], p. v.

[3] H. A. Wolfson, *Philo* (Cambridge, Mass. 1947, Harvard Press), 2 vols. The present chapter, though departing in places considerably from Professor Wolfson's own views so far as these appear in his work, is greatly indebted to it for the assembling of material in Philo, for references, and in many other ways.

already committed themselves to a set of revelations, but they could not shake off the impact of the tremendous force which was Greek reason. They accordingly attempted a reconciliation. And they drew on the whole of Greek philosophy, chiefly Plato but also to some extent Aristotle and the Stoics. Aristobulus, about 150 B.C., was the first name known to us of the Hellenizing Jews. He is only a forerunner of Philo, however, and not by any means up to his master.

The Jews had discovered much earlier that there was a super-natural law: that God does not rule capriciously but in accordance with Law. The Greeks later discovered natural law. Nature is God's world, and to be religious we need to know how God's world works. Both the Jews and the Greeks were accordingly rationalists. The theory of universals has been found implicitly in the Pentateuch. The creation of all things according to their kind[1] has been understood as *universalia ante res*. Then, too, there is the independent being of the Mosaic Law; do not these mark the appearance of the first avowed essences? Not for nothing did Moses become confused with Musaeus and the teacher of Orpheus, according to Eupolemius (*circa* 150 B.C.).[2]

Philo was the highest point of the movement to reconcile Greek philosophy with the Hebrew Bible, rationalism with revelation. He chose for this purpose the greatest of Greek philosophers, Plato. In so doing, he set the model for later theologians. Plotinus followed him first with Greek religion, then came Augustine with Christianity and Al-Farabi with Islam.

B. PHILO'S PROBLEM

Our aim here will be to examine the degree to which Philo adopted Platonic ideas and also, and by contrast, the degree to which he departed from Plato. But before we can pursue this

[1] Genesis i. 21.

[2] Quoted in Ernst Robert Curtius, *European Literature and the Latin Middle Ages* (New York 1953, Pantheon), p. 211.

aim we must first say a little about the way in which he conceived his problem and about what that implies.

Philo was a devout Jew and also a student of Greek philosophy. He set about reconciling these two main influences of his life. There were not many ways in which this could be done. To have gone all the way with Greek rationality would have meant abandoning revelation, for any attempt to subordinate the ideas found in the Septuagint to those found in the *Dialogues* must have failed. Rationality cannot on its own principles go against nature, whereas many of the events recorded in the Hebrew Scriptures are super-natural, and the super-natural is also a species of the unnatural. To have endeavoured to hold at one and the same time both the ideas of the *Dialogues* and those of the Septuagint would have satisfied the demands of neither reason nor revelation. Philo accordingly decided to subordinate reason to revelation. Evidently, his belief in Greek philosophy and in the Jewish religion was too strong to allow him to abandon either, and while his faith was primarily in Judaism it was not exclusively so, as his abiding interest and tremendous attempt at reconciliation ably testify.

What the Greek philosophy or, more particularly, the Platonic philosophy, is to which Philo was, partly at least, committed has been set forth earlier in this study. We should perhaps state also the Jewish beliefs to which he was even more strongly bound.

Professor Wolfson lists eight principles of Scriptural Judaism which he has collected in Philo's own writings. These are: (1) the existence of God, (2) the unity of God, (3) divine providence, (4) the creation of the world, (5) the unity of the world, (6) the existence of incorporeal ideas, (7) the revelation of the Law, and (8) the eternity of the Law.[1]

There are a number of other principles which could be added, but our aim is not so broad as to examine all of the relations between Greek philosophy and Judaism. We wish merely to set forth the degree to which Philo's conception of religion

[1] *Philo*, I, 164–5.

departed from religious Platonism, and so we shall not include in Judaism all that we think should be included but merely what Philo thought. There is nothing, for instance, in Philo's list as assembled by Wolfson concerning man and his nature, or his religious duties, or of the natural world as the material and the occasion for the display of the moral order,[1] although to be sure Scripture does treat of these questions and Philo does, too. They are evidently not a leading part of the Jewish theology but subordinate to it. As subordinate, man and his nature would be part of the fourth and fifth principles: man as created when the world was created and as part of the unity of the world.

But it might be parenthetically observed here that if this was the Scriptural presupposition, much in the Scriptures is thereafter inconsistent; for the importance of man, though driven from the Garden of Eden and full of guilt, far outdistances the rest of the world which was created by God and united, and had never sinned against Him. Man, in other words, by these principles should be no more or less important than the rest of nature, whereas this is assuredly not the case. It is the case, curiously enough, only with the Greeks. It was the Jews who continued the tradition, so consistent with Orphism, of placing man above the rest of nature, and who introduced it to the Neoplatonic tradition through Philo,

'The object of interest for the Jews is not nature, as it is for the Greeks, but man, for whom nature is subservient. The Greeks were interested in man mainly as part of nature; but the Jews were interested in him as an ethical being created by God and in nature because man lives nature.'[2]

---

[1] Ancient Judaism separated the moral order from the natural, and made of ethics something superior to nature. Not so the Greeks, for whom man and nature were inseparable, and for whom the moral order is part of nature. 'Nature' for the Jews meant of course the inhospitable desert; for the Greeks, it meant 'fertile Phthia', Greece and the eastern end of the Mediterranean.

[2] Cf. P. T. Raju, *East and West in Philosophy* (Jaipur, no date, University of Rajputana), p. 26.

The prominence of man in nature for religious considerations was Jewish but it was also Orphic. As for Orphism,

'certain elements, which seemed to have permanent value, were taken up by the philosophers, and so preserved in later ages. In this way Orphicism has profoundly affected all subsequent religions . . . and not least those which seem, at first sight, to be furthest removed from it'.[1]

Hence the Orphic message, which never took hold in Greece, was transmitted by Plato to the Neoplatonists, and so blended with Judaism in Christianity; while the essential Platonic realism of the Greek religion was not passed on.

Later books of the Hebrew Scriptures contain additional principles not mentioned in Wolfson's account of the presuppositions according to Philo, such as God's righteousness, His inextinguishable love, His essentially moral will; also the promise of resurrection. But since Philo did not emphasize these among the principles of the Hebrew Scriptures, we may neglect them.

It is clear that Philo overlooked one of the chief similarities between the Platonic tradition (other than its Orphic component) and the Jewish tradition; for he failed to point out that, in both, man's relations to God were mediated by nature, of which man was ingredient and in which he was created by God as an integral part.

There are of course other serious obstacles. Judaism for Philo was a religion, while the writings of Plato came under the heading of philosophy. To assert that Plato held religious as well as philosophical ideas—to say nothing of our contention that he held two irreconcilable sets of religious ideas—is to make a distinction that Philo did not recognize. Again, Philo drew heavily upon the philosophy of the Stoics, although opposing them on every point. Indeed it was the eclectic Stoic

[1] John Burnet, *Greek Philosophy from Thales to Plato* (London 1932, Macmillan), p. 32.

collection of Greek ideas with which Philo chiefly worked.[1] Now, Plato in this form is hardly Plato, or at least no better than a Plato badly warped. It would be no simple task to reconstruct Plato from what the Stoics derived from him.

We have just said that Philo's problem of how to reconcile Jewish Scripture with Greek philosophy, more particularly how to reconcile the Septuagint with Plato's philosophy, was solved by his determination to subordinate reason to revelation. For this purpose he made use of the allegorical method. It was a device which had been used before, notably by the Greek philosophers in their interpretation of Homer and Hesiod; but its subsequent use in the philosophy of religion owes its success to Philo. The allegorical method as developed and perfected by Philo holds that behind the primary and literal meaning of a text there is discoverable a second and more symbolic meaning.[2] The second meaning is hidden, but when laid bare it proves to be philosophical. In short, behind the concrete narratives of the Jewish Scripture there lie abstract points of a philosophical nature which can be uncovered. Revelations, then, do not have to be supported by adducing to their aid an extraneous philosophy; they contain their own philosophy which has only to be extracted.

Philo himself returned to remind his reader of his method with great frequency. A few passages shall suffice to illustrate how deliberately the allegorical method was applied. 'We shall fetch nothing from our own store', he said.[3] Speaking of Genesis ii. 8, he remarked, 'This description is, I think, intended symbolically rather than literally';[4] and he went on to add, 'Now these are no mythical fictions, such as poets and sophists delight in, but modes of making ideas visible, bidding us resort to allegorical interpretation guided in our renderings by what lies

---

[1] Cf. Wolfson, *Philo*, I, p. 112.

[2] For an excellent discussion of the allegorical method, see Wolfson, *Philo*, I, pp. 115 ff.

[3] Philo, *Opif.*, 5.   [4] *Ibid.*, 154.

beneath the surface'.[1] It was, however, not only a question of finding more general points beneath the particular narrative, but often in a way of making a truth out of what appeared to be a falsehood. At Genesis iv. 16, for instance, he was troubled. 'Let us here raise the question', he said, 'whether in the books in which Moses acts as God's interpreter we ought to take his statements figuratively, since the impression made by the words in their literal sense is greatly at variance with the truth.'[2] At the previous paragraph he had already decided: 'We must make up our minds that all such language is figurative and involves deeper meanings'.[3] Thus the allegorical method was not only a technique for eliciting a philosophy from the religious text, but it was also a way of justifying that which seemed otherwise unjustifiable.

We are here already a considerable distance from Plato as well as from Greek philosophy generally. Plato disapproved of the allegorical method,[4] and we have seen above,[5] Philo disapproved of the mythological method. The distinction was an important one, for Plato wished to illustrate the values which lay behind ideas by means of symbolic particulars, whereas Philo read abstract ideas behind particulars as though they were symbolic. Plato was in full control of his material, since both the ideas *and* the myths were his own. Philo was assuredly not, since the religious texts were those of revelations and the rational philosophy which he endeavoured to discover behind them had come to him from the Greek philosophers, and especially from Plato. On the basis of this comparison, Plato's method would seem to be the sounder.

It will have to be admitted that while Philo contributed no ideas to philosophy, he did contribute a method to the philosophy of religion in the attempt to solve his problem. The allegorical method in the expanded and elaborated form developed for it

---

[1] Philo, *Opif.*, 157. [2] *Ibid.*, *Post.*, 1. [3] *Ibid.*, *Deter.*, 167.
[4] *Cratylus*, 407A; *Phaedrus*, 229C; *Republic*, 378D.
[5] *Opif.*, 157.

by Philo is an original contribution to one branch of philosophy. What was original in Philo was the *defence* of revelation by philosophy through the allegorical method. Originality, however, cannot be equated with value or truth; and the only question is whether this original contribution has any truth or value to it. We have seen briefly, and we shall see further, that Philo departed from Plato; did he depart also from the Jewish Scripture in making the interpretation he did? Who is to say? On the face of it, he does seem to stretch the meaning of the text to a point far beyond what it will support, and often to a ludicrous extent. Yet there is no one able to speak authoritatively on its truth or falsity.

The historical importance of the allegorical method is undeniable. Philo's allegorical method was copied by Christian, Jew and Moslem, so much so that at least so far as theology is concerned, Philo may be said to have invented the Middle Ages. Lay versions of the use of the method, such as the bestiaries, abounded, but the profusion of religious interpretation that used one or another set of revelations and employed in its explication the writings of one or another Greek philosopher was even greater and was of course taken with greater seriousness. How far Philo misled the philosophy or religion in this wise, it is hard to determine; yet one thing is clear. Our theme is religious Platonism; and in so far as later religious philosophers thought they were employing the method of Plato when in actual fact they were following the Philonian interpretation, it is certain that they were disastrously misled. They were misled even more by Plotinus, but we shall see that Plotinus was second and not first in the Neoplatonic tradition. And it was the Neoplatonists that most of the medieval philosophers followed when they supposed that they were following Plato. The error, as we hope to show later on in this study, was a peculiarly persistent and insidious one, and we are not free of its influence even yet.

But before we can support these contentions, we must return

to our theme, and show some of the other ways in which Philo while using Platonic inventions departed from Plato's meaning for them. It is important to do this because of the Philonic stamp given to Plato's inventions by all later religious philosophers. We cannot here enter into a discussion of all of Philo's philosophy but only of some points in it, and chiefly those which will illustrate our main theme, and show the direction taken in the main by religious Platonism at this period.

C. THE THEORY OF THE IDEAS

'Now the starting point of Philo's philosophy is Plato's theory of Ideas'—so Wolfson stated,[1] and there is every reason to suppose that his statement, although a broad and sweeping one, is correct. Professor Wolfson detects three conceptions of the role of the Ideas in Philo, all of them somehow connected with a dependence upon the idea of God. They were: the Ideas as the thoughts of God from eternity; the Ideas created by God as incorporeal being prior to the creation of the world; and finally the Ideas as implanted in the world by God.[2]

When Plato discussed the theory of the Ideas, he was clearly not intending the gods, as our study in a previous chapter shows.[3] Moreover, even separating the two, he talked far more about the Ideas than he did about the gods. The Ideas had always existed,[4] hence they were not created, and they could not be destroyed,[5] hence they lay outside of God's power. Plato (or Socrates) discovered the Theory of the Ideas, but its development was left wanting, thus leaving the way open for subsequent investigators, such as Philo, to push their own prejudices, which were in this instance religious ones. But as the centre of interest shifted after him from philosophy to religion, God became more important than the Ideas, and the notion grew that they were His thoughts. Whether Philo was

[1] Wolfson, *Philo*, I, 289.   [2] *Ibid.*, 290.   [3] Ch. II.
[4] *Timaeus*, 29A; 52A.   [5] *Philebus*, 15B.

wholly responsible for this latter conception or not, it is hard to say; but his contribution certainly does mark a stage on the way. There is no record of the phrase, mind of God, before Philo.[1] For Plato, the Ideas had always existed; for Philo, God created them and then they existed both in His mind and outside His mind objectively in the divine Logos, and, as we shall see in a later chapter, for Plotinus they existed only in His thoughts.

The *demiourgos* of Plato mediates between the universal and the particular, operating, so to speak, between two worlds which already exist.[2] It would not take much interpretation, much twisting and turning, to reach from this conception to that of a God who followed in his effect upon the world the pattern which he already had in his mind, though this is not what Plato said. Another possible source of confusion which may account for the change from Plato to Philo, from the Ideas as independent Forms to the Ideas as thoughts in the mind of God, is contained in the notion of the *logos*. Despite Plato's rejection of three possible meanings of *logos* in the *Theatetus*,[3] the Stoics made much of the conception, taking the term, *logos*, from Heraclitus and making it over into a kind of universal world-mind, suggested, perhaps, more by Plato's *demiourgos;* and destined to be divided into the *logoi spermatikoi* of goodness and power which together made and patterned the world, according to Philo. Thus from Plato to Philo there is an understandable succession but also a clear shift, the shift from the abstract objects which were the Ideas of Plato, to the thoughts in the mind of God of Philo. The shift was a crucial one, and marks plainly the departure of Neoplatonism from Plato.

The notion of the Ideas as thoughts in the mind of God is to be found nowhere in Plato.[4] This important fact is somehow

[1] *Leg. All.* III, 9, 29.   [2] *Timaeus*, 29b–30e. See also *Laws*, 903c.
[3] 206c–208c. See Paul Shorey, *What Plato Said* (Chicago 1933, University Press), pp. 285–6.
[4] A. E. Taylor, *Plato* (London 1949, Methuen), p. 442.

crucial to the whole argument which is being advanced in this book. For the supposition that the Platonic Ideas were thoughts in the mind of God for Plato has belonged to most of subsequent philosophy and has permeated all Neoplatonism. As Ueberweg commented, 'the transformation of the ideas into divine thoughts . . . has interfered with the correct historical comprehension of Platonism even down to our own times'.[1] 'Plato apparently had no difficulty in conceiving this system of Ideas as self-existent; but for Philo, who, as a pious Jew, believed also in the God of Israel, it was natural to conceive them as in some sense the thoughts of God.'[2] The independent Ideas of Plato became the ideas in the mind of God for Philo.[3] Such a supposition was foreign to Greek philosophy of the classic period, and could not have arisen until later. It carries with it a decision in favour of the super-naturalism of the Orphic religion of idealism over the naturalism of the Greek religion of realism. But there is no evidence whatsoever for such a theory in Plato.[4]

Some authors, including Professor Wolfson, would read the passage in which Plato identified God with the idea of the good[5] in connection with the assertion that the good is the highest of the Ideas, as meaning that Plato had identified God and the Ideas.[6] But this still would not mean that Plato had reduced the gods to one in number: he speaks of God and the gods indifferently throughout the *Dialogues*; and it would not mean that he had reduced the Ideas to the Idea of the Good or that he had put either it or them in the 'mind' of God.

For Philo, it is ambiguous as to whether the Ideas existed in

[1] F. Ueberweg, *History of Philosophy*, trans. G. S. Morris (New York 1871, Scribner), 2 vols., Vol. I, p. 231.

[2] A. Seth Pringle-Pattison, *Studies in the Philosophy of Religion* (Oxford 1930, Clarendon Press), p. 251.

[3] 'Judaism and World Philosophy', by Alexander Altmann, in *The Jews: Their History, Culture, and Religion* (New York 1949, Harper), 2 vols., Vol. I, p. 630.

[4] See Paul Shorey's Introduction to the second volume of Plato's *Republic* in the Loeb Classical Library (London 1935, Heinemann), p. xx, note d.

[5] *Republic*, 379B–C.   [6] Wolfson, *Philo*, I, 201.

the mind of God, or were created by Him along with the Logos and then were employed as patterns for the creation of the sensible things.

In some passages, it is clear that Philo regarded the Ideas as in the mind of God. Thus 'God is a house, the incorporeal dwelling-place of incorporeal ideas'.[1] The 'active cause', we are told, is the 'Mind of the Universe' (*nous*);[2] and we are told further that God created the world out of His own nature.[3]

Far more frequently, however, Philo speaks as though God had needed two stages for the creation. He had created first the world of intelligible things, the Ideas, as patterns in the divine Logos and then copied the sensible things from them. When God 'willed to create this visible world He first fully formed the intelligible world, in order that He might have the use of a pattern wholly God-like and incorporeal'.[4] Accordingly, 'the universe that consisted of Ideas would have no location other than the Divine Reason' (*theion logon*).[5] Accordingly, it was 'after the pattern of a single Mind, even the Mind of the universe as an archetype, the mind in each of those who successively came into being was moulded'.[6]

There is good reason, then, to suppose that for Philo God created the intelligible world of Ideas and then used them as patterns in order to create the sensible world. In the latter case, He knew them, i.e. they were in His mind as they had been when He created them previously. Thus the Ideas for Philo were inseparable in one way or another from the mind of God, either as being in His mind eternally or as having been created by Him and then used by Him as patterns. But in either case or in both cases, Philo departed seriously from Plato. Plato did not seem to think of the Ideas in connection with any mind, divine or otherwise, except as they could be known by the human mind. And then such knowing had nothing to do with their creation or with their being. Thus in associating the Ideas

---

[1] *Cher.*, 49.   [2] *Opif.*, 8–9.   [3] *Ibid.*, 23.
[4] *Ibid.*, 16.   [5] *Ibid.*, 20.   [6] *Ibid.*, 69.

with God in the first place and with the divine mind of the Logos in the second, Philo took his own path of departure from Plato, even though it is certain that he like all others before and after him owes the theory of the Ideas itself to Plato.

The precise meaning of Plato's sunlight analogy is in doubt. For instance, in the cave allegory in the *Republic* the reality of the Ideas is reflected as shadows in the sensible things; whereas in the *Parmenides*[1] the sunlight which reaches the sensible things makes of them parts or fragments of the whole of sunlight, fragments which are as real as, though not as much of, the sunlight at its source. For Plato, in the trope it is the good which is the sun; but Philo substituted God for the good, 'God is the archetype on which laws are modelled: He is the sun of the sun, in the realm of mind what that is in the realm of sense, and from invisible fountains He supplies the visible beams to the sun which our own eyes behold'.[2] It is typical of Philo's method that having thus exaggerated Plato's usage, he was able to find Scriptural references to the same import: 'The Lord is a sun',[3] 'my light'.[4] The sun, for Philo, is God.[5]

On almost every point in his philosophy Philo employed some idea which had been previously employed by Plato, but also on almost every point Philo made something different of it; and the reason for this is not far to seek. For Plato's purpose and Philo's purpose were quite different. Plato's aim was the discovery of the truth; Philo's, the defence of a set of dogmas. Plato's purpose was essentially philosophical, despite his interest in religious ideas; Philo's purpose was essentially religious, despite his interest in philosophical ideas. Thus the ideas for Plato were abstractions: such forms as beauty, goodness, and the mathematicals. Philo's ideas were the laws of Scripture, although he had great difficulty in deciding just what in Scriptures were to be considered laws.[6]

---

[1] 131A.   [2] *Spec.*, I, 279: *Virt.*, 164. See also Wolfson, *Philo*, I, 201–2.
[3] Psalms lxxxiv. 12.   [4] *Ibid.*, xxvii. 1. See also Wolfson, *Philo*, I, 211.
[5] *Som.*, I, 72–114.   [6] Wolfson, *Philo*, I, 131.

The Logos doctrine of Philo only serves to mark a further departure from Plato. The Logos as conceived by Philo no doubt owes much to the *logos* of the Stoics, their 'world-spirit'. It may have owed something, too, to Plato's universal soul[1] or to his demiurge; but the differences are startling. There is no evidence that for Plato the demiurge was the collection of Ideas. In so far as the Ideas are concerned, to Philo the Logos meant what Wolfson sees that it meant: the totality of Ideas, but another meaning was involved, and in this second meaning the Logos was 'Philo's substitute for the term Nous'.[3] 'It is the mind of God, renamed Logos'.[4] There are then for Philo two divine minds, one, God's mind, which is sometimes called the Logos; and two, the totality of Ideas, created by God but dwelling outside Him and the objects of His contemplation as patterns.[5] Obviously, the model for such notions is the individual human mind.[6]

Let us listen to one of the recent Platonic realists on the topic.

'For all you know of "minds" is from the action of animals with brains or ganglia like yourselves, or at furthest like a cockroach. To apply such a word to *God* is precisely like the old pictures which show Him like an aged man leaning over to look out from above a cloud. Considering the *vague intention* of it, as conceived by the *non-theological* artist, it cannot be called false, but rather ludicrously figurative.'[7]

[1] *Timaeus*, 41D.　　　　　　　　[2] Wolfson, *Philo*, I, 252.
[3] *Ibid.*, 230.　　　　　　　　　[4] *Ibid.*, 231; also I, 253.
[5] Cf. Wolfson, *Philo*, I, 253: The Logos is used by Philo as 'the mind of God which is identical with His essence and as a created mind which is distinct from His essence'.
[6] For Philo, the Logos was a most confusedly-employed term, which if it meant anything, meant too much. Wolfson, for instance, is able to distinguish five meanings: a property of God (i.e. the totality of ideas), an incorporeal being created by God, a Logos immanent in the world, and one of its own constituent ideas. *Philo*, I, 258.
[7] *Collected Papers of Charles S. Peirce* (Cambridge, Mass. 1935, Harvard University Press), 6.199.

One thing is certain: if Philo's problem was how to adduce Greek philosophy to the service of Jewish Scripture, and if his method was the allegorical method and his starting point Plato's theory of Ideas, then so far as our theme of religious Platonism is concerned, no further departure under the guise of an adherence to the theory could be imagined. Again, what about Plato's own theories of religion?

He had several, as we have endeavoured to show in the fifth chapter of the present work, and it is rather remarkable, and perhaps indicative, that neither Philo nor any of the subsequent investigators of the problem of how to combine Greek rationalism with religious revelation kept very close to Plato's own religious suggestions. And, as we shall see, even Plotinus, who attempted to reconcile Plato's philosophy with Greek religion, did not stop to consider Plato's religion, for Plato evidently had in mind Greek religion and was, after all, himself a Greek.

Historically, the influence of Philo upon the philosophy of religion, particularly with respect to the theory of Ideas, has been to mislead scholars and others into supposing that whenever they understood the status of the Ideas as thoughts in the mind of God, they were following Plato.[1] This tradition has retarded the development of the theory of Ideas. It has linked them inevitably with the philosophy of revealed religion and so made them an object of disregard for empirically-oriented investigators.

D. FURTHER DEPARTURES FROM PLATO

All of the ways in which Philo departed from Plato were characterized by an increase in the use of God as an explanatory principle and an elevation and increased participation of the role played by God in things natural and human. Of these, some were of major consequent effect, while some were not. We may

[1] Cf. Wolfson, *Philo*, I, 294.

look at a few of these. The material world for Plato had always existed; like the Ideas, it was there as the receptacle[1] or space, and God as the Demiourgos could only implant copies of the former on the latter.[2] For Philo, on the contrary, God created both the Ideas and the material world, and these were no less His handiwork because He had created the former before the latter. The intelligible world was created on the first day of creation[3] and matter only later in the week. In the attempt to reconcile the Book of Genesis with Plato's *Timaeus*, much in the *Timaeus* had to be 'revised' or abandoned. And by the use of the term 'revised' throughout his study, Professor Wolfson evidently means every shading from 'changed' through 'radically altered' to 'opposed'. In the *Timaeus* God played a subdued role, since here He merely brought the two already existing worlds together, the world of intelligible Ideas and the world of sensible things, by copying the Ideas in the things. This would plainly not do for Philo, who had to credit God not only with the creation of the two worlds but also with bringing them together.[4]

There is a world-soul for Plato,[5] in the sense of a world-structure. The Logos served Philo in the double role of the totality of intelligible Ideas and of the soul which is in visible objects,[6] the immanent *Logos* which is the totality of immanent Ideas. Philo's Logos is closer to the world-soul of the Stoics than to that of Plato.

The nature of God was an important question to Philo as it had been to the Jewish tradition long before him. Could we suppose Plato as an absolute monist, or referring to God as 'the Prince of Peace'?[7] It was Philo who imprinted upon the idea of God the emphasis upon personality as opposed to the rationalism of Plato's conception. 'Thus mediaeval philosophers became heirs to a tradition in which emphasis had gradually

---

[1] *Timaeus*, 50D, 51A.   [2] *Ibid.*, 40.   [3] *Opif.*, 7, 29.
[4] Cf. Wolfson, *Philo*, I, Ch. V.   [5] *Timaeus*, 31E; 41B–D.
[6] *Mos.*, II, 25, 127.   [7] Philo, *Decal.*, 178.

shifted from the purposeful design of a cosmic principle to the arbitrary will of a personal God.'[1]

God for Philo is responsible not only for the natural laws but also and equally for their interruption. As with all those who followed him in religious philosophy, Philo used both the existence of regularity and the existence of irregularity as prime evidence for God. Needless to add, the notion of miracles had never occurred to Plato. Plato's God agreed to follow His own immutable law.[2] Philo's God could change anything He had ordered, even into its opposite.[3] Thus miracles are especially prized as evidence of the power which God exercised over nature.[4]

We have noted in a previous section that Philo was responsible for the conception of the mind of God. 'The mind of God' no doubt was suggested by individual human minds, since these are, according to Philo, the only two kinds.[5] For Plato, plants and animals and stars have souls;[6] for Philo, animals have souls, plants do not, and about stars he is uncertain.[7] With man, the terms, soul and mind, are used interchangeably.[8] For Philo, there are incorporeal souls, called angels, just as there are in Scripture.[9] In Plato, there were assuredly no angels in the sense of messengers of God, and the reference to the lighter souls which fly upwards, and the heavier souls which float downwards until they encounter and take hold of something solid,[10] is hardly comparable, not enough, certainly, to make the reconciliation of Plato and Scripture possible. In agreement with Plato, Philo held that there is a rational and an irrational human soul and that the rational soul is immortal.[11] Mind, in the sense of conscious thought, is what was meant by the rational soul,

---

[1] Raymond Klibansky, *The Continuity of the Platonic Tradition During the Middle Ages* (London 1950, Warburg Institute), p. 34.   [2] *Timaeus*, 41B.
[3] *Deus*, 19, 87.   [4] *Mos.*, I, 12, 65 ff.; *Mig.*, 15, 83 ff.
[5] See above, Sec. C. and Philo, *Leg. All.*, III, 9, 29.   [6] *Timaeus*, 77A–B.
[7] *Deus*, 7, 35–9, 45.   [8] *Leg. All.*, II, 95; *Deus*, 10, 45.
[9] *Gig.*, 2, 6; *Somn.* I, 22; *Conf.* 34, 174.   [10] *Phaedrus*, 246.
[11] *Timaeus*, 69C; *Gig.*, 3, 13.

although to be sure thought but not consciousness is mentioned. Both soul and mind were special Ideas for Philo as they were not for Plato. There are minds and souls, hence there must have been created previously the Ideas of mind and soul.[1] The mind is dependent upon the senses, and so susceptible to false knowledge.[2] The rational soul[3] is immortal, as in Plato. But, unlike Plato, man has to prove himself worthy of immortality by obeying the Laws of God. But Philo reserved a special status for the human mind which is akin to God's mind and to the Logos,[4] and for the human soul, which is also like the divine soul of God.[5] In short, having supposed God to have a mind analogous to the human mind, he then went on to assert the importance of the human mind because of its similarity to God's mind! In none of this, of course, is Plato's example to be found.

Plato allowed for three kinds of knowledge: opinion, based on sensation; knowledge, acquired through reasoning or dialectic;[6] and knowledge of the Ideas, gained through recollection. Philo recognized sensation and reason as sources of knowledge.[7] But where Plato had intended these as natural faculties, Philo ascribed them to God.[8] Now Plato's remembrance is inadmissible to Philo[9] who substitutes for it prophecy,[10] thus once again crediting to reliance upon God what was in Plato a natural function. Here, of course, Philo had his back to the wall in his effort to reconcile Plato with Scripture, for this meant bringing reason into consistency with revelation, for prophecy is divine revelation. But there could be no thought of abandoning divine revelation for human reasoning, or of substituting the latter for the former.

---

[1] *Leg. All.*, I, 9, 13, 21-2, 42.   [2] *Cher.*, 20, 65.
[3] *Leg.*, *All.*, III, 38; *Spec.*, IV, 15.
[4] *Ibid.*, I, 13, 42: *Decal.*, 15, 134; *Heres*, 48; etc.
[5] *Deter.*, 23, 86–7, 90.
[6] *Republic*, 511B.   [7] *Leg. All.*, I, 11, 29; *Conf.*, 26, 133; *Praem.*, 5, 28.
[8] *Ibid.*, II, 13, 45–47.
[9] *Mut.*, 16, 100–101; *Mos.*, I, 5, 21.   [10] *Qu. in Gen.*, IV, 90.

One of the radical departures from Plato was Philo's assertion that God is unknowable. The indescribability and unknowability of God was Philo's own discovery, a truth not asserted by any philosopher before him.[1] God cannot be known;[2] He is ineffable and incomprehensible.[3] It is not clear whether or not Philo understood that he was promulgating a new piece of knowledge; but he was nevertheless, for the assertion of God's unknowability is in effect the same as the proposition that God's unknowability is known, an assertion being a statement of truth. And if we have such knowledge, then it is self-contradictory, since if we know that God is unknowable, then He is not unknowable, since at least His unknowability is known. Despite the contradiction, the proposition as to God's unknowability had important consequences in the history of religion, as we shall see.

It is possible to know not only God's unknowability but also His existence. Here Philo has some antecedents. Plato, Aristotle and the Stoics had arguments for the existence of God or the gods. Philo's novelty here is his proof of God from revelation. Moses knew that the cause of the universe was the mind of the universe, because he had been divinely instructed.[4] The Neoplatonic character of the Philonic viewpoint is no better brought out than by his argument against the 'Chaldeans' that they should not look for the proof of God in the physical universe but in the mind of man.[5] Nature, non-human nature, we had better say, is irrelevant to the relations between God and man; and this is the Jewish tradition, and it was impressed upon Neoplatonism by Philo and hence upon all subsequent religious interest. Small wonder, then, that science had to grow up separately from religion and be opposed by religion. For where non-human nature is derogated and short-circuited by the direct relations of man and his God, that same non-human nature could hardly be counted as worthy of religious interest. And the part of man which belongs to nature, assuming it to

[1] Wolfson, Philo, II, 113, 150.   [2] Post., 48, 167.
[3] Somn., I, 11, 67.   [4] Opif., 2, 8.   [5] Migr., 32, 179.

be only a part, is to be evaluated as of little worth and left hastily behind and hence out of the grand account.

Considerations of space prohibit a full-dress comparison of Philo's ethical theory with that of his master, Plato. We shall mention briefly only a few of the significant differences. It has been said that religions are only absolutely authorized moralities. In this sense, Philo did what Plato did not: surrender completely to a revealed religion, and so to a well-formulated ethics. It might have been possible otherwise to show that on many points Plato and Philo were not too far apart. The principle of moderation is in both, and so is the ideal of the good life, as well as the general atmosphere of an ethics coloured by religion. But where Plato's religion is a combination of the acceptance of the state religion as a set of observances with his own philosophical convictions, Philo's ethics is dictated absolutely by Scripture. Apart from the fact that Plato had two philosophies, and that while we have been emphasizing all through that Philo's philosophy agreed more with the Orphic version of idealism than it did with the Greek version of realism, it could not in the end be said to agree with either because of the irrefrangible fact of revelation which Philo accepted without qualification.

The distinction between the presuppositions underlying Plato's ethics and those underlying Philo's hangs upon two points. For Plato and the Greeks generally, human good is a special case of the good, and the good is not confined to the human; whereas for Philo, nothing but the human could be good in the ethical sense. It is true that he insisted we should be good to other animals and even to trees, and he spoke of 'fairness in dealing with the unconscious forms of existence',[1] but he also approved of murder to right moral transgression.[2] In general, the world is a theatre in which the drama of the moral life of man is played. If the world is good, then it is good only because that makes it possible for man to obey the holy. For Plato and the Greeks generally, good and evil can be studied

[1] *Virt.*, 160.   [2] *Spec.*, I, 56.

by observing both the behaviour of man and the conditions of nature; whereas for Philo, nothing but the divine commandments can make the difference between good and evil.

Philo could never have agreed with the statement of Aristotle that 'the good is that at which all things aim'.[1] Philo could never have conceded that the senses must be satisfied in moderation, that evil is disorganization, that the good is not confined to God or man, that evil could be amusing, that reason is the best guide to the good.[2] In the Jewish tradition and in those religions which have derived from it, the good and hence also evil has meaning only in relation to man.[3] Philo's views on good and evil could be reconciled without too much difficulty with the Plato of the Orphic version of idealism;[4] they could not be reconciled with Aristotle's religion for in Aristotle reason is natural, whereas for Philo, it is revelation, not reason, which is the guide to conduct: what is natural has no special value for him. The body is the source of pleasure, and pleasure in turn is the source of all evil.[5] Using the language of Plato's *Laws*,[6] 'sowing in rocks and stones', Philo condemned the whole of Plato's *Symposium*, in which he can see nothing but pederasty.[7] From the Stoics, Philo learned the irrationality of the senses[8] and the rejection of all laws which favour pleasure.[9] The source of the good for Philo is God;[10] God is responsible for good but not for evil.[11] For Philo the good of the soul depends upon God in a way in which it did not for Plato, since it is a reward for the observance of the Jewish Law. Man's freedom to choose the good over evil is God-inspired.[12] This accords with Plato's idealistic version of religion more than it does with his realistic version, but in the end not completely with either, since for Plato there was more

---

[1] *Eth. Nic.*, 1094a2.   [2] See above, Ch. II and V.
[3] *Gig.*, 5, 20–1, *Immut.*, 10, 50.
[4] See above Ch. V (A); also Wolfson, *Philo*, I, 432 ff.
[5] *Leg. All.*, II, 18, 71–2 *et passim;* III, 21, 37, 68 *et passim.*
[6] 838E.   [7] *Cont.*, 57–62.   [8] *Spec.*, IV, 14, 79.
[9] *Ibid.*, 34, 179.   [10] *Opif.*, 24, 75.   [11] *Fug.*, 13, 70.
[12] *Conf.*, 35, 179.

human freedom. God leads us towards the good life, it is true, but God and the good are not one, for the good is an Idea and God only mediates between the Ideas and the actualities.

In political theory, as opposed to the aristocracy advocated by Plato, Philo proposed a theocracy, a government of Mosaic Law administered by king and high priest. Following the Stoics, Philo held that 'this world is the Megalopolis or "great city", and it has a single polity and a single law'.[1] The influence of Plato is still prevalent in the notion that this single law 'is the word or reason of nature, commanding what should be done and forbidding what should not be done',[2] and presumably leaving to humans little free will. Kingship is the preferred form of government.[3] The king is to be elected, but God will cast the deciding vote.[4] There was to be a high priest, selected by the same process from among the sons of Aaron who had been divinely appointed priests since the days of Moses.[5] There is no mention of an hereditary kingship but the priesthood is hereditary.[6] The king is as a guardian, while the priest is for the service of God.[7] There are in addition various judges and officers to be appointed by the king.[8] Following Scripture still, Philo mentions several times a council of elders, which could have been the seventy elders mentioned in the Pentateuch.[9] Thus Philo departed from the conception of an ideal society which was to be wholly the work of man, as in Plato's *Republic* or *Laws*, in favour of a religion-dominated society which was to be primarily the work of God. There is little doubt in this, as in all other cases, that the conception was suggested to Philo by a reading of Plato. The theory of the ideal society as such was not in the Septuagint but it was in the *Dialogues*. Having derived it from there, however, Philo found himself obliged to square

---

[1] *Jos.*, 29. [2] *Op. cit., loc. cit.* [3] *Spec.*, IV, 30, 157.
[4] *Op. cit., loc. cit.* [5] *Mos.*, II, 15, 28, 71 *et passim.*
[6] *Ibid.*, 34, 186. [7] *Virt.*, 9, 54. [8] *Spec.*, IV, 33, 170.
[9] Numbers xi. 16–17. For a thorough discussion of the derivation of Philo's political theory from Scripture, see Wolfson, *Philo*, I, Ch. XIII.

it with the Septuagint and so his version departed sharply from Plato's and for the usual reasons.

E. CONCLUSIONS ON PHILONIC PLATONISM

In so far as Philo followed Plato at all, and he did so whenever he was allowed to by his self-imposed criterion of consistency with the Jewish Scripture, it was Plato's idealistic philosophy and his Orphic version of idealism in religion that was chosen as a model. It was not his realistic philosophy nor his Greek version of realism in religion. These were followed only by Aristotle and were again neglected by the followers of Aristotle.

Plato, despite his interest in religion, was a secular philosopher, even though his philosophy of religion was freely put at the service of the Greek religion. Revelation was not involved in either; and although punishment was proscribed for non-conformity, it is clear for this reason that revelation did not already exist and hence did not apply to Plato's own speculations. The paradox is an old story in the case of Plato, whose philosophy, for instance, could never have been developed under the political system advocated in the *Republic*.

Philo, whatever else he was or was not, was a pious Jew, and hence dedicated to the subordination of all other religious influences to that of Scripture. He was a Platonist, too, but this meant only that he was forced to develop a method whereby the Platonic philosophy could be placed at the service of Scripture. Philo started with one set of revelations and with the notion that reason and the Greek contribution to reason are for practical purposes one (though of course there were other revelations in other religions at the time, and further discoveries have been made in reason since that time). He then looked for corroboration of his selected revelation by a selected reason. What he found inconsistent he blithely overlooked; what he found consistent he appropriated. Reason was not entirely harmonized with revelation; it was crushed by it. Where clashes occurred, it was not revelation which was to be changed but reason. But if reason were changed, could we still call it reason, reason being that method which could not be changed?

Reason as a method is of course inexorable, though its premises can be changed at will. And the inexorability is a question of the deduction from the premises: a statement is true, reason says, if and only if another statement or statements are true while the truth of the premises was held to be self-evident if examined at all. Philo radically altered this structure by substituting for the premises revelations which he regarded as also inexorably true, thus making of reason a locked system. In this way, dogmatism comes into existence, and dogmatism is not reason.

The remarkable feature of all thought before the advent of experimental science was the absence or rarity of the element of doubt. Many adverse views were held, but they were so *firmly* held by each advocate that scepticism became impossible, and so, under the Greeks, scepticism came to be just as firmly held by one school of thinkers. Consider, for example, the problem of the creation of the world. Many different views were advanced: that it had always existed, that it was created *ex-nihilo*, that it was created out of pre-existent matter, etc. Now, the evidence for any of these views, if we understand by evidence something both telling and empirical, i.e. found in the world itself, was entirely wanting. The only witness not called in to testify to the creation of the world was the world. Yet the advocate of each view was equally sure of the truth of his contention.

Now this characteristic of pre-Philonic thinking was raised by Philo into a prominent feature, even using the name of rationalism, though reason itself was never allowed to interfere. Thus, as we have noted, when evidence for God is wanted, the fact that there are laws in nature, and that they can be interrupted (miracles) are both taken—equally—as evidence, and the contradiction ignored. In this way speculation is permanently stifled, and reason as such eliminated. For the dogmatic is irrational and the speculative rational.

At this point Philo had recourse to a method of interpretation whereby Scripture, or reason, could be altered so as to appear to be in the required conformity. The allegorical method made it possible to read anything as anything else. Hence it constitutes in its way a fundamental betrayal of rationality. Philo thus made of philosophy a kind of religious exegesis, which it was not for Plato. On the whole, where Plato was interested in religious questions, it was an interest in everything religious except God. The number of passages devoted to a discussion of God's nature are few in proportion to those devoted to such other religious problems as good and evil, the nature of the human soul and its immortality, etc. The changes made in Plato by Philo are greater than those made by any later philosopher, as Wolfson himself observes.[1] Reason, one might say, has failed to see that reason is subordinate to revelation, and the reasons given for it are irrational ones. Moreover, the effort to support revelation by reason does not envisage further developments in either. If Philo was right, then philosophy ended with him. For in bringing together Plato and the Old Testament he had combined the perfect philosopher with the perfect Scripture, and thus left little to be added.

That the combination was not so perfect, emerges from a careful study. One serious alteration in subject-matter stands out prominently. In Philo, the grand triology of Greek philosophy: the divine, the natural and the human, is upset, and the natural allowed or compelled to fade into the background. The gods become God, and man advances into the foreground to deal directly with God without mediation. The primitive anthropomorphism which Greek religion fostered but which Greek philosophy and Greek literature sought to escape, was restored for another two thousand years. For the Greek, 'No sharp line is drawn between humanity and "inanimate" nature. Both move

[1] Wolfson, *Philo*, I, 112; II, 456.

in a certain regular pattern, and the pattern reveals, or is expressed by, the gods'.[1] Philo's understanding of the world of nature was in terms of human nature, whereas for the Greek the understanding of human nature was in terms of the world of nature. For the Greek, nature was of God or the gods and man was part of nature; for Philo, God was above man and nature beneath him. Nature mediated between God and man, according to the Greek. But for Philo, nature was pushed aside so as not to interfere with the relations between God and man. This can be put in another way. For the Greek, man was determined by nature and nature determined by God. For Philo and his followers, man was directly determined by God, and if nature interfered it could be set aside by God.

It is possible that in dividing man into body and soul, Philo was misled by the Orphic element in Plato, but in any case he made a distinction that Jewish tradition would not countenance. For according to that tradition, man's nature is a unity and so cannot be split into two disparate elements as Plato had it.[2]

The Greeks, then, studied the natural parts of the world by means of reason in order to understand the whole. Philo studied the meaning of the whole (God) through revelation in order to understand the part. But God is not, philosophically speaking, a category which can provide an explanation. To explain everything by one thing is to explain nothing, whatever that one thing may be. More than one category is needed for every explanation, if the explanation is truly to explain. Thus to say of everything that it is due to God may be true but is hardly worth saying, since it explains nothing of the differences between any one thing being explained and another. Explanation must always be made in terms of similarity and differences; but in religious explanations which depend upon only one thing, namely, God, the difference

---

[1] 'The Idea of God in Aeschylus and Sophocles', by H. D. F. Kitto, in *La Notion du Divin* (Geneva 1952, Fondation Hardt), p. 189.

[2] Rabbi Joseph Schecter, *The Social Nature of Moral Man*, Master's Thesis deposited at Tulane University (New Orleans 1956), Ch. II.

is omitted. Thus Philo, like all subsequent religious thinkers, could never have admitted that there are things in the world which are bigger than man yet less than God, e.g. galaxies.

Thenceforth we may say that the religious influence of Plato was conveyed in the distorted version of Philo, and even the purely philosophical influence of Plato was usually coloured in the same way. For what Philo taught was more Orphic than Greek, more irrational than rational (despite the apparent rationality), more infinite than finite, more religious than philosophical, more dogmatic than speculative, in short more Scriptural than dialectical. And, as Wolfson has been at pains to show in his study, the subsequent scholastic thinkers, Jewish, Christian and Moslem, followed Philo in his method and in many of his conclusions as well.

There is a strain of metaphysical realism in the Jewish Scriptures and in the Jewish tradition generally. It is possible that they could have been reconciled with the Greek version of realism as found in Plato. But Philo was plainly an idealist, and he found himself more at home in the reconciliation of Jewish idealism with the Orphic version of idealism in Plato. And so the realism of Scripture went begging in favour of the absolute idealism, which also, of course, exists in it.

Henceforth we shall call the philosophy of Philo and Plotinus early Neoplatonism, to distinguish it from that combination of Neoplatonism with Aristotle in the thirteenth century, which is here to be called later Neoplatonism. Early Neoplatonism shares with later Neoplatonism the syncretic and analogic properties which consist in trying to make something old mean what it did not intend to mean and thereby to seem to make something new. In the words of Zeller, 'the shrewdness which it [Neoplatonism] exhibited in its attempt to harmonize all that is thought into a comprehensive unity should not deceive us as to its lack of real originality'.[1]

[1] Eduard Zeller, *Outlines of the History of Greek Philosophy* (London 1934, Kegan Paul), p. 290.

CHAPTER VIII

PLOTINUS' PHILOSOPHY OF RELIGION

A. THE PHILOSOPHY OF PLOTINUS

Ammonius Saccas was a disciple of Philo and possibly a teacher of Plotinus. If so, he did not learn to hold to the theory of the complete agreement of Plato and Aristotle from Philo nor did he succeed in conveying it to Plotinus. He was in all probability not the founder of Platonism but the route whereby Philo became the founder. There is evidence for other routes from Philo, such as through the *Hermetica* or via Albinus and Nemenius. It is quite possible that in these and less indirect ways, such as the reading of Philo's own works, Plotinus was heavily influenced by Philo. Let us look at a few of the resemblances which lead us to this opinion.

It is difficult to know precisely what Plotinus intended to say in his writings. The main outlines, however, seem discernible.

First, as to method of approach. Absoluteness of belief could almost be a definition of religion, which is perhaps only another way of saying that Plato did not hold a religion so much as an interest in religious questions.

The same certainty that we found in Philo, in contrast with the tentativeness of Plato, is to be found also in the pronouncement of Plotinus. The probing of the dialectical method as practised by Socrates is nowhere to be discovered in the *Enneads*. It is characteristic of Plato's followers (all, that is, except Aristotle) until modern times, that where he wondered, they asserted. Socrates eliminated the wrong solutions to crucial problems by a series of questions, at the end leaving the issue open. At all events, Plato's suggestions, when he makes them at all, are not the didactic establishments of dogmatism, which is what Philo and Plotinus and their successors achieved by adducing to the aid of super-naturally revealed truths the defence of an absolute rationality.

Next as to subject-matter. The world for Plotinus came from the One through intermediaries. The intermediaries were the Ideas of Plato, in their totality named *Logos* by Philo and *Nous* by Plotinus.[1] For Plotinus the notion that the Ideas were thoughts in the divine mind was more prominent and firmly established than it was in Philo, by whom it was first suggested.[2] In placing Plato's Ideas in the mind of God exclusively, Plotinus was following the Neo-Pythagoreans, who interpreted Plato after this fashion; but he had the opposition of Longinus, who did not and who actively opposed such an interpretation by Plotinus.[3] According to Plotinus, God could know the Ideas, as in Plato and Philo; but they emanated from Him in Philo alone.

The emanation theory of generation whereby all things flow from the One by a process of spilling over of His abundance, provided first the One alone, then the divine mind and finally the all-soul. The One is the One of Plato,[4] and the Good of Plato.[5] The divine mind is the *Nous* or the *Demiourgos* of Plato.[6] Or, in Plotinus again, first the One comprehensively, then the Divine Thoughts and finally the Universal Soul. Then there is man, with his tripartite soul: intellectual, reasoning and unreasoning. Here is the end of the process of emanation, the light can penetrate no farther. Just beyond its reach, and almost identical with non-being—since all being is from the One—is matter. Evil is simply and by itself rooted in matter. Matter lies on the borderline of being, evil just beyond it. It is at this point

[1] *Enneads*, V. 4. 1.   [2] *Ibid.*, V. 1. 4.
[3] Cf. Eduard Zeller, *Outlines of the History of Greek Philosophy*, trans. L. R. Palmer (London 1931, Kegan Paul), pp. 282 and 292.
[4] In the *Parmenides*, 128a; *Sophist*, 244.
[5] In the *Republic*, 509a.   [6] In the *Timaeus*, 29d ff.

that the process turns and starts up again, and the upward contemplation of the soul leads to its reversion to its source in the
One. Since everything existing owes its being to the overflow of
the plenitude of the One, each strives upwards towards the source
of its being. The human soul is half attracted to the world, and
so to darkness and evil (we are not told why these are so attractive)
and half to the timeless eternity of the Godhead. Salvation is
involved in making the right choice, in denouncing the pleasures
of this world for a mystical union of ecstatic contemplation with
God.

The emanation theory, and the image of God as the source of
light, i.e. being, came from Plato's sunlight analogy, refracted
so to speak, through Philo.[1] For Plotinus, God is unity, the
first, and above the realm of the ideas;[2] yet 'all is God'.[3] The
divine mind comes into being by 'circumradiation—and may be
compared to the brilliant light encircling the sun and ceaselessly
generated from that unchanging substance'.[4] Again, 'the One is
perfect and, in our metaphor, has overflowed, and its exuberance
has produced the new'.[5] After the Divine Mind, the place of the
Ideas, comes the soul.[6] The human soul borders on the supreme
soul and emanates from the Divine Mind.[7] The soul reasons
only when it resides in the body.[8] The existence of free will
leads to the path towards matter, to evil through the unreasoning
soul by a rebellious act of self-assertion.[9] Plants are even more
rebellious and self-assertive.[10] Matter is without body;[11] it is
closer to non-being.[12] Evil is connected with the sense-world
and with matter, in so far as these approach the condition of
non-being,[13] but it serves the good by furnishing a contrast

[1] See above, p. 113.   [2] *Enneads*, VI. 9. 2.
[3] *Ibid.*, V. 1. 4.   [4] *Ibid.*, V. 1. 6.   [5] *Ibid.*, V. 2. 1.
[6] *Op. cit., loc. cit.*   [7] *Ibid.*, V. 1. 3.   [8] *Ibid.*, IV. 3. 18.
[9] *Ibid.*, V. 3. 9.   [10] *Ibid.*, V. 2. 2.
[11] But see *Enneads*, II. 4. 6., where something close to Aristotle's primary
substance seems to be posited, a neutral but enduring ground capable of taking
on form but unaffected by changes in form.
[12] *Enneads*, III. 6. 7.   [13] *Ibid.*, I. 8. 3.

with it: evil is opposed to the good.[1] The return of the soul to God of which it is part is accomplished first through a demontration of the worthlessness of earthly things and secondly by reminding the soul of its true place.[2]

B. THE INFLUENCE OF PHILO

Plotinus thought that in the main he was following Plato, although the influence of Aristotle and the Stoics is evident enough. His many explicit references to Plato are sufficient evidence.[3] Much in Plotinus, however, is simply an elaboration of what Philo had already exaggerated from Plato. This would follow from the method which Plotinus adopted. For, as he says, in defence of the reality of being, motion and stability, 'if they are thought, they exist'.[4] Philo enlisted philosophy in the aid of religion, in such a way that reason was not abandoned but only reconciled by having its axioms shifted to the revelations. Plotinus made of philosophy a religion, in such a way that reason was identified with *his* reasons and these regarded as revelations. Plotinus did not subscribe to a given set of revelations institutionally established; he had his own insight, so that philosophy and revelation (or rather its surrogate) became one. In so doing (and it was an adventurous and speculative step), he abandoned both reason and revelation in the way they had existed separately and established them in the way they were to exist together, which was, as it happened, the way in which Philo had brought them together.

The Plotinian system marked a curious phase in the history of both Greek philosophy and the Philonic method; for although Plotinus had learned his philosophy from Philo's own peculiar distortions of Plato, Plotinus himself did not follow the Philonic method. He seemed to have no set of orthodox revelations he

[1] *Enneads*, III. 2. 5.
[2] *Ibid.*, V. 3. 9.
[3] E.g. *Enneads*, V. 1. 8; VI. 2. 2.; VI. 2. 22; VI. 3. 1.
[4] *Enneads*, VI. 2. 8.

wished to promote, and was simply advancing in philosophic dress his own religious intuitions; yet subsequent thinkers have given him credit for much that existed first and only in Philo.

Let us glance quickly at one or two significant pieces of evidence for our thesis that what Plotinus established was an exaggeration of the Philonic version of Plato.

Plotinus accepted the Philonic version of the two-storeyed world of Plato, and in Philo's terms: the 'sensible and the intellectual realms'.[1] He followed Philo rather than Plato in holding matter to be closer to non-being than to formless matter or space. But he went further than Philo in declaring matter to be almost non-being. Nature in the Greek trilogy of the natural, the divine, and the human, is successively depressed by Philo and Plotinus. The divine and the human alone are highly regarded by them with nature playing either no role at all (Philo) or else a negative one (Plotinus).

The absoluteness of God is Philonic rather than Platonic. Again, however, Plotinus went further than Philo, for where Plato had never admitted that God was unknowable, and Philo had insisted He was unknowable,[2] Plotinus insisted that He was ineffable. Thus unknowability is the first departure from Plato, and ineffability is a departure from the departure. This is significant, for Philo was still making a rational although a different point than Plato; but Plotinus turned the rational point into an emotional one.

Philo, like Plato, was still looking up towards the pyramid of being to a God who for Philo, at least, was very much concerned with the world and its creatures, as the Scriptures had insisted; Plotinus in the emanation theory which was his own looked down, as it were, instead, as if from a remote and indifferent God whose character has been suggested by Aristotle,[3] and to whom the world and its creatures owed their existence to whatever degree of being had managed to spill over to them. The triple

---

[1] *Enneads*, VI. 2. 11.   [2] Cf. e.g. Wolfson, *Philo*, II, 111, 150, 160.
[3] Cf. *Enneads*, VI. 1; VI. 8, and *Metaphysics*, Λ, 7, 9.

being of God could have come from Philo, it is true,[1] but the theory of emanation could not have except in a vaguely suggestive way. Philo was always preaching the glory and power of God but not the rest of being as emanations from Him. God is the good for Plato, once, at least; for Philo, God is good but there are, as in Plato, other and lesser goods; but for Plotinus there is only one good and it is God.[2] Nothing else can be good except as part of God. The sunlight analogy which Plato had suggested, was, as we have noted above, elaborated by Philo; but it was almost erected into an entire cosmology by Plotinus.[3] The first emanation is from the One to the *Nous*.[4] The *Nous* from God is like the light from the sun.[5] 'Plotinianism may be considered as a revision of the Philonic version of the Platonic theory of ideas', wrote Wolfson.[6] Once again, in Plato God did not create the Ideas, which had already existed. In Philo, the *Logos* was the name for the totality of the Ideas, while in Plotinus it is called *Nous*.[7] For Philo, the Ideas exist separately as the *Logos* but also in the mind of God, a typically un-Platonic notion. For Plotinus, they remained in God as the 'divine thoughts'.[8] For Philo, God created the *Logos* in order that afterwards, using it as a pattern, He could create the world. This betrays more trouble about the world than Plotinus could ever have credited to God, for whom it was the limit of being, set by the non-being of matter, and containing only part of the human soul as real being.

For Plato the proper life for man so far as religion was concerned—and there were clearly other considerations, such as the state—called for sacrifices to the gods and the pursuit of goodness, beauty and truth. For Philo, it meant obedience to the Jewish Law and the following of the prescribed ritual. For Plotinus, it

---

[1] *Quaestiones et Solutiones in Genesin*, IV, 2; *Abr.*, 121 ff.
[2] *Enneads*, I. 8. 1.   [3] *Ibid.*, IV. 3. 11.
[4] *Ibid.*, III. 2. 2.   [5] *Ibid.*, e.g. I. 7. 1; 12; VI. 8. 18.
[6] *The Philosophy of the Church Fathers* (Cambridge 1956, Harvard University Press), I, p. 202.
[7] *Enneads*, V. 9. 8.   [8] *Ibid.*, V. 1. 4.

meant to aspire to make his way to The One of which his soul is part and from which it has become quasi-separated because of an interest in earthly things.[1] Although for Philo the religious life was all-enveloping, as it was not for Plato, he thought that the good life could be lived here, and indeed constructed the blueprints for a Theocracy for that purpose. For Plotinus, there were no abstract institutional problems, and here he left Philo well behind. All for Plotinus was individual, since separation was not complete; 'the souls are separate without being distinct',[2] and 'the particular souls merge into one soul'.[3] Sympathy, then, is but a symptom[4] and so no social structure is needed; it would exist were it to be established, only in a world which was darkness anyway, and from which the best part of the human souls were seeking to free themselves. There are signs in Plato of belief in a divinely-inspired frenzy.[5] In Philo, too, it is possible to become 'maddened by heavenly love', actively[6] or passively.[7] So in Plotinus, again with the aid of the sunlight analogy to being, the soul reaches actively towards it,[8] or passively awaits divine illumination.[9]

C. CONCLUSIONS ON PLOTINIAN PLATONISM

Since, as we have seen, it is clear that Plotinus thought of himself as a Platonist, a number of interesting questions arise.

The first and perhaps the foremost of these is the question of why Plotinus thought it necessary to write a religious philosophy at all. The Greek religion, if that is what he had in mind, existed also in Plato's day and Plato was well aware of it. His pronouncements on the topic are scattered all through the *Dialogues*. Presumably, if Plato had wished to bring the philosophy of his ideas on religion together, he would have done so—assuming he did not do it completely, for he certainly did do it to some

---

[1] *Enneads*, V. 1. 3.   [2] *Ibid.*, VI. 4. 4.   [3] *Ibid.*, IV. 9. 5.
[4] *Ibid.*, IV. 9. 3.   [5] *Phaedrus*, 244–5.   [6] *Her.*, 69–70.
[7] *Ibid.*, 264–5.   [8] *Enneads*, V. 3. 14; VI. 7. 35.
[9] *Ibid.*, V. 3. 17; V. 5. 8.

extent—but he would not have done it in the way in which Plotinus did it, for Plotinus departs from him far too often.

In Plotinus, in fact, the separation from Greek realism in religion, as it exists, for instance, in Plato, is complete. The motive, for one thing, is quite distinct. Where Plato's motive would seem to be that of pure inquiry, a theoretical concern, Plotinus wishes to save his own soul, a more practical preoccupation. For assuredly the detached desire for knowledge is a far purer thing than anxiety over salvation. The contrast is nowhere more sharply drawn than by introducing the Plato of the *Euthyphro*, which is a satire on popular religion. How could the solemn and portentious Plotinus ever have reconciled his interest in religion with this?[1]

How the difference occurred is easy to detect. The derogation of the world, elements of which certainly are to be found in Plato, is accelerated in Philo but brought to completion in Plotinus. The world of existence may be real only in so far as it can contain copies of essences, but is real to that extent, and Plato is at pains in more than one of his longest dialogues to occupy himself with the question of how the ideal society can be established here. In Philo, as we have noted, this concern is still present, but by the time we reach Plotinus it all but vanished completely. It is true that according to Porphyry Plotinus at one time sought to establish a city which was to be called Platonopolis and in which he, his disciples and the population generally were to live under Plato's laws.[2] A project from which he was saved by opposition—perhaps fortunately. But Plotinus excluded society from religious consideration, whereas Philo had not. An interest in the founding of an ideal society is a good index to the reasonable evaluation of life in this world. Plotinus had none. The Roman Emperor, Gallienus (260–268), encouraged Plotinus to found a Platonic city, a 'Platonopolis',

[1] Cf. Paul Shorey, *What Plato Said* (Chicago 1934, University Press), p. 79.
[2] Plotinus, *The Enneads* (Boston no date, Branford), trans. S. Mackenna, Vol. I, p. 12.

in Campania; but there is no concern for actual life or for the conditions of existence to be found in the *Enneads*.

'He thus has no interest in the State; the "Platonopolis" of which Plotinus dreamed is a hermitage rather than a *polis*. Indeed he has no interest in *any* form of society (unless it be a philosophical conference or circle). He is non-social as well as nonpolitical; he has no feeling for community, and no feeling for any voluntary association or society, any more than for the State and its political organization.'[1]

The 'life of gods', Plotinus has informed us, is 'a life taking no pleasure in the things of earth, it is rather the passing of solitary to solitary'.[2]

The Chthonic gods have vanished utterly, and in their place is the nothingness and the darkness of non-being where matter and evil and worthlessness reside. For the Greeks, it is true, the earth was dark and evil, while Olympus was nearer to the sun and hence bright and also good; but the earth and the dark and the evil were *real*, they were not nothing, not close to nonbeing. The propitiation of the earth gods through ritual avoidance was as positive and forceful an activity for the Greeks as was the ritual tendance of the Olympic gods. Plato wavered on this a little, but Plotinus did not; he held the earth to be almost nothing. Hence the Chthonic religion which was so strong a force in Plato is missing altogether from Plotinus. The spilling over of The One, which provides all the being there is, fell short of that domain. Plato thought enough of this world of shadows to want to build a good society and a good life in it. In this his realism came to the fore. He lived, like a good Greek, in the present, with reason dominant over feeling and both guiding action.

In Plotinus, the Icarus fallacy is intensified and justified; for

[1] Ernest Barker, *From Alexander to Constantine* (Oxford 1956, Clarendon Press), p. 333.   [2] *Enneads*, VI. 9. 11.

him the decision of Icarus to fly to the sun would have to have been the right one, and his doom was not previsioned. If all things flow from, and strive to return to, the absolute unity of The One, which is God, if the phenomenal world and its concerns are errors, then asceticism, relieved only by ecstasy, is the only approved course.

The distinction in regard to the theory of the Ideas is relevant in this latter connection. For Plato, the Ideas can be known only through reason, whereas Plotinus' *Nous* is reached through the emotions. The knowledge of the Ideas is not the same as the love of God. And where in Plato does the 'love of God' appear? All was not well, evidently, even in Neoplatonism, with regard to this question, for Longinus, for instance, defended against Plotinus the theory that the Ideas exist apart from the divine mind.[1] Again, Plato did not deduce the other Ideas from the Idea of The One or the Good, whereas Philo and Plotinus did.[2]

There are further differences between Plato and Plotinus, including some which are more prevalent and pervasive than those we have enumerated; but they will be somewhat harder to show.

The first of these concerns the prevailing tone and texture of the writing in the work of the two authors. A difference of this sort is perhaps inevitable between a rationalist and a religionist. Plato's preoccupation was with the truth, and his debates were for the most part bent towards this end.[3] He trusted, he said, only reasoning which on consideration seemed to him best,[4] and so had to abandon the quest for a teleological explanation, after having been a failure at it.[5] Now does this sound like Plotinus or for that matter like any other religionist of whom we have any record? There is a certitude to Plotinus' writings which

[1] Cf. Eduard Zeller, *Outlines of the History of Greek Philosophy* (London 1931, Kegan Paul, Trench and Trubner), p. 292.
[2] Cf. Paul Shorey, *Platonism* (Berkeley 1938, University of California Press), p. 31.
[3] *Philebus*, 14B.   [4] *Crito*, 46B.   [5] *Phaedo*, 99C–D.

can issue only from the absolutist and the dogmatist. For Plotinus, like Philo before him, *knows*: he knows God and God's workings. Here we find none of the hesitation, the humility, the uncertainty, and even the failure, to which Plato was so admittedly subject. Plato was too much concerned with planning good government to have been persuaded of the advantages of the method of *epistrophe*.

Plato's philosophy, in short, is a method in search of an understanding; Plotinus' is a theology in search of a religion. Plato found Aristotle; Plotinus, despite his dislike of the Christians, was discovered by their Church. If he does have doubts, they are finally resolved by him to his complete satisfaction, even when they concern so troublesome a topic as eternity.[1]

In short, we think that we have Plato when we have Plotinus. But the elaboration and distortion of the part is not the whole— it is not even that part as Plato himself would have had it. For Plotinus, as for Philo, God is the all in all. For Plato no such conception is even implied. For Plato

'God is a supreme category of the moral ideal and a word of edification, and that is all there is to it. He does not identify God with the Idea of Good, the idea of unity, the idea of pure being, the mythical Demiourgos of the *Timaeus*, or any other abstraction, principle, or symbol in his philosophy'.[2]

It is more the influence of Orphism that we see in Philo and Plotinus than that of Plato himself.

The Plato the Neoplatonists adopted and adapted was a highly selected one.[3] It included the more didactic of points combined with the more mystic of elements, while the strong rationality of other passages and the down-to-earth concerns are overlooked as though they had not existed. It may be

---

[1] *Enneads*, III. 7. 3.   [2] Paul Shorey, *Platonism*, p. 30.
[3] It is succinctly set forth in *ibid.*, pp. 45–7.

possible to conclude that Philo furnished the *form* of the scholastic theology by inventing the allegorical method and along with it the entire conception of the philosophy of religion. Plotinus, by contrast, furnished the *content* by suggesting a qualitative type of objective idealism which was later to be interpreted by that method. Henceforth, Plato was to mean Neoplatonism, and Neoplatonism was to mean a philosophy constructed on the framework of metaphysical objective idealism, suggested by one of Plato's two philosophies but extending far beyond it in directions Plato could not have envisaged and would probably not have sanctioned. Platonism was not to be represented by metaphysical realism, the philosophy in which two storeys of the two-storeyed natural world are equally weighted as to their reality and equally valued. And indeed metaphysical realism in religion was not to be tried for many millenia. It might have turned out quite differently, and it might have represented Plato in some ways in which he has not been adequately represented.

The social effect of Plotinus' philosophy was not to further rational speculation but rather to sanction an irrational type of mysticism. Plato's name became one to conjure with,[1] while the Platonic elements which existed in the *Enneads* were reduced in importance.[2] The magic and mysteries of wonder-workers, the popular sense of superstition and sin,[3] had found their champion. His disciple, Porphyry, was unable to hold back this torrent of unreason which in his name swept over the Hellenistic world. After Porphyry there was his pupil, Jamblichus, in whom fully for the first time philosophy serves theology: the task of the philosopher is to expatiate in intellectual terms upon the multiplicity of gods. Proclus called Plato and Aristotle divine. In both Iamblichus and Proclus, or from Syria to Greece, the foreshadowing of the thirteenth-century synthesis is to be seen,

---

[1] Jacob Burckhardt, *The Age of Constantine the Great* (Garden City 1956, Doubleday), p. 179.

[2] *Ibid.*, p. 182.   [3] *Ibid.*, pp. 151, 168, 181, 195.

for both Plato and Aristotle are accepted in sanctified terms, and the combination of Plato in Neoplatonic dress with Aristotle is attempted. But, as Erdmann remarked, 'Doctrines of emanation and of ascetic morality can, if necessary, be united with the letter but never with the spirit of Platonic and Aristotelian philosophy'.[1]

[1] Johann Eduard Erdmann, *A History of Philosophy*, trans. by W. S. Hough, 3 vols. (London 1922, Allen and Unwin), Vol. I, p. 236.

CHAPTER IX

RIVALS AND SUBSTITUTES
FOR PLATONISM

A. MITHRAISM

Mithraism was an ancient religion, and it survived to challenge Christianity from an unknown origin in the early Aryan authors of the Vedic hymns and the Persian Avesta. In the post-Hellenic religious struggle, sun-worship found its strongest defender not in the Orphic cult but in the worship of Mithras. That there might have been a connection is suggested by the importance in the liturgy of both religions played by the role of the bull and its ritual slaughter.

Philosophically, Mithraism combines objective idealism with nominalism, in calling for ritual avoidance of the evil forces as well as ritual tendance of the good. There was the struggle which was unremitting between Ormuzd and Ahriman, and this dualism did not admit of an ontological ascendance of either god over the other. There are many features of the Mithraic mysteries which are reminiscent of the Orphic and Dionysiac cults. But the later religion of Christianity shared even more striking parallels with it. The use of the idea of brotherhood, purification by baptism, communion, a Lord's Supper, a birth of the saviour on December 25th, a sabbath on Sunday, an asceticism of abstinence and continence, a heaven and a hell, a flood early in history, immortality of the soul, a last judgment, a resurrection of the dead, a mediating *Logos* which was one of a trinity, and many other resemblances which have often been noted.[1]

[1] Franz Cumont, *The Mysteries of Mithra* (New York 1956, Dover), pp. 190 ff.

Like Christianity, Mithraism was introduced into Rome as a religion of the proletariat, where it met with enormous success and at about the same time. Both made an emotional appeal to the ignorant masses rather than to the aristocracy, and did not employ reason to convert the intellectuals until centuries later. Commodus (A.D. 180–192) was a member. After Constantine had proclaimed Christianity as the official religion of the Roman Empire, Mithraism suffered persecution but returned again under Julian the Apostate (A.D. 331–353). This was its last victory. As soon as the Christians were securely in power, they invoked the same kind of violence against their enemies, chiefly in other religions, especially Mithraism, that those enemies had invoked against them. Mithraism never again achieved the position of power it held in the third century. By the fourth century Christianity was sufficiently entrenched to enable it to do unto others what had been done unto it, and 'the Christians, in order to render places contaminated by the presence of a dead body ever afterwards unfit for worship, sometimes slew the refractory priests of Mithras and buried them in the ruins of their sanctuaries, now forever profaned'.[1] The victory of Christianity was arranged through violence and fixed by establishment, won by the sword and made permanent by philosophy. For the fourth century that saw the ruthless destruction of Mithraism by the Christians saw also the adoption of Platonism by St. Augustine.

The doom of Mithraism and the triumph of Christianity were spelled out in advance in their relations to Platonism. Mithraism had no relations with Greek culture[2] and so was never able to avail itself of the support of rationalism in general and of Platonism in particular. It could not meet the challenge of a rival—and strikingly similar—religion which availed itself of these supports. Religious Platonism seems to have been responsible for the divergent fates of these two mystery cults, so that the one perished altogether, and quickly, after an ancient career, while the other, brand new, was successful for centuries.

[1] Cumont, *ibid.*, pp. 204–5.   [2] *Ibid.*, pp. 33–4.

At the risk of repetition, the point is worth emphasizing. The religion of Mithras illustrates as much for philosophy in general, for Greek philosophy in particular, and, more specifically for Platonism of whatever variety, that where there is no establishment there can be no survival for an institution. There is no telling with what philosophy Mithraism started and maintained itself through those millenia before it appeared upon the Western scene and in Rome challenged its rival and twin, Christianity. Mithraism, we do know, was even then very old. Now a theology is what enables a religion to be handed down by a church, and a theology is a philosophy which has been called into the service of a religion. The religion of Mithras was transported to Rome in the first century B.C. by the Cilician pirates Pompey had captured, and when pirates transport a religion they are apt to do so in the lightest fashion, that is to say, stripped of all such impedimenta as a theology and the philosophy it contains. It evidently succeeded in maintaining the struggle with Christianity quite successfully, until Christianity incorporated Greek philosophy, and then the struggle was all over. What defeated Mithras was not the exclusion of women from his cult but the neglect of philosophy: establishment requires rationalism. The trick would have been easy enough to turn, inasmuch as Mithras was a sun-god, and the tradition of that other Eastern sun-god, Orpheus, was waiting off stage as the image of The Good and The One, and in the cave allegory of Plato's *Republic*. But the fact is that nobody turned it, and so Mithras is remembered now merely for a striking similarity to the much later religion of Christianity.

B. STOICISM

We shall be obliged now to have a look at the fate of Plato in the Hellenistic world in the three centuries from the beginning of the fourth century B.C. to the establishment of the Roman empire by Augustus. We shall find that Plato meant, in this period and long after, what is called Neoplatonism; that is to say, Plato as adapted and adopted by Philo and Plotinus.

Culturally, the Hellenistic period is marked by a number of obvious characteristics. It was a super-national culture based on the national culture of the Greeks. From being social in the limited sense of the society of the city state, it became both international and individual: it sought a world society in which each man was the limit of his own concern. Politics became a struggle between rich and poor rather than a division along less crucial economic lines. This struggle may well account for the insecurity and sense of haste that the Hellenistic world of Alexandria felt but which had been so alien to the Greek world of fifth and fourth-century Athens. For the Hellenistic Age lasted just as long as the Golden Age of Greece and was beset by no greater threats to its stability and peace. Lastly, Hellenism gave up the pursuit of pure knowledge for the down-to-earth maxims of a practical interest. In this last characteristic Stoicism emerges triumphant over Neoplatonism as a philosophy to meet the current needs. The 'culture-Greek', the Asiatic who adopted Greek culture, never understood the reason for pure theory. He willingly avoided the *cosmetes*, the teachers of order who were influenced by Plato, for the *sophronistes*, the teachers of self-control whose concern was with personal morality.[1]

The western culture did not originate in the height of Greek culture, but rather took off from that culture in decline. The importance of this fact has been obscured or overlooked. Another feature which has not had the prominence it deserves is the derivation of Stoicism from the Cynics. Asceticism is the moral concomitant of idealism; if matter is derogated, then we should not profit from desiring material things. Hence the rejection of material goods and also of that narrow society which produces material goods. Other people are the source of our pleasures as well as of many of our pains; the pains we can have by ourselves

[1] W. W. Tarn and G. T. Griffith, *Hellenistic Civilization* (London 1952, Arnold), pp. 96, 160.

but more rarely the pleasures. They write the books we read as well as furnish the sensual pleasures we enjoy. Stoicism rejected society as an arena of individual effort towards the good life. The ideal of the intellectual life devoid of social participation, a life of pure contemplation as envisaged by Plato and Aristotle, was the Stoic preference. Curiously, it combined the Heraclitean metaphysics, and the logos doctrine in particular, with the ascetic ethics of Socrates and Plato. The Socratic love of sensual pleasures and the Platonic republic are both ignored. It was a half Greek world that influenced the Christians, and the Stoics had the influential half; but it was only half.

Zeno, the founder of Stoicism, taught at Athens but was himself an Asiatic, specifically a Phoenician, though he may have had some Greek blood. His teacher, Crates, was devoted to Cynicism, and it was by way of Cynicism that Zeno was influenced by Socrates, for Antisthenes, the founder of the Cynic school, had been a pupil of Socrates. The Stoics ran away with the Platonic notion that the senses were irrational, and included even the pleasure of being good. The virtue, of which Plato had made so much, became a matter of the will, of which he had not. Where Plato had sought to bring together custom and nature, and so to eliminate the distinction, the Stoics emphasized the distinction: all social institutions were contrary to nature. Later Roman Stoicism embraced the state but only as a concession which was necessary. The relation of man to God became prominent in a way in which it had not in Plato. The austerity of the Platonic ethics as avowed (not, assuredly, as practised by Socrates as depicted in the *Symposium*) was picked up by the Stoics and made central to their doctrine, in accordance with the shift from the concern with the truth to a concern with the practical. The ethics of Plato was never central in Plato, and metaphysics had never been subordinated to moral interests by him as it was with the Stoics.

In short, although the Stoic philosophy represents in a way the application of Plato's philosophic idealism, and more specifically

Plato's first religion, the Orphic version of idealism, it is even more true that Stoicism represents a distortion of the elements taken from this philosophy and this religion as these are to be found in the Platonic *Dialogues*. We shall see that the spread of Neoplatonism stood for Platonism in a way in which Stoicism most assuredly did not.

CHAPTER X

EARLY NEOPLATONISM

A. THE THREE PRINCIPLES OF NEOPLATONISM

We have now left Plato and the Neoplatonists behind, and we are about to trace, all too briefly, the history of their influence. Plato, of course, has received the credit and the blame for both; for where the credit is not explicitly acknowledged it is still often due, and where the blame is not always due, it is still acknowledged. If it is true that fame consists in a sufficient number of misunderstandings, then the influence of Plato has often extended beyond the limits of his known effects. Plato's work casts a long shadow, and his name has not always been written on it.

Neoplatonism derived from Plato, but it emerged as a separate and quite distinct philosophy. In an earlier chapter, we endeavoured to set forth six ways in which Neoplatonism as a philosophy differs from the philosophy of Plato.[1] These were diffused throughout the work of Plato and the Neoplatonists. Now we shall be more specific and endeavour to spell out three precise principles in respect to which Plato holds one position and the Neoplatonists another. There have been numerous attempts to pass over the differences and to insist on the similarities, in order to claim the authority of Plato for Neoplatonism. But it only adds to the confusion to play down the distinction. For it was Neoplatonism rather than the philosophy of Plato which was taken over by, and incorporated into, the established religions, first through the Jewish philosophers, then through

[1] Ch. VII (A).

the Greeks, and finally by the Moslems and Christians. As a consequence, the flat statement can be made that Plato's own theology has never been tried in religion.

The institutional religious effects of Neoplatonism have been somewhat different from what the adoption of Plato's own theories of institutionalized religion might have been. And as we shall see if we consider the prospect of the adoption of that second religion of Plato, which was the one Aristotle adopted, they might have been far different indeed.

The study of the work of Philo and to a lesser extent of Plotinus reveals the emergence of a distinct philosophy of religion called Neoplatonism. It is not a complete philosophy in the sense of Plato's, since unlike his it is devoted exclusively to one of the many divisions of philosophy, namely, to the philosophy of religion.

An important point to remember throughout the remainder of this work is that while unquestionably Neoplatonism as a separate philosophy owes much to Plato, it is nevertheless a corruption of his philosophy and can by no means be allowed to stand for it. We shall note that throughout the Middle Ages as well as in the Renaissance and modern periods it will be repeatedly claimed that Platonism is adequately represented by Neoplatonism, especially where the claim to be the inheritors of the best that is in Plato would be very much embarrassed by any irrefrangible indication of a sharp division between the two.

Neoplatonism is a difficult and subtle philosophy. Let us see whether, for the purposes of tracing its influence, we can reduce it to a very few principles. We shall do so not on the assumption that these are all the principles to which Neoplatonism subscribes, but rather on the quite different assumption that they will be the easiest to trace. We are selecting large and highly visible principles in order that we can view them as strong evidence for the incorporation of much else in Neoplatonism wherever they emerge.

Neoplatonism can be indicated by the following three proposi-
tions: (1) that the reality of things as the many is due to the
spilling over of the being of God as The One; (2) that the
Platonic Ideas are thoughts in the mind of God, and (3) that
matter is the source of evil.

In selecting these three principles to stand for Neoplatonism,
we are not only selecting the most prominent of the Neoplatonic
principles as these are carried forward into the western theologies
but we are also sharpening up the distinction between Platonism
and Neoplatonism. For none of these three principles of Neoplatonism is to be found in Plato. Neoplatonism, then, is not
merely a minor emendation of Platonism—it is a distinctly
different philosophy.

(1) The emanation theory, which Plotinus emphasized so
greatly, was suggested in a way by Plato but was strengthened
by Plotinus far beyond Plato's usage. It can always be detected
by the image of the sun and of sunlight. The One is likened
to the sun, and its emanations to sunlight. The One pours out
its essence with no diminution in itself, until every existence is
actualized.

(2) The Platonic Ideas, which for Plato existed co-eternally
with God or the gods, were placed by Philo in the mind of the
one and only God and in the Logos after they had been created
by God; and that is where Plotinus found them and how he
regarded them as existing. Subsequent speculators made something else of the Logos and limited the ideas to the divine mind.

(3) The matter which accounts for evil is hardly an emanation;
and though itself almost nothing, is through privation the cause
of evil. The physical universe is the last emanation, and the
light by this time is very dim, matter itself being almost gathered
up in darkness. It can still serve the good purpose, however,
of making a contrast with spirit and the good.

We are now in a position to examine each of these three
principles at some greater length. All three of them, though
collectively indicating the tradition from Plato, mark serious

departures from the Platonic philosophy. In so far as they are Platonic, they belong to the religious part of Plato only, more specifically to that one of Plato's two religious philosophies which we have earlier named the Orphic version of idealism. They have nothing at all to do with his other religious philosophy which we named the Greek version of realism. They thus continue the influence of Orpheus as it was brought through the Greek world by Plato and handed on to later cultures. In so far as the three principles can be said at all to be due to Plato's influence—and there is of course some justification for the debt—it has been entirely transformed and exaggerated into a version which Plato himself, judging by the whole corpus of his extant writings, could hardly have endorsed or even admitted.

Our discussion, then, will take a number of forms. We shall discuss the historical association of the principle, its logical refutation, and the nature of its influence.

B. THE EMANATION THEORY

We have noted already that the sunlight analogy began with Plato, was used by Philo with a religious meaning, and became finally in Plotinus' hands the theory of emanation. It is possible now to return to an earlier theme and see that this particular strain in Plato was Orphic.[1] From Orphism certain elements were transmitted by the philosophers to the early Christian theologians where they became an integral part of Christianity. Specifically, the elements of Orphism to be found in Christianity are: the belief that all things owe their being to God (from sun-worship via the emanation theory); asceticism; the sacraments (from rites of purification); ritual (from the ritual formularies); the dichotomy of body and soul; the immortality of the soul; salvation through otherworldliness; posthumous retribution: bliss or purgatory; the emotional and ecstatic overtone (in contrast with the rational Greek and moral Hebrew).

[1] See above, Ch. IV and V (A).

Admittedly, some of these influences met others of a like nature, and older, which had been transmitted from the Jewish tradition, especially the Scriptures, both via Philo and via the Scriptures themselves. But we are here concerned with the Greek tradition and with Plato rather than with the Jewish tradition, and we must indicate their influences especially.

If there is any solid lesson to be learned from the history of ideas it is that a system of ideas may be successfully adopted and pass into the general current of belief without even its name being remembered. Orphism was known to the fifth century B.C. because of its peculiarities and its differences from ordinary Greek cultural beliefs. It was lost in the Hellenistic period for the very reason that its fundamental ideas became so prevalent that no particular name was needed for it. Other mystery-religions furnished the same basis, and one of them: Christianity, eventually triumphed. Dean Inge had a clear picture of the succession of idealism. From Asia to Greece and southern Italy came Orphism and Pythagoreanism, converting Socrates and Plato, who were rationalists, but finding more mystical expression in Plotinus and Neoplatonism, in which form it passed through Augustine into Christianity.[1] The three western religions, Judaism, Christianity and Islam, made up their theologies out of Hellenistic rather than Hellenic philosophies, out of Neoplatonism rather than Platonism, which is to say, out of Philo and Plotinus. Plato has been read customarily by the Christians as a Neoplatonist, almost as a follower of Plotinus. Perhaps the widest of the mark that such a tradition can get is exemplified in the contention that Plato and Plotinus, 'with their roots in the Oriental philosophy of the Hindu' gave us 'the concept of a spiritualistic Absolute' and 'the outcome of the doctrine of the Absolute was the search for Nirvana'.[2]

The opposition of the early Christian fathers to the Greek

---

[1] *The Platonic Tradition in English Religious Thought* (London 1920), Ch. I.
[2] 'The Supreme Continuum', by Ralph Tyler Flewelling, in *The Personalist*, vol. 37 (1956) p. 229

pagan religions does not furnish any index of their borrowing, which was heavy. Indeed, 'The early Christians owed some of their noblest impulses to Orphism',[1] that 'Thracian wizard',[2] as Clement of Alexandria called Orpheus. Then there is Paul's Orphic metaphor of the body as a tent in which the soul has its transient habitation.[3] 'We detect', wrote Farnell, 'in the Orphic service the idea, prominent in the liturgy of Catholicism, that the souls of the departed can be released from penance by ritual performed by the living.'[4] There is, too, the common protest against suicide, alone of Greek cults, to be found in Orphism.[5]

It should not be forgotten that Plutarch was a member of an Orphic cult, and that Orphism had by this time contributed a number of ideas to the common culture.[6] The fact is that the implicit dominant ontology of the Hellenistic culture, in which atmosphere of ideas Christianity took its start, contained a large admixture of the Orphic mysteries; and a great deal of the background was sure to be absorbed by any starting-institution, such as a new religion, without acknowledgment or even—to be perfectly fair—without awareness.

Henceforth, philosophy was to be identified with religious philosophy, and the appeal to the emotions was to be clothed in, and for the most part disguised as, the language of reason. Religion could not defeat Greek rationality but it could subordinate it, and make of it a handmaid. In the West, after the discoveries of Neoplatonism, the best explanation of anything was to attribute it to God if it were logical, and to attribute it to His approval or disapproval if it had anything to do with values.

But it may be asked, to what extent are we justified in attributing to the whole the reality of the parts? As an emotional attitude

---

[1] Harrison, *Proleg.*, p. 504.   [2] *Exhortation to the Greeks, I.*
[3] II Corinthians v, 1.
[4] *Greek Hero Cults*, p. 382.   [5] *Ibid.*, p. 385.
[6] *Ibid.*, pp. 388–9; and Ch. XIV *passim.*

towards religion, the doctrine of emanation with its epistrophe may do very well; but as a rational explanation the case is far different. For God is a single category, rationally speaking, and a single category may account for the similarities of things, but it assuredly cannot account for their differences. We need two or more categories—many philosophers seem to think three— if we are to engage in explanation. For if the distinctions and differences that we are able to detect both empirically and logically are illusions and unreal, then we do not need rationality at all, and to the contrary must learn to distrust it. Those who can settle for such a conclusion have taken another path: we cannot hope to refute logically what will not allow itself to subscribe to the rules of logic. If we are to conclude that they are real, then they, too, call for explanation; but to attribute everything to God may be good for worship but amounts to a poor explanation. The doctrine of emanation does something which Plato never did: it attributes to the One the reality of the many, to the capstone among Ideas the reality of all other Ideas. The doctrine cannot justify such an attribution logically, and so the theology in which the attribution is made cannot justify itself as a theology, not, at least, so far as its use of reason is concerned.

C. THE IDEAS AS THOUGHTS OF GOD

In Plato's theory of the Ideas, the One or the Good was the most inclusive; yet there was no evidence that the other Ideas were reducible to it. Each Idea stood in isolation, and each, though more or less inclusive than the others, had its own independence. The Ideas existed eternally, every one on its own ground; and if together they constituted a system, it was because each part of the whole was a whole to its parts. Yet Plato had never made much of the system of the Ideas. This was left to his successor, Philo, and Philo did so only on the compromise basis that the Ideas were thoughts in the mind of God, created separately by God; whereupon they continued as elements of the Logos. Philo succeeded in uniting the Ideas only by theologizing them.

Plato and Socrates had only just established knowledge upon a firm rational foundation by setting up a second natural order of logic consisting of the Ideas, when Philo, and after him Plotinus, reduced them to the second grade ingredients of a super-natural order by asserting them to be the thoughts in the mind of God or created by God, or both. Reason, too, was thereby dethroned in favour of feeling: reason treated of the Ideas, but feeling was called out in connection with God. And the gain through the establishment of the Ideas, which might have led to natural science, and even to other developments of the application of abstract reason applied to the data of experience, was set back several thousand years.

The argument for the Ideas can be made from logic and from sense experience. The argument from logic consists in the evidently endless recurrence of the similarities of the abstractions. The argument from experience consists in the evidently endless recurrence of the similarities among the sensed elements. It is as true of a relation which is thought about as of a function which is experienced by means of overt action, that it resembles all others in the past which have been of the same class—and the same class does recur. The Ideas are the forms of the most universal of abstract thoughts, they are the forms also of the most individual of concrete things. And we can hold best to a metaphysical as well as to an epistemological realism by maintaining the balance between the two worlds: the world of the Ideas and the world of the concrete individual things. And since realism provides the best explanation of what there is, there is reason to preserve it and to validate it. Now, once identify the Ideas with thoughts in the mind of God, and the balance between the two worlds is upset. For the belief in God which is of this tradition can be supported only on the assumption that while God made the world, the world is not part of God; and so God becomes of importance far beyond the importance of the world, and metaphysically an objective idealism replaces the realism.

These arguments by no means exhaust the arguments for the being of the Ideas. But it is time to pass on to the arguments against the being of the Ideas as thoughts in the mind of God. These consist in two sets: negative and direct, and positive and indirect. We shall give a negative and direct argument first.

Apart from revelations, there is no evidence that the Ideas are thoughts in the mind of God. And since the entire theory was added to at least two of the western religions, namely, Judaism and Christianity, after the revelations, and evidently not known to the promulgator of the third set of revelations, namely, those of Mohammed and Islam, there is no contention which has to be met that the theory of Ideas as thoughts in the mind of God was revealed. Hence there is no evidence in connection with religion, either through revelations or apart from them.

The positive and indirect argument against the Ideas being thoughts in the mind of God consists in the fact that those who believe in the unity and exclusivity of God are led to make distinctions and divisions which eventually challenge the claim to both. The unity of God is contradicted by the separation from God of the created ideas (Philo's Logos) and the created world, and so by the Trinity. The exclusivity of God is contradicted by the very transcendence which was supposed to elevate the conception of Him. Whenever God is said to be absolutely transcendent, as with Philo, then there have to be intermediate beings to bridge the gap between so remote a God and the world. Hence Plato's *demiourgos* in the *Timaeus*, the *logoi spermatikoi* of Philo, and the *Logos* doctrine of Plotinus. God's authority is not exclusively God's when it is delegated, even though it is God's delegating; it is ever so slightly divided. And the remoteness of God, when He is apart from the world, requires for the world intermediate beings. And in this way the unity and exclusivity of God if not abandoned is at least severely modified. Three-in-one has its aspect of trinity as well as unity, and to call three-in-one exclusively one is no more justified than it would have been to call it exclusively three; for otherwise, the one or the three must have gone unmentioned.

It would be a mistake to forget at this point what Kant[1] taught us, namely, that the conception of the mind of God leads to two errors. (1) It turns us away from the investigation of nature on the assumption that the only place to learn about the laws of nature is in the mind of God; and (2) it is a crude, anthropomorphic conception. The more we learn about the laws of nature, the more we shall know about the reasons for the world, which are God's. And, in the second place, it is hard to suppose that God is just a great man, or that great men are almost God-like. This is a human presumption which it would be difficult for rationality to accept.

There is no doubt of the persistence of the error that Ideas are thoughts in the mind of God. Wrong though it may be from a rational point of view, and thoroughly un-Platonic, it has survived.[2] Of course, mere survival is no argument for its validity. Astrology has a longer history than astronomy but is no more to be preferred for that reason. The ideas as thoughts in the mind of God passed into Christianity. For St. Augustine, it is the divine mind in which abide the Platonic Ideas, the forms, archetypes or essences. Albinus in A.D. 200 held that the Platonic Ideas are the eternal Ideas of God, and John Scotus Eriugena in the ninth century still held that God had created the world according to the eternal Ideas in the divine mind.

D. MATTER AS THE SOURCE OF EVIL

In Plato, assuredly, matter is not evil. Matter is lesser in reality, it is true, than the Ideas, or matter is space; matter is even

[1] *Critique of Pure Reason*, A602, A641.
[2] Paul Shorey's translation of Plato's *Republic*, Loeb edition, Vol. II, p. xx, noted.

sometimes a kind of non-being, though non-being is not nothing, it is positive otherness, at least in the *Sophist*.

By the time we reach Philo's and Plotinus' interpretations of Plato, matter, in their estimation, grows steadily worse. It is connected with evil and darkness, and to concern oneself with it is to turn away from God.

Another important element which is played down in Plato by Philo, and completely omitted by Plotinus where he does not in fact deplore it decisively, is concern with society. The good life for Plato was the social life, and the planning of political institutions concerned him in more than one dialogue. 'The main thesis of the *Republic* is that virtue is its own reward and needs no external sanction in this world or the other.'[1] If matter were evil, then the planning of the actual social institution which has regard for economic affairs would be either a waste or an unholy concern. The good life for Plato was the social life, yes, but not for his successors, the Neoplatonists. Philosophy may be a social enterprise; indeed, conceived in the way in which Plato and Socrates conceived it, it was social, for the dialectic method of inquiry was always engaged in by a number of persons. But religion, at least the western religions of the group with which we are concerned, was an individual affair, one strictly between the individual and God. For Philo the social life was possible but only in the restricted sense of a theocracy, while for Plotinus the situation was more restricted still, and the famous 'flight of the alone to the alone'[2] was hardly a social statement. Philo does not treat of society at any great length and Plotinus ignores it except to warn against any preoccupation with its concern.

We have two theses here which, though related, ought not to be confused. One is the contention that matter is evil or connected with evil, and the other a subordinate contention that actual societies and their organizations are connected with

[1] Paul Shorey, *Platonism*, p. 65, referring to Plato's *Republic*, 612B ff.
[2] *Enneads*, VI. 9. 11.

matter and hence with evil. Let us examine these logically one at a time.

The contention that matter is evil must meet the argument that no good things can be done without it. The means to a good end, though material, cannot be altogether evil if they are, successfully, the means. Consider, for example, faith, hope and charity. Faith may be faith in salvation, hope may be hope for another and a better world, but charity is the giving of property, and property consists inevitably in material of some sort. If it is possible for the soul to escape from the material body it must be somehow by material means, and the symbolic sacraments, for instance, do employ wafers and wine.

Another argument against the evil nature of matter comes from the standpoint of recently acquired knowledge. Matter is not entirely what the ancients thought. It can be analysed into particles of energy, and energy can be made to do work, good as well as bad. Matter, it would seem, so far as the higher values are concerned, is neutral: it can serve a good just as well as an evil purpose, and is equally necessary to both. It is the *sine qua non* of action, and there is assuredly such a thing as good action.

Let us turn now to the second thesis, namely, that societies are connected with matter and hence evil. The good life is an individual life in the next world, why not in this? God is not many but one—at least for the Neoplatonists, though not definitely for Plato. The soul flies back to God: where is the need for human society? Social life thus becomes a model for actual life, for life as lived in this world of matter. There is nothing holy about social organization.

The contention that society is not needed for the good life must meet the argument that the individual cannot live his life at all in total isolation from society. He needs other people, or at the very least their artifacts. It has been maintained that a man without a language is not a human being, and there is some evidence for the statement; and language is the product of many generations of social life.

A second argument can be made from the theory of the Ideas as held by Philo and Plotinus. If God created the Ideas and set them aside in the system of the Logos, and then used them as archetypes for the creation of the world, so that they existed in His mind as well as apart from His mind in the Logos, then there must be an Idea for every actual thing, societies and social organizations included. And nothing altogether or predominantly evil could have existed in His mind or have been created by Him in the Logos.

Zeller said that 'in one respect Neoplatonism shows a far-reaching modification of real Platonism. The social and political ideals to which—in the *Republic* at least—Plato had sacrificed the individual are replaced in Neoplatonism by an individualistic tendency. The kernel of philosophic thought lies no longer in knowledge of the object, but in the state of soul of the subject which is exalted to its highest bliss, the ecstatic union with God by means of asceticism and pursuit of knowledge. This Neoplatonism, with its need of revelation instead of independent investigation, carried to its end the development begun in Neopythagoreanism and the Greek-Jewish philosophy, and thus completed the suicide of philosophy.'[1]

The subsequent history of the Christian Church as a social institution after its absorption of Neoplatonism can tell us much about the theory that matter is evil and that societies are connected with matter and hence also are inherently evil.

One profound difference ought to be noted first off between Platonism and Christianity, and its significance cannot lightly be overlooked. Christianity rapidly became an institutional affair, whereas neither Platonism nor Neoplatonism ever was institutional. The religious speculations in the Platonic *Dialogues* were unique and unaffiliated; and while Plato often advocated the support of existing Greek religious institutions, his own thought was original and free. Indeed if Plato has left us any

[1] Eduard Zeller, *Outlines of the History of Greek Philosophy* (London 1931, Kegan Paul), p. 291.

unified impression of his own views as to social action, it is that intellectual inquiry ought to be conducted in isolation from existing institutions although approving of adherence to them. On the other hand, the Christianity which sought to incorporate Platonism through Neoplatonism was already heavily organized and institutionalized. The picture we have of the social world of the early Church fathers is hardly one of monks in the desert but rather of deeply engaged institutional men working tirelessly among their fellows to bring them in to what they regarded as the proper social organization. If matter is evil, then so is wealth and power in this world, and the admonition of Jesus to render unto Caesar the things that are Caesar's never met with much practical adherence despite the extent of the lip service which has been accorded it. A wealthy and powerful Church and one with a high degree of social organization has been the result of the view that matter and society are connected with evil.

To what extent could one argue that the structure of the Roman Catholic Church—and the Roman state, too, for all that—was like Plato's *Republic*? The Roman Church has been political and militant, an historical result, perhaps, of the fact that where the Byzantine Empire was overrun by a people with a high degree of social organization, the Roman Empire was overrun by German tribes with relatively little organization, and so the Church in order to survive in the confusion was obliged to take over the role of the state, a task which it has never willingly relinquished. The conflict between Church and State, which has happened to so many churches in so many states, was never more sharply antagonistic than in the West where the Roman Catholic Church engaged in politics and the acquisition of wealth.

It is easy to see where and how the Neoplatonic if not the Platonic admonitions were applied in the Church. The highest form of action for the Church would have been refraining from action: the action of the saint. Then the problem became rapidly one of how to develop an institution to provide for action when interest lay somewhere else. The Roman State was the form chosen, and it was constructed in terms of the most violent action. Thus the low regard for matter held by Plato and emphasized by his successors to the point of recommending its neglect, was a notion not incorporated into the western religions as a practice even if it was adopted as a principle. And this holds true of all three western religions, of the Jewish and Moslem as well as of the chronologically intermediate Christian.

E. THE HISTORIC FAILURE OF PLATO'S SECOND RELIGION

If you wish to know how powerful the Platonic philosophy is, you have only to recall that the Academy which Plato founded lasted almost a thousand years and survived three conquests. First the Macedonians, next the Romans, and finally the Germans were in possession of Athens. Perhaps we owe to the influence of the Academy not only the preservation of the *Dialogues* but also the influence of Neoplatonism. It is significant that Hypatia who had retained the secular view of Plato and Aristotle was in A.D. 415 killed by a Christian mob.[1] And when, two generations after the death of Proclus, who, as head of the Academy, had revived Neoplatonism, Justinian in A.D. 529 closed the Academy that Plato had founded more than nine hundred years earlier, it was Justinian and not Proclus who might have been acting in Plato's name. For it was no longer a recognizable Platonic philosophy whose teaching in one place Justinian thus brought to an end. The Neoplatonism of Proclus bore little relation to the philosophy of Plato.

And so today when a modern scholar wishes to compare Neoplatonism with Platonism not altogether to the detriment of the former, as we have seen, it is Plato's first generation pupils and not Plato himself who must be brought into the comparison

[1] See Zeller, *op. cit.*, p. 311.

which would otherwise be too cruel an indictment of the Neoplatonists and—what is perhaps more strategically important —of the religionists who followed doctrinally in their wake.[1]

We have noted that the Platonic religion which the Neoplatonists transmitted to the western religions was the Orphic version of idealism. The Greek version of realism was, as we have also noted, the one chosen and developed briefly by Aristotle. That it was not, so far as we know, developed more fully, as fully, say, as psychology and politics were developed by being assigned separate and complete treatises in the Aristotelian corpus, is something of an index of the way in which Aristotle must have regarded religion. Yet there was a genuine field of inquiry waiting there. For it was the realistic theology of Plato, the religion of Socrates as exemplified in the drama of his life to which Aristotle wished to subscribe. Plato's metaphysical realism has never been presented in the theological version which is appropriate to it. Who knows what effects it might have had, when it has never been tried? This particular philosophy of religion, it is safe to assert, has not yet even received adequate formulation.

Much of course had passed into the unconscious beliefs of the average man of the fifth and fourth centuries B.C. and after. Along with the Orphic beliefs went the Stoic and Epicurean realistic reactions. For they were religious and ethical nominalisms, and it requires the metaphysical excess of nominalism in religion to right the opposite excess of idealism in order to produce a balance of realism. Greek rationalism, as represented by the theology of Plato's second religion and Aristotle's version of it, has never been officially (or even informally) adopted by any institutionalized religion.

Now when there are two such powerful strains as we have endeavoured to distinguish, and one is adopted as formally and as completely as the Orphic version of idealism has been by becoming incorporated into the western religions: Judaism,

[1] Cf. Philip Merlan, *op. cit.*, *loc. cit.*

Christianity and Islam, the other must exist somewhere and somehow, ready to appear if called upon. For the moment it was eclipsed; and we shall see that this moment lasted for several thousand years. Yet systems of ideas are imperishable: even if lost they may be rediscovered in all their purity; and they may be applied at any time. Later, with what success we shall see, the attempt was made.

Meanwhile, however, our concern shall be with the post-Neoplatonic adventures of Plato's first religion, which we have named the Orphic version of idealism. We have seen it begin to pass into the Judaic tradition in the hands of Philo. There it was never official. It became official in Christianity, and to this development we must soon turn our attention.

F. PAGAN NEOPLATONISM

But before we do so, it will be advisable to say a word about the fate of the Orphic version of idealism in the hands of those who wished to make it into a formal Greek religion, something it had never been. One difference between Plato and Neoplatonism is that Plato wrote philosophy while Neoplatonism was directed towards religion. Plato may have in the course of presenting his speculative philosophy touched upon many religious ideas, and even, as in the case of the immortality of the soul, for instance, discussed them at length and in a number of dialogues; but it was still speculative philosophy. Neoplatonism, beginning with Plotinus, had in view specifically religious ideas, and if any philosophical ideas were broached other than those specifically connected with religion, it was in connection with religion that they were mentioned at all. Plato is first and foremost philosophy, lay philosophy, unconnected with the religion of the day; Neoplatonism is above all the theory and practice of religion, using some of Plato's ideas and exaggerating them.

There are reasons to suppose that Neoplatonism in this sense did not begin with Philo but, much earlier, with Plato's successor in the Academy, Speusippus. Professor Merlan would have it that Speusippus, before Plotinus, taught that the One is above being and goodness.[1] However, we are concerned with Neoplatonism in this section as it bore on religious ideas, and more specifically with the establishment of Neoplatonism as an institutional religion.

We have already noted how Neoplatonism received its formal beginnings with Philo who, while not wishing to establish Neoplatonism as a religion, did intend to establish it within the theology of an already-existing religion. If Philo had had his way, or if the Jews had been more inclined towards the establishment of principles of a philosophical nature than they were, Judaism as a religion would have shown more of the influence of Hellenism than it does, and more of the influence of Plato in particular.

After Philo we have the interest expressed in Greek religious ideas under the influence of Plato by a number of philosophical thinkers of the second century. Plutarch preferred to be a priest at Delphi than a Roman consul and 'devoted his life to making of Hellenism a cult of civilization which could survive the loss of national sovereignty'.[2] Maximus of Tyre was an avowed Platonist at Rome in the same period, A.D. the second century. Many of his Orations are on specifically Platonic themes, although his interest in the religious questions was more marked than it was in Plutarch. Numenius of Apamea (circa A.D. 170) not only saw a resemblance between Plato and Moses[3] but traced the philosophy of Plato back to what he considered its sources in Oriental and particularly in Jewish wisdom. His Platonism was in this regard more Neoplatonic. Numenius in the same period, judging of those fragments of his which have survived, made a sort of Neoplatonic fusion of Plato with the Old Testament,

---

[1] *From Platonism to Neoplatonism*, Ch. V.

[2] Moses Hadas, *Ancilla to Classical Reading* (New York 1954, Columbia University Press), p. 309.

[3] Clement of Alexandria, *Stromateis*, i, 342.

the latter, probably, only in the references of Philo; his concern, too, is with theological questions.

The chief author of the attempt to found a theology on Plato was of course Plotinus, whom we have already discussed. After Plotinus, it becomes very difficult to distinguish between Plato and Neoplatonism, and the attempt is rarely undertaken. The chief attempt to found a religion on Greek philosophy was made by the Emperor Julian, some hundred years after Plotinus. Julian wished to arrest the spread of Christianity and to establish in its place a version of Greek religion in which sun-worship was central. He wished to put together a sort of cult of Mithras under the influence of Platonism, but he did not live long enough to carry his plan into effect, although he had certainly made a start. After Julian, Christianity triumphed in such a way that the issue could not be brought up again for a very long time. By the fourth century Neoplatonism was part of the equipment of the Roman gentlemen, and the chosen philosophy, under which a compilation could be made of knowledge. For Macrobius, for instance, Plotinus is of equal importance with Plato.

G. ROMAN CATHOLIC NEOPLATONISM

The transition from Platonism to Latin Christianity is not easy to trace. For example, Judaism probably owed to Zoroastrianism the idea that the resurrection will see the body restored and reunited with the soul so that the whole man may stand at the bar of judgment before God and receive reward or retribution for the deeds of the mortal life. Did Christianity derive this idea from Zoroastrianism via Judaism, or from Orpheus via the Greeks? That there is evidence of some Christian ideas in Plato has been noted. It is difficult to establish that these were taken from Plato but only that chronologically they could have been, and that it would be difficult to discover where else they were to be found. In any case, the similarity has to be accounted for, and anticipations tie us to nothing definite. Among the anticipations are: Augustine's City of God, in the *Republic*, 592A–B; the saying of Jesus, that 'whosoever shall save his life will lose it', in *Gorgias*, 511B; the Holy Spirit, in the world-soul of the *Timaeus;* and there are others. It is possible now to draw up an astonishingly large list of parallels between Plato and the Christian Bible, both in the Old and New Testaments.[1] Yet Plato was neither Jewish nor Christian. The parallels are never read to Plato's credit but only as reinforcements of Christian truth. Origen, for instance, was painfully aware of the anticipation and of the contrast, and struggles mightily (if not too logically) to read it in favour of the Christians.[2] The attempt to constrain Greek rationalism, as represented by Plato, into a subordinate religious role has been a persistent one.

The two great schools of Alexandria showed a marked difference in that one was Christian and one pagan. The Christian fathers and the Neoplatonists were not only friendly but attended each other's lectures; but this amiable relation was brought to an end when the conversion of Constantine to Christianity and the apostasy of Julian from Christianity changed the field of controversy from an academic affair to a bloody political one. But they were both learned and there was only one learning. Both quoted Plato and both thought of Neoplatonism as the direct inheritance of Platonism. The *Isagoge* of Porphyry, the disciple of Plotinus, was a Neoplatonic interpretation of Aristotle.[3] That the early Christian fathers were very familiar with Plato is amply attested by the writings of Clement of Alexandria and of Origen. Clement admired Plato immensely, and made many direct quotations from the *Dialogues*. He was equally familiar with the Hebrew Scriptures, and in fact thought that he saw influences of the Hebrew conception of God in Plato.[4]

[1] A. Fox, *Plato and the Christians* (London 1957, S. C. M. Press).
[2] *Contra Celsum*, VII: 58 ff.
[3] Cf. R. R. Bolgar, *The Classical Heritage* (Cambridge 1954, University Press), p. 176.   [4] *Exhortation to the Greeks*, Ch. VI.

Christianity was never truly Greek. It was an uneasy amalgam of religion (as set forth, for instance, in the Apostles' Creed) and Neoplatonism; and Neoplatonism was not Greek, either, but Hellenistic. The articles of the creed eventually triumphed over the philosophy, and the emotions (as in the gospel of love) over reason.[1] Christianity had, in fact, tried to reconcile Jewish and Greek elements. But the Hebraism that Christianity took over was already saturated with Hellenism, chiefly though not altogether Plato, acquired during Hellenistic times.[2] It ended by defending Jewish elements by means of Greek rationalism, and applied the result with a dynamic western use of force alien to both. To love thy neighbour[3] and to be persuaded that one should do so (Plato) are in the same spirit. The story of the relations between Christianity and Platonism is one in which Platonism, under the guise of Neoplatonism, was first defeated and then incorporated. Hippolytus, already in the second century A.D. had ascribed the Platonic ideas to the mind of God. He proclaimed that 'the exemplar, which he [i.e. Plato] likewise called ideas, is the intelligence of the Deity',[4] even though on God and the nature of matter he is a more faithful Platonist. Tertullian shouted that the Christianity which had Jesus Christ and the Gospel needed no curiosity and no inquiry.[5] The *Logos* of Philo finally became Jesus Christ in the beginning of the Gospel According to John. The distinction drawn so much earlier by Plato between opinion and knowledge, the opinion gained from the sensing of particulars, and the knowledge from reasoning about the Ideas, was given at the hands of the Christians a different meaning. Opinion was based on the sensual life,

---

[1] Plato and Aristotle were, above all, rationalists, while Christianity substituted faith. See e.g. Frederick Copleston, *Contemporary Philosophy* (London 1956, Burns and Oates), p. 155; especially the passage about Catholicism, which 'never surrendered to rationalism'.

[2] 'Plato in Hellenistic Fusion', by Moses Hadas, in *Journal of the History of Ideas*, Vol. XIX (1958), p. 6.   [3] Leviticus xix. 18.

[4] *The Refutation of All Heresies* by Hippolytus, translated by Salmond (Edinburgh 1868, Clark), p. 49.   [5] Cf. Shorey, *Platonism*, p. 82.

while knowledge, which was of Jesus Christ and God, was obtained through revealed Scriptures. This was quite a different turn, and it contained an asceticism which Plato had not put in it. For his ladder of love went *through* the stage of carnal love, not around it or despite it, and 'through' meant 'by means of it'. The most generally used metaphor for *gnosis* was 'light'. See for instance also 'the light of life'[1] and the 'light of the world'.[2]

'The allegorical explanation of the Scriptures as introduced by Philo became an indispensable means of combining the new faith with the older revelations, and the Logos-Doctrine of Philo, which was fused with the Jewish-Christian messianic belief, formed the centre of the dogmatic movement in Christian theology for centuries to come.'[3] From the fourth century on, so far as Christianity was concerned, there were three authorities in Greek philosophy: Plato, Aristotle, and Plotinus.[4]

We can see the evidence of the transition of the three principles of Neoplatonism, namely, the emanation theory, the Ideas as thoughts in the mind of God, and matter as the source of evil, from their Jewish and pagan versions to Christianity, in the writings of the early Church fathers. In tracing that philosophy of religion which was Neoplatonism into the Christian form which it was to occupy for millenia, we must not fail to weigh the effects upon it of the peculiar forces which were now brought to bear. Let us give as examples the transition of the three principles together with the type of reinforcement which was added to each when it was adopted by the Church.

In the first place, the new religion of Jesus Christ wished to preserve the divinity of Jesus as part of and yet also apart from God. From the very beginning, the Gnostic sects made a definite

---

[1] John i. 4.   [2] John viii. 12.

[3] Cf. E. Zeller, *Outlines of the History of Greek Philosophy* (London 1931. Kegan Paul), p. 262.

[4] See e.g. Nemesius of Emesa, *Treatise on the Nature of Man* (Philadelphia 1955, Westminster Press), pp. 224–5.

though complex set of emanations their doctrine, and they reinforced also the belief in the essentially evil nature of the world. Even the soul of man might have been lost had not Jesus, that mightiest of emanations, descended in order to retrieve her. Clement would have the Son the divine mind of the Father. And for Origen, too, Jesus was divine. Origen, for instance, wrote that 'we do not separate the Son of God from Jesus';[1] 'it was the divine Logos and Son of the God of the universe that spoke in Jesus'. The words of Jesus on this point are not clear. There is the peace of consistency[2] but there is also the conflict of difference,[3] the doctrine of love, and also the reforming sword; and there is also the clear statement of supernaturalism: 'My kingdom is not of this world',[4] and the equally clear statement of naturalism: 'I am come that they might have life, and that they might have it more abundantly'.[5]

Consider the reinforcement which such a belief must lend to the theory of emanation. Since Origen could not have read Plotinus for chronological reasons, Wolfson speculates that both derived the conceptions which they undoubtedly held in common from their teacher, Ammonius Saccas.[6] The emanation of the Logos from The One becomes in Origen the derivation of the Son from God; and just as the Logos which was created by The One exists apart from The One yet has its own being also as part of The One, so the Son was created by God and exists apart from Him yet has His being also in Him.

In the second place, the new religion of Jesus Christ was being endowed with a firm organization, an institution the justification for which, at least in its most political and militant form, was not to be justified anywhere in Scripture. There was no social order in heaven, or, at least, even where there was, no conception of what the heavenly social order could mean was

---

[1] *Contra Celsum*, II: 9.   [2] Matthew xxii. 35–40.
[3] Matthew x. 34–7.   [4] John xviii. 36.   [5] John x. 10.
[6] H. A. Wolfson, *The Philosophy of the Church Fathers* (Cambridge 1956, Harvard University Press), I, 202 ff. and references.

ever detailed. And this remains true despite the Pauline 'conversation in heaven'.[1]

Jesus was the last of the early Christians who looked towards the future in this world because He looked forward to the end of the world. The remainder of Christianity has looked back to the past, towards the lifetime of Jesus. It is true that Jesus had said of Peter, 'upon this rock I will build my church';[2] but He could hardly have envisaged the kind of Church it would prove to be, as it rapidly developed politically under the pressure of the disintegrating Roman social organization and the incursion of the far less well organized German tribes. And He could not have envisaged, either, the lengths to which the Apostolic Fathers would go in order to justify such a Church; He could not have envisaged, for instance, the concept of the pre-existent Church, which, in the words of Clement, was 'the first Church, the spiritual one which was created before the sun and moon'.[3]

Consider the reinforcement which such a belief must lend to the theory of the Ideas as thoughts in the mind of God. For as there was to be no Church on earth as there was to be no earth, so there was to be always the Church there had always been, the spiritual Church which dwells as an Idea forever in the mind of God or in the Logos.

Neoplatonism won over Platonism only after a struggle. The Nicene Creed, by incorporating the doctrine that the Son was 'one substance' with the Father, supported the super-natural over the natural religion by reinforcing the conception of the Ideas as thoughts in the mind of God.

In the third place, the new religion of Jesus Christ was not one which it was supposed would endure forever upon the earth. Human life—existence itself—was believed to be nearing its end. 'These are the last times', wrote Ignatius.[4]

---

[1] Philippians iii. 20. See also the discussion in Ernest Barker, *From Alexander to Constantine* (Oxford 1956, Clarendon Press), pp. 398 f.

[2] Matthew xvi. 13-20.

[3] II Clement, xiv, 1.   [4] To the Ephesians xi. 1.

Consider the reinforcement which such a belief must lend to the theory of matter as the source of evil. The only hope for the end of evil must then be some theory of the end of matter.

Augustine, the first of the great Christian theologians was heavily influenced by Neoplatonism, and he may have been chiefly responsible for incorporating it in Church doctrine.[1] Augustine accepted the second and third of the Neoplatonic principles, namely, the Ideas as thoughts in the mind of God,[2] and evil as nothing positive but instead the privation of the good.[3] He rejected the emanation theory, though there are distinct echoes of it. We have, for instance, 'that Light which is distinct from it and created it, and by whose intelligible illumination it enjoys light in the things intelligible',[4] and again 'he who knows the truth knows that Light and he who knows that Light knows Eternity'.[5]

'Augustine had set the ideas he had borrowed from pagan sources within a Christian framework and had avoided developing their implications.'[6] Again, 'Neoplatonism was for Augustine much more than the bridge by which he passed over to the church; it entered into his religious experience, and its influence on his thinking was pervasive and permanent'.[7] But he gave Neoplatonism and with it Christianity a psychological turn which was most alien to all of Greek thinking. He derived the notion of original sin from the evil nature of matter. He also developed the emphasis on faith, free will and the doctrine of grace. The philosophy of theology in his hands became the psychology of religion.

[1] *City of God*, Ch. VIII.

[2] *De Ideis*, 2. Cf. Raymond Klibansky, *The Continuity of the Platonic Tradition during the Middle Ages* (London 1950, Warburg Institute), p. 23.

[3] *De Moribus Eccl.*, 2, 2, 2.   [4] *City of God*, X, 2.

[5] *Confessions*, VII, x, xvii.

[6] R. R. Bolgar, *The Classical Heritage* (Cambridge 1954, University Press), p. 175.

[7] George Foot Moore, *History of Religions* (New York 1949, Scribner), II, 194.

The Roman state had been a republic, then it became an empire. It was destroyed, but in its destruction gave rise to a third type of state: the Roman Church, which thus played the role of the third act in the Roman drama. How could the Church under those circumstances have failed to assume the trappings as well as the authority of political power, thus in a sense abdicating in the very hour of its birth as an institution from just those values for which it had been founded: the abjurgation of violence and the rule through love. Its greatest leaders thought in political similes. Plato's theory of Ideas and his political blue-prints in the *Republic* were combined by Augustine in his *City of God*. His *civitas terrena* had been destroyed by the Goths but not his *civitas coelestis* which was safe from harm even though not readily available for citizenship by the living. In this way Augustine marked the distinction between State and Church and foretold the replacement of the one by the other.

As late as the ninth century, we still have theologians defending the Philonian-Plotinian doctrine of emanation. John Scotus Eriugena discriminated four stages in 'the divine unfolding' whereby the universe emanates from God. But he tried— unsuccessfully—to show that there were no quarrels between reason and revelation and sought in this way to retain the supremacy of reason, thus retaining within the predominantly super-natural interpretation one of the most naturalistic elements. The evidence of another tradition off-stage, so to speak, was never altogether lacking. We have Wolfson's testimony that 'Marius Victorinus as well as John Scotus Eriugena were under the influence of Neoplatonism'.[1]

Post-Augustinian Christianity is, however, largely the story of the clarification of the dogma, and of the establishment of the Church as an institution. The two are not unrelated: to increase in institutions has meant also to increase in the firmness of dogma, for dogmas are the ground on which institutions are

[1] H. A. Wolfson, 'The Muslim Attributes and the Christian Trinity' in *The Harvard Theological Review*, Vol. XLIX (1956), p. 10.

established; they carry an inertia of belief, which welcomes reasons in favour of what is accepted, to continue its acceptance, and rejects reasons not in favour. Institutionalizing has always meant dogmatizing (though the question of whether it has to is open to discussion). And so it has been with the western religions, including Christianity. In adopting a dogmatic theology which stemmed originally from Plato, they departed from Plato in at least two ways: one, by dogmatic acceptance, and, two, by Neoplatonism. Both Neoplatonism and dogmatism are involved, and neither is Platonic.

Unfortunately, the fact is that Christianity was never truly Platonic. When arguments are made to the contrary, they rest on two pieces of evidence: the existence in the Middle Ages of an indirect tradition of Platonism, and the existence of an authentic though thin direct tradition consisting of Chalcidius' version of a portion of the *Timaeus* and of versions of the *Meno* and the *Phaedo* made by Henricus Aristippus in 1156.[1] Let us consider how much weight there is to these factors.

Who is to estimate the strength of an indirect tradition? More importantly, what is an indirect tradition worth when it is endeavouring to carry the precise and technical ideas of a thinker of the eminence of Plato? Verbal traditions are never known for their accuracy, and in this case, the indirect tradition of Plato had to meet the direct tradition of Neoplatonism in the writings of Plotinus. The argument for the continuity of the Platonic tradition during the Middle Ages seems more intent on saving the hypothesis than it does on saving the phenomena.

As to the direct tradition, we have garbled versions of portions of three Platonic dialogues out of at most twenty-five. How strong a tradition is that? Of course, it is something; but even if all the Platonic dialogues had existed, it would not necessarily have had the effect of continuing the Platonic tradition. Neoplatonism, because of its dominant emotionalism, fits

---

[1] Raymond Klibansky, *The Continuity of the Platonic Tradition During the Middle Ages* (London 1950, Warburg Institute), pp. 27–8 *et passim*.

with religion better than the rationalism of Plato; and even after Plato's dialogues were translated into modern European languages and studied in the Renaissance and after, Plato himself continued to be read Neoplatonically! There are theologians alive today who are still under the illusion that Plato supposed that the Ideas are thoughts in the mind of God.

H. GREEK ORTHODOX NEOPLATONISM

Of Byzantine Christianity we in the west know far less than we should. Its history has been neglected in the West in favour of the Roman Catholic Church. The Greek Orthodox Church had the bad luck to be overrun by intolerant and dogmatic movements as strong as itself: first by the Moslems and then by the communists. In the West, the Roman Catholic Church had better luck, for the Protestants who struggled against the Church for survival have permitted the Roman Catholics to exist and to practise their religion under conditions of absolute equality, and so the Church has had no difficulty in surviving. That the tolerance has not been returned is well known, and wherever the Catholic Church succeeds in regaining political power, for instance in the 1950's in Spain and Colombia, the Protestants have not been granted equal religious rights. The result of the survival of the Roman Catholic Church in the West is that the West knows little of the history of the Greek Church, which has always been blamed for being schismatic, though not heretical like the Protestants. We need a good history of Byzantine Neoplatonism.

The conquests of Alexander of Macedon accomplished something which the historians of religion are apt to overlook. They insured that the culture of Greece in general, and of Athens in particular, would be known in the East, especially in the area we now refer to as the Middle East, centuries before Rome as a power existed. The spread of Greek culture into Persia under the Seleucids, intended by them as a support for their reign, included artists and philosophers, and helped to preserve Greek culture in the Middle East where it was later picked up by the Greek Orthodox civilization and afterwards taken over by the crusading Arabs and by them retained until Europe was able much later to receive it. Many a Persian prince, such as Shapur in the third century A.D. and Chosroes I in the sixth, encouraged the translation of Greek philosophy.[1]

By the third century A.D., Plato had become the subject of miraculous tales. For instance, he was the son of Apollo,[2] he claimed the possession of a third eye,[3] etc. Origen complained that for the uneducated Plato's writings were too difficult, and the *Crito*, he held therefore, was far inferior to the Gospels of Jesus although on some points saying much the same things.[4]

Nemesius of Emesa mixed Aristotelian arguments and Biblical expressions, and, although attacked by more orthodox Neoplatonists, such as Aeneas of Gaza, probably showed the way to the later combination of Aristotle with Neoplatonism. For Dionysius the Areopagite in the fifth century the ineffability of the One and the doctrine of emanation and the return of the soul to God were doctrines that indicated clearly the influence of Plotinus and Proclus.

Of course all those thinkers in the East who supposed that they were being faithful Platonists were actually—as in the West—Neoplatonists.

The name of Plato, his reputation and some of his works, probably passed into the Byzantine culture through the medium of that great repository of Greek culture, Alexandria. Unfortunately, however, Alexandria was also the centre where Neoplatonism was born, Philo and Plotinus lived and wrote there. And so it was also the place where Plato began to be subjected to Neoplatonic interpretation. It is safe to assert that the Platonism possessed by the Byzantines was what we would call Neoplatonism,

---

[1] Cf. e.g. R. Ghirshman, *Iran* (Middlesex 1954, Penguin Books), pp. 224 ff., 294, 304, 340.   [2] Origen, *Contra Celsum*, I: 37.

[3] *Ibid.*, VI: 8.   [4] *Ibid.*, VII: 61.

a Plato heavily suffused with his own mystical elements, accorded the three principles of Neoplatonism and forgiven for having lived before the Christian era.

From the very liberal teachings of Photius and the opening of Bardas' university in the ninth century, to the reintroduction of Plato to western Europe by Pletho via the founding of the Platonic Academy at Florence in the fifteenth century, Plato was known and admired. By the eleventh century, John Mauropus could say that Plato must have been a Christian because he was such a fine philosopher.[1] The outstanding names of Michael Psellus in the eleventh century, of John Italus in the twelfth and of Nicephorus Blemmydes in the thirteenth, are the best known, though of these Psellus was the chief Platonist. The others knew Plato but preferred Aristotle, and most saw a deep cleavage between the two. Italus is credited with having separated philosophy from theology and of maintaining that opinions could be held in either study independently of the other.[2]

Photius read and commented on the Platonic dialogues at length, and it may be largely due to his interest in Plato that our editions have survived. Together with George Hamartolos, Photius kept alive the controversy between the Platonists and Aristotelians, arguing in favour of Plato. Photius, and his pupil, Arethas, thought of Plato and the Neoplatonists together and saw no distinction between them. He was, in short, a Neoplatonist and not a Platonist. Politically powerful, Pletho lacked the disinterest in actual affairs, and especially in political matters, which sharply distinguished the Neoplatonists from Plato, and even sought to apply some of the principles of Plato's *Republic* to settling the unrest in southern Greece.[3] But Plotinian mysticism overcame him in the end, and such impulses as he may have had of a rational nature were drowned in pagan theology.

[1] Bolgar, *The Classical Heritage*, p. 74.
[2] A. A. Vasiliev, *History of the Byzantine Empire* (Madison 1952, University of Wisconsin Press), p. 474 *et passim*.
[3] Ernest Barker, *Social and Political Thought in Byzantium*, (Oxford 1957, Clarendon Press), p. 23.

After Photius the interest in Plato sputtered along, and the next great name in this connection does not occur until the eleventh century. Michael Psellus revived that interest, and after that date Platonism (in the name of Plato) never lacked a champion. The eleventh century and the following saw an intellectual revival in which the attainments of the Greek Orthodox culture reached its height. The founding of a university in Constantinople occurred during Psellus' lifetime. Psellus himself was more interested in concrete humanity than he was in abstract thought,[1] and he saw in the Platonic dialogues just so many anticipations of Christian truth. He was most emphatically a Neoplatonist rather than a Platonist. The Neoplatonic version of Psellus' Platonism is well brought out in many passages of his writings. Two illustrations may suffice. Psellus referred to 'the hidden meanings' contained in the Platonic allegories,[2] and he gave almost equal place to Plato and Aristotle, Plotinus, Porphyry and Iamblichus.[3] He gave an important place also to the dialogue which many scholars consider spurious, the *Epinomis*.[4] Yet he seems to have been responsible none the less for a revival of Plato in Byzantium and thus may have contributed heavily to the survival of our knowledge of him through the offices of Pletho.[5]

Pletho, the last of the three great Platonists of Byzantium, was, like his predecessors, a Neoplatonist. Theoretically, Pletho sought to demonstrate the superiority of Plato to Aristotle. Practically, he sought, as the Roman Emperor Julian had many centuries before him, to found a Neoplatonic religion with Zoroastrian elements to replace Christianity, an attempt which failed. His chief service to Platonism seems to have been performed through a political opportunity. Having been designated as one

---

[1] See the quotation in Barker, *op. cit.*, p. 133.

[2] Michael Psellus, *Chronographia*, trans. E. R. A. Sewter (London 1953, Routledge and Kegan Paul), p. 40.

[3] *Op. cit.*, p. 128.   [4] *Op. cit.*, p. 128.

[5] See e.g. F. Ueberweg, *History of Philosophy* (New York 1871–3, Scribner), 2 vols., Vol. II, pp. 8–9.

member of the Greek delegation to the council which met in Florence in 1438–39 to consider the union of the Eastern or Greek Orthodox Church with the Western or Roman Catholic, he seems to have spent his time lecturing on 'Platonism' (i.e. Neoplatonism). Inspired by hearing him, Cosimo de Medici founded the Florentine Academy, through which Plato's fame was spread in Europe.

That the Byzantine scholars towards the end were not confined to the individualistic mysticism which so characterized the Neo-platonists is clear from Pletho's work and influence. He planned a social system for the Greek mainland which suggested strongly the reading of the *Republic*. There was also the defence of Plato undertaken in writing by Bessarion of Trebizond. Both he and Pletho were at work in Italy when Constantinople fell to the Turks in 1453.

I. JEWISH NEOPLATONISM

Before Judaism encountered Hellenism, it was a religion which would have been most consistent with the second of Plato's two religions, the one we have called the Greek version of realism. For the emphasis of Judaism was on the moral order and its maintenance in this world. Justice, kindness,[1] humility,[2] and peace;[3] love,[4] and the knowledge of God[5] were the touchstones of the prophets. The demand for justice above all virtues appears over and over again;[6] Deuteronomy was nothing more than a detailing of the charter for justice, and the Commandments a moral code. History was the dramatic exemplification of the moral order. Super-naturalism was maintained but not at the expense of this world; God was a personal God, a sort of powerful extension of this world and its operator, who laid down the law and then observed carefully its execution or failure; He was always present and watchful, an immanent though eternal God.

---

[1] Leviticus xix. 18.   [2] Micah vi. 8.   [3] Micah iv. 3.   [4] Hosea vii. 6.
[5] Hosea iv. 6   [6] Isaiah i. 10–17; Hosea x. 12; Amos v. 21–24.

The prophets spoke of Him, they quoted Him. Judaism looks forward to a golden age in the future in this world, when there shall be a Messiah and a resurrection of those among the dead who have led good lives.

Here, then, is a religion and a theology consistent with metaphysical realism. God is real, He is eternal; but the world is, too. And the drama of good and evil has to be played out on the stage of space and time and matter, has to be illustrated in events. The punishment for those who have led evil lives is that they shall remain dead, they shall not arise on the day of resurrection; they are forbidden to return. Life is good, and those who have lived it in a good way will be bidden to return again just as they were.

Such was the Judaism of the two kingdoms and of the dispersion. But then Judaism had encountered Hellenism before the first century B.C. and was not thereafter free from its influence.

The similarity in many respects of the Hebrew and Greek traditions is evidenced in two ways. There was the contention, which was supported for centuries, that Plato had learned his philosophy from the Hebrew prophets,[1] and there was the influence of Hellenism on Jewish life and thought.

As to the first way, the passport of Plato to Christian circles was predicated upon the fact that he was not a pagan entirely but well within the Biblical tradition. If the Torah and Wisdom were one and the same, and if Plato had wisdom, then somehow Plato had come under the influence of the Torah. All that remained was to trace this influence, and the rest was simple. He had met Jeremiah on his visit to Egypt and learned from him the Mosaic Law. It may have been Aristobulus, who had made allegorical interpretations of passages in the Bible, and who had appealed to the Jewish doctrines incorporated in Orphic poems to support his contention that the Greek philosophers

---

[1] 'Judaism and World Philosophy', by Alexander Altmann, in *The Jews: Their History, Culture, and Religion*, edited by Louis Finkelstein (New York 1949, Harper), 2 vols., Vol. I, pp. 626–7.

had learned from an early translation of the Pentateuch,[1] to whom Philo owed something of his doctrine and the suggestion of his method.

As to the second way, there is an immense amount of evidence of a symbolic kind that a Hellenizing of traditional Judaism took place during the Greco-Roman period.[2] Professor Good-enough has collected sufficient artifacts to prove that the 'Jews were so Hellenized that they could borrow for their amulets, charms, graves, and synagogues the mystic symbols of paganism, even the forms of some of the pagan gods. For no error of induction or fancy in my own thinking can obscure the fact that Jews did borrow this art, not sporadically, but systematically and for their most sacred and official associations'.[3] The influence of Hellenism must have been strong upon Judaism to have pulled it out of its orbit to the extent that Goodenough's monumental work shows that it did.

Evidently, Philo, the greatest of the Hellenizing Jews, grew up in an atmosphere in which the Jewish concern with things Greek was hardly a novelty. Philo was simply the most important of those who tried to reconcile Judaism and Hellenism. We have already seen that Neoplatonism in the sense in which the western religions adopted it was chiefly (though not exclusively) a Jewish invention. For while the philosophy of the Academy after the death of Plato certainly exerted an influence and while the Stoics and Epicureans did also, Neoplatonism owed more to Philo than to any other single force. Philo gathered into his work the influence of the Stoics also, from Panaetius and Posidonius, both, incidentally, stout Platonists.

There were many serious distinctions between the way in which Neoplatonism affected Christianity and the way in which it affected Judaism, however. In Christianity it became

---

[1] Cf. Friedrich Ueberweg, *History of Philosophy* (New York 1871, Scribner), 2 vols., vol. I, p. 223.

[2] Erwin R. Goodenough, *Jewish Symbols in the Greco-Roman Period* (New York 1953–56, Pantheon Books).   [3] *Op. cit.*, iv, p. 62.

incorporated into the official theology and helped to shape part of the dogma. In Judaism there was and is no official theology, and hence neither Neoplatonism nor its influence could possibly become dogmatic.

A second serious difference consisted in the fact that while the Roman Catholic Church and the Greek Orthodox Church were institutions in the formal sense of deliberately organized and centrally directed organizations, the Jewish religion has not been, and its peculiar character still escapes definition, as even recent commentators have noticed.[1]

At all events it is clear that in such theology as there was among the Jews, with whatever institutional status we wish to assign it, there was a shift due to the influence of Neoplatonism. And it was a shift from an interpretation of Judaism which left alone might have accorded with Plato's Greek religion of realism but which under the influence of Neoplatonism after Philo shifted to the kind of interpretation of Judaism which was far more in accord with the Orphic religion of idealism. Post-Philonic Judaism, theologically speaking, is Orphism reasserted.

It is a curious fact that Philo invented Neoplatonism but that the chief influence of Neoplatonism on Jewish thinking did not issue directly from Philo. Not so curious, perhaps, in the light of the points made in the foregoing paragraphs of this section. For a religion lives in the atmosphere of ideas of its times. The religion of a minority is bound to be influenced to some extent by the religious ideas which are prevalent among the majority, especially when the minority is a relatively small one. In the early centuries of the Christian era Judaism lived in an atmosphere of Neoplatonism for which Plotinus was more responsible than Philo. Plotinus' debt to Philo was never acknowledged as part of the consideration. Under the influence of a

---

[1] Cf. Reinhold Niebuhr in *The New York Times Book Review* for August 19, 1956: 'the phenomenon of the Jewish people, as a race, a culture, and as the bearers of a religion, does not fit simply into any of the categories by which we try to comprehend historical phenomena.'

synthetic syncretism of Greek religious philosophy which was guided by adherence to the doctrines of Plotinus in particular and of Neoplatonism in general, the age was bound to impinge upon Judaism. A fragment of Artapanus from the first century B.C. relates that Musaeus was simply the Greek name for Moses who was the teacher of Orpheus.[1]

The rabbinical interpretation of the Bible in allegorical form was one result; but another and more important one was the Kabbala. In written form it probably dates from the ninth century and was certainly composed under the influence of Neoplatonism, as is evidenced, for instance, by the doctrine of emanation. The alleged esoteric teachings of Simeon ben Yohai (second century A.D.) in the form of a commentary on the Pentateuch reveals Neoplatonic doctrine. God is the absolute, there is a gradually descending series of emanations from God, and a disposition on the part of the soul to return to God. Asceticism is not omitted. There are definite Neoplatonic elements in Saadia Gaon (882–942) and in Isaac ben Solomon Israeli (850–950). There is Neo-platonism also in the next century, in the work of Joseph ibn Saddik. (d. 1149). But the greatest of the Jewish Neoplatonists is Solomon ibn Gabirol (Avicebron) (1021–1070) whose work derived possibly from Philo but most certainly from Plotinus and Proclus. The Ideas are still thoughts in the mind of God, the universe was still created by a series of emanations, and the corruptible world was still the source of evil. Like so many Jews in Spain, he was brought by the Moslems into contact with Greek thought. Although he died early, he lived long enough to write a religious classic, the *Fons Vitae*, which, like his earlier poems, showed strains of definite Neoplatonic influence.

In the twelfth century, there was a reaction against reason and philosophy in Judaism, in the person of Judah ha-Levi, who argued that the basic beliefs of Judaism rest on revelation. Creation *ex nihilo*, providence, and the immortality of the soul, are neither to be supported nor denied by reason or fact. Judah

---

[1] 'Hellenistic Jewish Literature', by Ralph Marcus in *The Jews*, Vol. II, p. 750.

ha-Levi was, however, also strongly influenced by Neoplatonism, although himself opposed to the doctrine of emanation and the theory of the Logos. Ha-Levi saw Judaism triumphant over Greek as over Christian and Mohammedan philosophy, and evidently did not see that Greek philosophy had already wrought subtle changes in his own version of Judaism.

J. MOSLEM NEOPLATONISM

Alexandria in Egypt was of course the prime source for the spread of Greek philosophy eastwards, and the additions there made to it, notably the contributions of Philo and Plotinus, played as a consequence no small role. As a matter of fact, when the Moslems first encountered Greek culture, they came upon it in the form of Neoplatonic doctrine, however falsely attributed. Alexandria as a centre of scholarship had its imitators which were substantially branches. First the one founded at Caesarea in Palestine by Origen, and, more importantly for the purposes of tracing the Neoplatonic religious philosophy, the one founded at Antioch in Syria by Malchion as early as A.D. 270.[1] The school at Nisibis founded about 320 and the one at Edessa in 373 brought Greek learning to the Syriac communities and with it of course Greek philosophy. Christianity was the fertilizing agent. 'The great importance of the Syriac speaking Christian communities was as the medium whereby Hellenistic philosophy and science was transmitted to the Arabic world'.[2]

The ideas of Greek philosophy, and in particular of Neoplatonism were ready and waiting in the Middle East. The Arabs were already engaged in expansion and conquest when Mohammed first appeared;[3] they were in one of the periodic outbursts in which the Semitic desert folk had been engaging for millenia[4] and needed only the rationality of a cause, in this case a religious

[1] De Lacy O'learn, *Arabic Thought and Its Place in History* (London 1922, Kegan Paul), p. 25. For much of the information in this section I am indebted to this excellent work.

[2] *Ibid.*, p. 53.   [3] *Ibid.*, p. 60.   [4] *Ibid.*, p. 61.

revelation, to spur them to greater efforts. From A.D. 635 to 641—
six years—they had conquered Syria, Iraq, Egypt, and Persia.[1]
The first masters of the new world of Islam were the Arabs;
under the Umayyads the intellectual impulse to the establishment
of theology was wanting. Where it existed at all, it came in the
form of criticism of the conventional outlook of Muslim theology.
Within eighty years after the Arab 'Umayyads had been replaced
by the Persian 'Abbasids, much of Aristotle, some of Plato,
and a great many of the Neoplatonic commentators, were available
in Arabic translations. The Persian Shi'ites had a leaning towards
Greek philosophy, and they furthered the allegorical interpretation of the Qu'ran in the light of Neoplatonism.

Aristotle's logic, and the last three books of the *Enneads* of
Plotinus, under the name of 'Aristotle's theology', together
with some abstracts from Proclus and from Alexander of
Aphrodisias, were the chief influences in forming the Neoplatonic
ideas of the Muslim culture.

Gradually, the translators became commentators. The first
large movement which lent itself to Neoplatonism was Sufism.
From a start in primitive Moslem notions of a mystical nature,
the Sufis, led by Dhu al-Nun Misri, by the ninth century had
acquired an intellectual content for their doctrine largely acquired
from Neoplatonism. In the Essays of the Ikhwan al-Safa, the
unity of Plato and Aristotle seen through Neoplatonic commentators was taken for granted by the society at Basra. The Platonic
virtues, the definition of virtue as a mean between extreme
vices from Aristotle, much of the *Nichomachean Ethics* and
Neoplatonic ideas of the nature and destiny of the soul, came
together here, and remained together subsequently in Moslem
theology. For instance, the doctrine of emanation, which is to
be found neither in Plato nor in Aristotle, was assumed for both.

The first important Arabic philosopher was al-Kindi who
died in 870. This translator turned philosopher was thoroughly

[1] De Lacy O'learn, *Arabic Thought and Its Place in History* (London 1922,
Kegan Paul), p. 64.

indoctrinated with Neoplatonism, and the beginning of a long line of Moslem philosophers who relied on Greek texts for their information. Al-Kindi revised the translation of the portion of Plotinus which had come to be known as Aristotle's theology, and gave it a new authority. Already in al-Kindi we find the Neoplatonic version of the doctrine of emanation and a variety of interpretations of the human soul which accords very closely with it. The world-soul is the first emanation, and the human soul is an emanation from the world-soul.[1] He recognized Aristotle as the master, acknowledged himself an Aristotelian, and made a thoroughly Neoplatonic interpretation of Aristotelianism. The intelligence of God is the cause of the existence of the world. There is a world-soul intermediate between God and the world. The world-soul is an emanation from God, and the human soul is an emanation from the world-soul.

The Muslim theologians, like the Jewish and the Christian, had to deal with Greek rationalism; but the Muslim differed from the others in at least one important respect: they possessed and valued highly the Greek scientific works. The Christians and Jews left out of their account the scientific works of Aristotle, and the mathematics of other Greek thinkers; the Moslems did not. The necessity of grounding metaphysics on a study of nature is at least as old as the Arabian school, and it began with al-Kindi and from him was passed on to other Muslim theologians. But they, like the Greeks, still lacked the study of nature on which to ground metaphysics. They preserved the Greek scientific findings in astronomy, in physics and in medicine, and used such knowledge *practically;* it never occurred to them to use it *theoretically* as well. Hence the discovery of the natural sciences and their method had once again to wait. The preservation of those elements which were necessary to science were received by the Arabs from the Greeks, and passed on by the theologians, most of whom also practised medicine.

[1] Cf. T. J. De Boer, *History of Philosophy in Islam*, trans. E. R. Jones (London 1903, Luzac), pp. 97 ff., esp. 101.

The Neoplatonists did not always have things their own way. The men the Arabs called *falasifa* were considered quite unorthodox, and there existed figures of reaction who wished to return to the problems posed by orthodoxy. The greatest of these was al-Ghazali (1058–1128) but the most famous of the earlier names was that of al-Ashari (d. 935), trained by the Mu'tazalites and devoted to the destruction of the kind of rationalism which the Neoplatonists had introduced. He opposed interpretation with literalness, thought with observances, and held that revelation was sufficient to stand alone.

The greatest of the Muslim philosophers was al-Farabi (d. 950). For him Plato and Aristotle were in perfect agreement, and neither contradicted the Qu'ran. In effect, he did what all other philosophers, both eastern and western, had become accustomed to doing: he made a Neoplatonic interpretation of Aristotle without recognizing how much both had become transmuted in the process. The chief interest of al-Farabi lay in logic, and he studied and commented on Aristotle's logic, without, however, adding much to it. Al-Farabi has the Neoplatonic tokens, especially the world as the last emanation. For him the lowly state of matter is what renders it intractable; evil belongs to the finite and the individual. His influence on later Muslim philosophers, on Avicenna and Averroes, was very great indeed.

Ibn Sina (or Avicenna 980–1037) in particular departs very little from the teachings of al-Farabi. He discussed philosophy in distinction from Moslem theology but did not set up a doctrinal distinction between them. Avicenna followed Plotinus in believing that God is One and that from the One only one can develop. Therefore form and matter cannot emanate from God but only form. The process of emanation consists of an unfolding of trinities, e.g. World-Spirit, Sphere-Spirit, Spirit.[1] In his justly famous solution to the problem of universals which had been

[1] Cf. De Boer, *History of Philosophy in Islam*, p. 135; also Raymond Klibansky, *The Continuity of the Platonic Tradition During the Middle Ages* (London 1950, Warburg Institute), p. 17.

bequeathed to the philosophical world by Porphyry, Avicenna had ruled that universals do exist apart from physical things and human minds, but only as thoughts in the mind of God. His statement, more specifically, is that the genus, or universal, has three stages of existence, the first of which is 'before the many, when it is in the wisdom of God'.[1] This, as Professor Wolfson has pointed out, is a reproduction of the exact words used by Ammonius in his commentary on Porphyry's *Isagoge*. The retention by the Muslim philosophers of the principles of Neoplatonism is here precisely traced.[2] Al-Farabi held similar views, and neither he nor Avicenna had any conception that they were departing from Plato and Aristotle, but, quite to the contrary, thought that they had found a means of reconciling Plato and Aristotle.[3] Avicenna was the last of the great eastern theologians; after him, the wave of orthodoxy flowed back, and we must look to the west for the continuance of the Neoplatonic tradition.

It is curious that in Islam the formulation of orthodoxy was contemporary with its interpretation. The author, so to speak, of Muslim orthodoxy was al-Ghazali. By his own account, he first went through a period of scepticism during which he would not admit anything to belief except on the basis of necessary truths and the evidence of the senses.[4] After this, he went carefully through the writings of the philosophers,[5] only to become convinced that the way of the mystics was the only true path to God and eternal life. Thereafter, al-Ghazali remained an enemy of philosophy. His *Destruction of the Philosophers* was a blast aimed at the Neoplatonic rationalists, the Plotinian interpreters of Aristotle. He ended the formation of Muslim scholasticism by strengthening and confirming the work of al-Ashari and

---

[1] Quoted in H. A. Wolfson, 'Avicenna, Algazali and Averroes on divine attributes', in *Homenaje a Millas-Vallicrosa*, Vol. II (Barcelona 1956, Consejo Superior de Investigaciones Cientificas), p. 548.

[2] *Op. cit.*, pp. 548–9.　　　　　　　　　　　　　　[3] *Ibid.*, pp. 549–50.

[4] *Deliverance from Error*, translated in W. Montgomery Watt, *The Faith and Practice of Al-Ghazali* (London 1953, Allen and Unwin), p. 22.

[5] *Op. cit.*, pp. 30 ff.

al-Baqilani: philosophy is not necessary to religious thought; truth is not attainable through revelation alone. As Plotinus had shown, there is in addition a final intuition of God possible to those who maintain an ascetic discipline: mysticism can be added to reason and revelation as one of the paths to God. Al-Ghazali was a personal force, much given to the interpretation of religion in emotional terms. Religion is subjective, we can understand the next world through feeling much better than we can this one through reason.[1]

In returning to Plotinus, al-Ghazali illustrated clearly that the dominance of the emotions over the reason produces a sum which is distinctly anti-rational, and with it he was able to oppose Plato and Aristotle, in whom the reason is dominant over the emotions. In all subsequent western philosophy the attempt to make a Neoplatonic (instead of a Platonic) interpretation of Aristotle meant the attempt to subordinate reason to emotion in matters of institutionalized religion and theology. 'A positive religion can never be content to recognize the leading position of philosophy in the realm of truth. It was only natural that the theologies of the West, like their brethren of the East should seek to profit by the favour of circumstances, and take no rest until they had reduced the mistress to the position of the handmaid of Theology.'[2] This position achieved considerable endorsement, and in the East at least philosophy went out of favour.

---

[1] Cf. De Boer, *History of Philosophy in Islam*, pp. 154 ff.
[2] *Op. cit.*, p. 199.

CHAPTER XI

LATER NEOPLATONISM:
THE MIDDLE AGES

A. GENERAL CHARACTERISTICS

We are now to consider the fate of Plato's philosophy in the later Middle Ages, the period which reached its culmination in the thirteenth century. Later Neoplatonism may be characterized in general by the recognition that theory had got off the ground altogether and left almost no contact with practice, a situation in theory which ill accorded with daily experience. We live in this world at least, even if we also live in and for another world; and to neglect in thought the things of this world to the extent to which Neoplatonism had led the theologians of western Europe to do, allowed appalling conditions to prevail. The swing of the pendulum was many centuries later to bring about equally appalling conditions in the realm of speculation, when concentration on practice led to the neglect of respectable theory; but in the later Middle Ages this was not yet true, and it was not to be true for a long while.

Excesses of otherworldly consideration led to the theological attempt to get back somehow to solid ground. This consisted in the effort to recapture, in the name of Aristotle, something of the religious ideas which were contained in the Greek version of realism according to Plato. Plato had discovered the theory of the Ideas, but Aristotle was credited with the restoration of the importance of substance, and it was a doctrine of substance which was sorely needed. However, the restoration of the theological aspect of the values of this world proved to be self-defeating, for they took the form of a Neoplatonic interpretation. The twelfth and thirteenth-century philosophers managed somehow to see Aristotle through Neoplatonic spectacles which had by that time become commonplace. The combination of the Ideas with substance made an uneasy synthesis, yet provided the two poles whereby vacillation could give the illusion of a width of range: from fact to mysticism, it seemed, though only mysticism was truly covered. The result was a further hardening of the dogma and a confusion of presentation. The syncretism of St. Thomas was not broad enough to sublate the endlessly restless and inconsistent elements which it endeavoured to include, and the attempt to make it do so brought about an intellectual revolt and a new form of Christianity.

Platonism in the Middle Ages was not represented by the works of Plato, which were almost unknown. It is a Roman Catholic historian of philosophy to whom we owe the statement that Plato was a philosopher 'of whom the mediaevals really did not know very much'.[1] Plato was nowhere, but Platonism was everywhere during the Middle Ages, Etienne Gilson observes.[2] Indeed, 'The *Timaeus* is the only work of Plato's that the Middle Ages possessed'.[3] 'Since none of Plato's works with the solitary exception of a Neoplatonist translation of the *Timaeus*[4] were available in the West before the twelfth century (and such dialogues as made their appearance after 1100 were few in number and rarely copied) while the doctrines of Plotinus, or extensions of them, could be exhaustively studied in Macrobius or Dionysius, any philosopher who sought to advance from the Augustinian position by drawing more heavily on ancient sources was bound in practice to end up as a Neo-

[1] Frederick Copleston, S.J., *A History of Philosophy* (London 1953, Burns, Oates and Washbourne), 3 vols., Vol. II, p. 4.

[2] *Philosophie du moyen age* (Paris 1944), p. 268.

[3] Ernst Robert Curtius, *European Literature and the Latin Middle Ages* (New York 1953, Pantheon), p. 544.

[4] In the Latin translation of Chalcidius, see Paul Shorey, *Platonism*, p. 89, 91, 105, and notes.

platonist'.[1] The *Meno* and the *Phaedo* were translated in the twelfth century by Henricus Aristippus, and then so far as we know there was nothing more for several centuries.

The ignorance of Plato's *Dialogues* in the Middle Ages was perhaps no accident. Platonism except for its rare practical aspects would not have been well received. For in the Middle Ages, curiously enough, only those studies were fostered which offered some practical advantage. 'Law, medicine and theology were the three foci of mediaeval thought'[2] for the reason that keeping out of trouble, recovering health, and last and most important, surviving death, were practical ends. Despite the otherworldliness of the western religions and their elaborate Neoplatonic theology, personal considerations were prominent: the longest life was the one to be lived in the next world, and so actions leading to the best treatment there were chiefly to be exercised here. Hence the almost total absence in scholastic thought of what might be described as detached inquiry. What concerned the fate of the soul could hardly be described as disinterest. Now, Platonism as such, if we mean by it the philosophical inquiries of Socrates and Plato, is concerned with the detached and disinterested search for truth, which is theoretical rather than practical in the narrow sense of the word. That there is also a broader sense in which the theoretical proved practical had to await the advent of experimental science to be revealed.

Now, the Neoplatonism of Philo and Plotinus consisted in just those changes and altered interpretations of the Platonic doctrine which would lend themselves to practical theological concerns. Platonism was available in the Middle Ages chiefly through the works of Proclus, who is known to have exercised a heavy influence on Aquinas. But in general we may define the Neoplatonism of the later Middle Ages as the theologically-interpreted combination of Neoplatonism with the newly discovered Aristotle. A thousand years of Christian Europe

[1] R. R. Bolgar, *The Classical Heritage* (Cambridge 1954, University Press), p. 175.   [2] *Ibid.*, p. 133.

without philosophy—and then stimulated to it only by the Moslem revival of Greek philosophy, such is the plain record. And then to get it in the form of a Neoplatonic interpretation of Aristotle, is also peculiar. Surely Philo and Plotinus, both of whom were very late in Greek culture, did not properly represent it; and as for Aristotle, there is clear evidence of three doctrines which were dead against the corresponding doctrines of the three revealed religions of the West. Professor Moore has put this very well. 'The great stumbling-blocks in the genuine Aristotle to Moslems, as well as to Jews and Christians, were, *first*, the eternity of the universe, which was the necessary corollary of his conception of God as the First Cause; *second*, the limitation of God's knowledge to universals, which excludes particular providence; and, *third*, his denial of immortality of the individual soul. All these theories are integral parts of Aristotle's system, and they are in flat contradiction to the fundamental doctrines of all three religions, creation, providence and retribution.'[1]

By the time Aristotle reached Europe, he had been through the hands of the Hellenistic Neoplatonists and the Moslem theologians. He had become in many respects hard to recognize. Gone was the old Greek conception of man as part of nature and of God or the gods as the cause, first or final, of nature, a conception in which nature, not man, is central, and man counts only as an element in nature. Instead, the Jewish, Christian and Moslem preference for God and man to the exclusion of nature from the theological account, had asserted itself. A current Catholic historian expresses the point of view very well when he asserts that for the Christian 'each human person is ultimately of more value than the whole material universe'.[2] It is important to emphasize at this point that the influence of Aristotle on the western religions came from his secular metaphysics and ethics, and not from such strands as could be separated out of his

[1] George Foot Moore, *History of Religions* (New York 1949, Scribner), 2 vols., Vol. II, pp. 453–4.
[2] Copleston, *History of Philosophy*, II, 428.

religious views.[1] A necessary though hardly a highly-regarded substance in combination with the Ideas conceived as thoughts in the mind of God and also outside God in the divine Logos was the result.

The formula of the Neoplatonic interpretation of Aristotle was adopted by all three western religions—for by now Judaism and Christianity had been joined by a third: Islam. In the twelfth century Averroes introduced Aristotle to the Arabs and Maimonides introduced him to the Jews, both in Cordoba. In the thirteenth century, Aquinas introduced him to the Christians. All three employed the familiar Plotinian type of Neoplatonism and through it saw their similar versions of Aristotle. There was little Plato in any of this, if we mean by Plato the philosophy contained in the *Dialogues* by him, and there was little of Aristotle either, if by Aristotle we mean the probative secular philosophy of the *Metaphysics* and the *Nichomachean Ethics*. In this sense it is safe to say simply that the religious ideas of Plato and Aristotle have never been applied to any organized and institutionalized religion, though there is no good reason why they could not be or should not be.

B. AQUINAS

Since the theology of Aquinas is now official in the Roman Catholic Church and Aquinas himself a saint, it is fair to consider him as typical of the Neoplatonism of the later Christian Middle Ages. We shall therefore search in his writings for the evidence of Neoplatonism.

The issue between nominalism and realism (and idealism) had been occasioned by the question in Boethius' commentary on the *Isagoge* of Porphyry as to whether the genera and species of Aristotle were to be interpreted realistically or nominalistically, and had been discussed for many centuries and settled shortly

[1] See for example above, Ch. VI.

before Aquinas' day by some theologians, at least, in a form in which it was taken by Aquinas; specifically by Abelard and by John of Salisbury. 'Moderate realism' left the Ideas in the mind of God but insisted that human minds derive the knowledge of them from things, thus justifying all three of the alternatives but, oddly enough, leaving out the theory of Plato. For well before Aquinas, the doctrine of creation had established for the Christian tradition both the supposition that creation took place by successive stages in emanation and that actual things were copies of the Ideas as these were in the mind of God. There were no Platonists among the later scholastics, but there also were no thinkers who were not Neoplatonists. Neoplatonism made up the core of all western theology, and Christian theology was no exception. A tradition of particularistic inquiry which had lasted the thousand years from the time in the third century when Boethius had raised it,[1] through the support nominalism had received occasionally, as for instance by Berengar and Roscellinus, until the thirteenth century when it was decided to the satisfaction of Aquinas, can hardly have been traceable any more to the source some seven hundred years before Boethius when Plato had first discussed through the character of Socrates in the dialogues the theory of the Ideas. There was a tradition of rationalism among the scholastics, and it would have been more in agreement with Plato's own views; but it received no encouragement, and in the end was submerged. The names of John Scotus Eriugena and of Hugh St. Victor, for instance, for whom reason was the final authority, must be mentioned, although, to be sure, they left no impress of any strength upon Aquinas or the Catholic tradition.

In a recent article reference was made to 'the indispensable role of certain Platonic—or more accurately Neoplatonic—

[1] See e.g. Allard Pierson, *Disquisitio Historico-Dogmatica de Realismo et Nominalismo* (Amsterdam 1854, Kemink); Helen M. Barrett, *Boethius* (Cambridge 1940, University Press), pp. 41 f.; Henry Osborn Taylor, *The Mediaeval Mind* (London 1927, Macmillan), 2 vols., Vol. I, p. 305.

elements in the philosophical synthesis of St. Thomas'.[1] The distinction is still often carelessly drawn or blurred over, yet it is crucial. It is blurred over when, despite the fact that Aquinas' 'knowledge of Plato and of Platonism came, certainly for the most part, from other sources', it is still held possible to discuss Platonism as 'the Platonism described and criticized in the Thomistic texts themselves'.[2] It is crucial because of the differences between Plato and the Neoplatonism which Aquinas partly accepted and partly rejected. For as we have seen, Plato was all but totally unknown in the Middle Ages and so his true influence rendered ineffective; while the philosophy of Philo and Plotinus, the forms in which 'Plato' was taken over into the Christian theology, was a distinctly different affair.

When we come to consider Aquinas, we find that no one makes any argument against the Neoplatonic and Aristotelian influences. The example of the way in which Aristotle could be read Neoplatonically and then combined with Neoplatonism had already been shown in the Jewish and Moslem traditions by Maimonides and Averroes respectively. Perhaps Aquinas had read Averroes in the translation made by the Christian Archbishop of Toledo. It was easy enough to see that Averroes had made the kind of Neoplatonic interpretation of Aristotle which could be harmonized with the Koran. Aquinas had only to make the same kind of interpretation *mutatis mutandis* for Christianity. This he did; and to show how what he did is still acceptable to those who know better about the scholarship involved but still prefer faith to truth in the face of truth, no better evidence could be needed than this passage from a leading contemporary Catholic historian of philosophy. 'St. Thomas was anxious to rescue Aristotle from the toils of Averroes and to show that his philosophy did not necessarily involve the denial of divine

[1] 'The Platonic Heritage of Thomism', by W. Norris Clarke, S.J., in *The Review of Metaphysics*, Vol. VIII (1954), p. 106. It is interesting to compare the above quotation with the title of the article, which was allowed to stand.

[2] R. J. Henle, *Saint Thomas and Platonism* (The Hague 1956, Martinus Nijhoff), p. xxi.

providence or of personal immortality, and in this he succeeded, even if his interpretation of what Aristotle actually thought on these matters is probably not the correct one.'[1]

Thus we have in Aquinas the emanation theory, though in somewhat disguised form. Aquinas rejected the literal doctrine of emanation, on the ground that God did not act from will and design if it were true, for if He had acted from will and design, then the process of emanation would not have been needed.[2] But there are other doctrines of a more purely Scriptural nature which could be read as being similar to if not identical with the doctrine of emanation. It should be recalled here that Plotinus was not a Christian but a pagan enemy of the Christians, and that he did not draw on Old Testament sources, but that Aquinas did; and so we may be justified in recognizing God's act of creation as the Christian version of emanation. God did not spill over from His own substance, but He did create the world out of nothing and He alone could create and He could create freely,[3] a view of creation towards which the Neoplatonic Augustine had clearly shown the way.

The doctrine of participation implies the theory of emanation. For Aquinas, participation means to receive from another a part of his perfection.[4] It is possible for Father Little to say on one and the same page both that 'Plotinus and Augustine had already emended Platonism by finding a doctrine of participation' and to refer to 'the Platonic principle of participation'! So the participation of Aquinas, which is the version of emanation which was found acceptable, stems from Plotinus and Augustine —clearly Neoplatonic rather than Platonic.[5] Despite Gilson's

---

[1] Frederick Copleston, *A History of Philosophy* (Westminster, Maryland 1952, Newman Press), 3 vols., Vol. II, pp. 426–7.

[2] *Summa Contra Gentiles*, II, 21–24. See also Wolfson, *Philo*, I, pp. 283–4.

[3] *De Potentia*, 3, 1–7; *Summa Theologica*, Ia, 45, 1–3.

[4] *De Coelo*, Lect. 18, No. 6, and *In De Hebdom. Boetii*, cap. 2, quoted in Arthur Little, S.J., *The Platonic Heritage of Thomism* (Dublin no date, Golden Eagle Books), p. 38, q.v.

[5] *Op. cit.*, p. 279.

clear assertion that ' "to participate in God" means "not to be God",'[1] which would eliminate from consideration any Platonic connection whatsoever, since Plato had neither a doctrine of emanation nor any such doctrine of participation, the commentators on St. Thomas continue to father on to Plato some connection which would justify them in speaking of a 'Platonic Participation'.[2] A *via Platonica* is still attributed to St. Thomas, even though it is admitted that he worked *entirely* with secondary sources; whereas Plato is considered difficult enough even for those who work with the original.

We certainly do have in Aquinas the notion of the Ideas as thoughts in the divine mind, *necesse est ponere in mente divine ideas*. He said flatly that 'It is necessary to suppose ideas in the divine mind . . . There must exist in the divine mind a form to the likeness of which the world was made. And in this the notion of an idea consists.'[3] And again, 'And therefore we must say that in the divine wisdom are the models of all things, which we have called ideas—i.e. exemplary forms existing in the divine mind. And although these ideas are multiplied by their relations to things, nevertheless, they are not really distinct from the divine essence, inasmuch as the likeness of that essence can be shared diversely by different things. In this manner, therefore, God Himself is the first exemplar of all things'.[4] By the 'divine wisdom' Aquinas clearly does not mean the Logos, for in the first of the two passages quoted above from the *Summa Theologica* he said 'God does not understand things according to an idea existing outside Himself'.

As for the third Neoplatonic principle, namely, that matter is the source of evil, we find in Aquinas no ultimate principle of evil, but we do find the privation of the good. Matter as

[1] Etienne Gilson, *The Philosophy of St. Thomas Aquinas*, trans. by E. Bullough (London 1929, W. Heffer), p. 140 and note 18.

[2] R. J. Henle, *Saint Thomas and Platonism* (The Hague 1956, Martinus Nijhoff), Ch. VII.

[3] *Summa Theologica*, Part Ia, Q. 15, Art. 1.

[4] *Ibid.*, Part I, Q. 44, Art. 3, *Ad. Resp.*

characterized by quantity is the principle of individuation, and this is impossible for pure spirits. Creation, for Aquinas, was a descent.[1] In the hierarchy of unequal essences, some are outside the reach of evil, but others are subject to evil and corruptible. Now, the matter of the celestial spheres is incorruptible,[2] and matter is good and was created by God.[3] But it is none the less the ground for evil, for evil is negation within a substance.[4] It is difficult to see how one could believe in the doctrine of emanation and not accept the connection of matter with evil, even if, as in the case of Aquinas, matter was not evil in itself.

Aristotle was condemned as late as 1210, when the teaching, both public and private, of the natural philosophy of Aristotle was forbidden by the Council of Paris for the University. Exactly one hundred and thirteen years later, the theologian who had introduced Aristotle into Roman Catholic Christianity was canonized. And some five hundred years later—in 1879— with the Encyclical *Aeterni Patris* of Pope Leo XIII, Thomism became the official philosophy.

The vogue of Aristotle in the Roman Catholic Church since the days of Aquinas neglects three important facts.

The first of these is that Aristotle was a Platonist. He differed with his master on many points, in particular on the interpretation of the theory of Ideas; but he owed him a very great debt. Much of Aristotle, especially the metaphysics, the psychology and the logic, consists of a selection and rearrangement of material which is to be found also in the Platonic *Dialogues*.[5] Now, what Aquinas did, like Averroes and Maimonides before him, was to attempt to square Aristotle with Neoplatonism. Platonism was left out of the account, and no small wonder: Plato's own writings, with one rare exception, were unknown at the time. But the point is that since the recovery of Plato no adjustment

---

[1] *In lib. de Divin. Nomin.*, c. I., lect. I; *Cont. Gent.*, IV: 7.
[2] *Sum. Theol.*, I, 68, 4.   [3] *Ibid.*, I, 47, 2; I, 65, 2.
[4] *Cont. Gent.*, III: 7; *De Malo*, I. 1; *De Potentia*, III. 6.
[5] See e.g. Shorey, *Platonism*, p. 125.

has been made in the theology, which most certainly would have been established on a quite different basis had Plato been known then. Had Aquinas possessed as we do now a knowledge of the Platonic dialogues, his philosophy might have turned out quite differently. It is not as though he had to hand the writings of Plato, Aristotle and the Neoplatonists, and preferred the Neoplatonic interpretation of Aristotle introduced by the Moslems. We do not know what Thomism would be like had Aquinas known Plato, but we may be sure, judging by the degree to which his thought was affected by the philosophers he did know, that it would have been different.

The second important fact is that Aristotle had his own religious ideas, as we have tried to show in an earlier chapter.[1] Now, nothing in Aquinas can be shown to be in accord with the religious ideas of Aristotle, only with some of his other ideas. But what about his own religious ideas, did they count for nothing simply because they could not have been brought into accord with revealed religions? To use Aristotle's lay ideas in revealed religion and to neglect his own religious ideas is to use him in something of an irregular fashion—irregular, that is, so long as he is claimed in the way, for instance, that Aquinas claimed him.

A third important point is that while Aristotle was not an absolutist but, on the contrary, put everything in a suggestive and probative rather than a finalistic way,[2] Aquinas subscribed to the dogma of a revealed religion, and the only possible way in which he could hope to reconcile a probative philosophy with a dogmatic religion was to render the philosophy as absolute as the religion by fusing them into a new and absolute synthesis, which, in so far as it failed to be tentative and probative, meant not only a surrender of the philosophy to the religion (which was, as a matter of fact, in this case called for) but a distortion

---

[1] Ch. VI.

[2] 'Aristotle as Finite Ontologist', in *Tulane Studies in Philosophy* (New Orleans 1953, Tulane University), Vol. II, p. 39.

of the philosophy to the extent to which it is involved with its own method.

C. MAIMONIDES

The Neoplatonic interpretation of Aristotle was discovered and developed for the western religions by Jewish and Moslem theologians. Soloman ibn Gabirol in the eleventh century quickly followed up the rediscovery of Aristotle by the Moslems with a Neoplatonic interpretation. The doctrine of emanation is to be found in Solomon ibn Gabirol and also in Judah ha-Levi in the twelfth century.

It was Maimonides, however, who in the twelfth century completed and perfected the synthesis of religion and philosophy for the Jews. Like his predecessors in Neoplatonism, he definitely subordinated philosophy to theology, making philosophy subservient to Scripture.[1]

Maimonides, like Aquinas after him, rejected the emanation theory to the extent to which it denied that God acts by will and design.[2] But there is an emanation theory inherent in the revelations, and Maimonides was careful to expand it into a series of ten emanations, under the influence of Avicenna. The last of the ten consisted in a kind of actualizing intelligence which presided over the world and man. For if God is not only the highest but also the source of everything, if in paying compliments to God it is impossible to deny Him all the qualities and properties deemed good, then everything is assumed to have emanated from God. And the denial of His emanation by design is assumed and emanation rejected as a consequence, when it need not have been assumed in the first place; emanation as a theory being much broader than that would allow.

Like all other good Neoplatonists, Maimonides had no other understanding of the Platonic Ideas than as thoughts in the

---

[1] See the quotations in Wolfson, *Philo*, I, p. 157.
[2] See Wolfson, *Philo*, I, pp. 283–4.

mind of God.[1] Conventionally, in those terms, he also held that 'the species have no existence except in our own minds. Species and other classes are merely ideas formed in our minds, whilst everything in real existence is an individual object, or an aggregate of individual objects'.[2] The absolute oneness and unity of God in the Hebrew Scriptures would preclude the separate being of the Ideas.

That matter is the source of evil, the third principle by which we have decided to flag Neoplatonism as opposed to Platonism, was well understood and accepted by Maimonides.[3] God created evil only by producing the 'corporeal element'. What does not possess this corporeal element is not subject to evil. The human being with his 'dark and opaque body'[4] is of course subject to evil. Shades of Plotinus!

But the figure of Philo stands out from behind that of Plotinus, and we have the allegorical method vigorously defended. The imaginative faculty is the organ of prophecy, we are told.[5] The figurative interpretation of the language of the Scriptures is defended just as it was by Philo.[6]

Just as Philo sought to reconcile Plato with Scriptures, so Maimonides sought to reconcile Aristotle with Scriptures. But he thought of it as the reconciliation of reason with revelation, for he knew no reason other than Aristotle and he recognized no revelation other than the Hebrew Scriptures. The same task had been fulfilled by Averroes in his own time for the combination of Aristotle with Moslem revelation, and was to be fulfilled a century later by Aquinas for Aristotle and Christian revelation. In all three cases, the actual position of Plato had been left far behind.

The *Talmud* contains evidence of Neoplatonism sufficient for us to suspect that it may be part of the Neoplatonic tradition.

[1] *Guide of the Perplexed*, Ch. LXVIII.

[2] *Moses Maimonides, The Guide for the Perplexed*, translated by M. Friedlander (New York 1956, Dover), p. 289.

[3] *Op. cit.*, pp. 266–7.   [4] *Op. cit.*, p. 264.

[5] *Op. cit.*, Ch. XLVII.   [6] *Op. cit.*, Ch. IX.

It would probably be fair to say that Neoplatonism ended in the mysticism of the Kabbala. Here, the Pythagorean side of the Orphic tradition met with the underground tradition of primitive agricultural magic and merged with it. The Kabbala is definitely Neoplatonic, as most authorities agree. Maimonides was the last Jewish thinker in the Neoplatonic tradition. With Hasdai Crescas something else was born, a criticism of Aristotle and of the Neoplatonic interpretation with which his work had become by then traditionally encrusted. For Crescas, Aristotle was not perfect; and in argument after argument, he tried to take the Peripatetic philosopher apart.[1] He modified Aristotelianism in the direction of the unity of all nature and of atomism, thus helping to prepare the way for Spinoza and Bruno, and empiricism. As with Eriugena and Hugh of St. Victor in the Christian tradition, we get a faint suggestion of the naturalism which existed in Plato himself and even in Aristotle, but which had been lost since the Neoplatonic tradition had come to replace all previous Greek thought.

D. AVERROES

Of all the later scholastics, it was the Arabic physician and metaphysician, Avicenna (Ibn Sina) who was most responsible for introducing Aristotle to Jewish and Christian thinkers in western Europe, though of course other scholars in Islam had studied and preserved his work long before. Undoubtedly, Averroes derived much of his knowledge of Aristotle from al-Farabi and Avicenna.

Avicenna is credited with having solved the problem of universals, which had occupied theologians ever since the question of their status had been raised by Porphyry. Universals, Avicenna asserted, existed *in* things epistemologically, were derived from things and hence existed *after* things psychologically,

---

[1] Harry A. Wolfson, *Crescas' Critique of Aristotle* (Cambridge 1929, Harvard University Press).

but had always existed *before* things ontologically. But their existence *before* things, he went on in the then already traditional manner, is as thoughts in the mind of God.

It was Averroes in the twelfth century who established the final synthesis in the practice of making a Neoplatonic interpretation of Aristotle for the Moslems. Maimonides accomplished the same task in the same place and at the same time, but quite independently, for the Jews. Aquinas, following Maimonides, did the same thing for the Christians about a century later.

Of the three principles which we have chosen as sufficient to indicate the presence of Neoplatonism: the emanation theory, the Ideas as thoughts in the mind of God, and matter as the source of evil, it is clear that Averroes accepted the first. He admitted, for instance, that the theory 'that out of the one all things proceed by one first emanation is generally accepted',[1] i.e. by the Moslem philosophers. His own theory amounts to much the same thing.[2] Van Den Bergh believes that Averroes combines Aristotle's astronomy with the emanation theory of Neoplatonism.[3] There is some reason to suppose that in accepting the emanation theory the Arab philosophers thought they were following Plato. Among them also 'Plato and Platonism seem to have been confused'.[4]

As to the second principle, namely, that of the Ideas as thoughts in the mind of God, according to 'the Arabic philosophers (Averroes included) the Platonic Ideas, i.e. the universals, exist eternally in the mind of God'.[5] Could Plato have ever used a phrase such as 'divine intelligibles'?[6] Or does this not sound

---

[1] Averroes' *Tahafut Al-Tahafut* (London 1954, Luzac), edited by Simon Van Den Bergh, 2 vols., Vol. I, p. 107.   [2] See *Ibid.*, Vol. II, p. 73.
[3] *Ibid.*, Vol. II, p. 75.   [4] *Ibid.*, p. 203.
[5] Van Den Bergh, *ibid.*, Vol. II, p. 88.
[6] *Averroes' Commentary on Plato's Republic*, trans. E. I. J. Rosenthal (Cambridge 1956, University Press), p. 125. In this and all subsequent references to this book, it should be remembered that, as Dr. Rosenthal has reminded us, the *Commentary* has come down to us only in an Hebrew translation, and may not represent the exact words of Averroes. The general tenor, however, seems clear, particularly when it is compared with other writings of Averroes.

more like Philo and Plotinus? Plato never made the subject of political science free will and choice,[1] nor could Plato have ever said—as Philo or Plotinus could have—that 'What the religious laws in our own time think of this matter is what God wills'.[2]

As to the third principle, that matter is the source of evil, Averroes wrote, 'it is most fitting to relate evil to the representation of matter, rather in the manner of those who attribute evil to deprivation or non-existence'.[3] It would be difficult to discover a sharper contrast between Neoplatonism and Plato.

It is clear enough that Averroes was making an Aristotelian interpretation of Plato. It was Aristotle's metaphysics that Averroes combined with Plato's politics, and not Aristotle's *Politics* nor the metaphysics of Plato's earlier dialogues. The distinction between the sensible and the intelligible was not meant in Plato's sense, and indeed came from Aristotle's 'First Philosophy'.[4] Averroes quite frankly declared his choice in the matter of authority, for in one connection he said, 'If this is not the opinion of Plato, it is nevertheless the opinion of Aristotle, and is undoubtedly the truth'.[5]

Before Averroes, a Neoplatonic version of Aristotle represented Greek philosophy to the Muslim culture as it did to the Jews and the Christians. After Averroes, the Neoplatonic interpretation of Aristotle took its place as separate from theology. Averroes, like al-Farabi and Avicenna before him, became a leading Muslim authority. But it was Averroes who gave back to philosophy an authority of its own while holding theology inviolate, thus resolving all the contradictions between them by keeping them apart. Averroes 'spurned the subterfuges by which Aristotle was harmonized with the religious dogmas of creation, providence, and immortality. Science and philosophy are one thing; religion is another. Each should confine itself to its own

---

[1] *Averroes' Commentary on Plato's Republic*, trans. E. I. J. Rosenthal (Cambridge 1956, University Press), p. 111.   [2] *Ibid.*, p. 185.
[3] *Ibid.*, pp. 126–7.   [4] *Ibid.*, p. 192.   [5] *Ibid.*, p. 153.

sphere, and not intrude on the other'.[1] He was bitterly opposed to al-Ghazali who sought to prove the truths of religion, and insisted that philosophy did not stand or fall upon its ability to support the faith; and similarly that the faith stood alone but also that there were reasons for it. Hence his rejection of al-Ghazali's rejection of philosophy, the *Destruction of the Destruction*. By the time of Ibn Khaldun, not many years later, Aristotle and Averroes were the supreme authorities in matters of metaphysics, and Plato and al-Farabi in matters of theoretical politics.[2]

[1] George Foot Moore, *History of Religions* (New York 1949, Scribner), II, p. 455.
[2] Muhsin Mahdi, *Ibn Khaldun's Philosophy of History* (London 1957, Allen and Unwin), pp. 32–3, 79, 126.

CHAPTER XII

LATER NEOPLATONISM:
THE RENAISSANCE

The Renaissance has been characterized so many times and in so many ways that one more can hardly help. We are concerned chiefly with its effect upon the history of religious Platonism. But we can not overlook the interplay of Church and State in that connection. The Renaissance reversed the Roman process; for just as we saw that the birth of Christianity in the West meant the replacement of State by Church in the third act of the Roman drama,[1] so the Renaissance saw the replacement of the Church by the State. Society seems able to tolerate only one leading institution at a time. In the Renaissance, as the national states arose, the Church declined. For now there was a series of revolts against the Roman Catholic Church: Luther, Calvin, Zwingli, resulting in a series of Protestant Churches. The Counter-Reformation marked the attempt to hold the line, and it certainly did have the effect of forcing the ever-present political activities of the Roman Catholic Church out into the open, and employed such force in the hands of the newly created order of the Jesuits so ruthlessly that the Pope was compelled to disband them for a time. Institutions neither die nor decline quickly; but it was clear after a while that religion had given way to politics in the western world.

Curiously, Plato was introduced into the West through the medium of a religious conference. His popularity, or perhaps it would be more correct to say the popularity of Neoplatonism, was a result of its usefulness in the overthrow of the rigid

[1] See above, Ch. X(E).

structure of Roman Catholic dogmatism. It must not be forgotten that the conquest of Catholicism by Aristotle was complete. It may have been a Neoplatonic interpretation of Aristotle that was adopted, but it was Aristotle who was so interpreted. Plato came as a new voice to shatter the hard mould with his novelties. Thereafter, Neoplatonic interpretations of Plato replaced those of Aristotle.

A. THE REDISCOVERY OF PLATO

The big news of the Renaissance was the rediscovery of Plato, after more than a millenia of ignorance of his works, in the West at least. The East had not forgotten Plato, and, as we have seen, it was the lectures given by the Greek, Pletho, who had been sent to attend a council of eastern and western Churches, which first aroused the West to Plato's importance. Were it not for Greek Orthodox Christendom, Plato might have been lost. But the success of Pletho's lectures to Italian audiences led to the foundation in Florence of a Platonic Academy and was the reason why Cosimo de' Medici had the son of his physician, Ficino, educated in Greek, and specifically as a Platonist. The result was not only a considerable stirring of interest in things Greek and in Greek philosophy but also a huge and intense revival of Plato. Marsilio Ficino translated the *Dialogues* into Latin in 1482. The first French translation was made in 1541 and the first English one in 1592. Plotinus has proved Plato's evil genius, accompanying him closely and persisting in the obfuscation of his ideas and point of view. Not long after Ficino had translated Plato into Latin, a Latin translation of Plotinus also was made.

There is no doubt that Platonism was introduced into Europe by Pletho and the founding of the Florentine Academy devoted to Plato. But the Italians, who led the revival, nevertheless never understood Plato nor had anything of an intimate understanding of Greek culture generally.[1] For Renaissance humanism, Plato

[1] Leonardo Olschki, *The Genius of Italy* (London 1950, Gollancz), p. 264.

meant a way of thought, an atmosphere, rather than a systematic and didactic philosophical structure.[1] Ficino's Platonism was mysticism; there is no trace of Plato's metaphysics nor of his politics.[2] It was, besides, atmosphere and mysticism, sentiment and emotion,[3] and, logically, at the most a feeling for order and symmetry.[4] The Biblical God was replaced by the human souls striving to rejoin the divine source[5]—in short, by Neoplatonism.

A number of points must be made about the religious import of the rediscovery of Plato. In the Renaissance it was the occasion for his use as a tool against the scholastics![6] Ficino, who not only translated Plato but also wrote a *Theologica Platonica*, in which he identified the philosophical thought of Plato with that of Plotinus and Christianity in general, had no notion of doing anything unchristian. He wished to be approved by orthodoxy, and to remain a good member of the Church.

A third and most important point is that the effect of Neoplatonism was not to be thrown off so easily, not even by the rediscovery of the original writings of Plato. The interpretation of Plato as a Plotinian was continued, and everyone thought he saw in the *Dialogues* a confirmation of this unconscious view. The practice of reading Plotinus and Neoplatonism back into Plato did not end with the Middle Ages. It was revived in another form by the Florentines in the Renaissance, and was to be continued into the eighteenth century.[7] Florentine Renaissance Platonism, despite the new translations of Plato, was more Neoplatonic than Platonic. Dionysius the Areopagite played too large a role, and mysticism still held sway over rationalism.

The type of Renaissance Neoplatonism which was to prevail was set by Ficino and by Pico della Mirandola. The latter combined with the usual Neoplatonic elements a strong and enthusiastic belief in the mysticism and wisdom of the Kabbala.

[1] Leonardo Olschki, *The Genius of Italy* (London 1950, Gollancz), p. 268.
[2] *Ibid.*, p. 272.   [3] *Ibid.*, p. 275.   [4] *Ibid.*, p. 300.   [5] *Ibid.*, p. 277.
[6] See Bolgar, *The Classical Heritage*, p. 285, and note on 436.
[7] Cf. Werner Jaeger, *Paideia* (New York 1943, Oxford University Press), trans. G. Highet, II, pp. 77–8.

The amount of pure Platonism was accordingly reduced as the occult took over from the rational. These men had an enormous influence within and without their own country, and once again the understanding of Plato had to wait. The Swiss, Paracelsus, as well as the Cambridge Platonists, absorbed Kabbalism along with their Neoplatonism.

It has been argued by Huntington Cairns that one finds in Plato what one comes to him to find. Contradictory positions no doubt abound in the *Dialogues;* and by a careful process of selection and interpretation, by considering as axioms what one prefers and as theorems what can be interpreted to mean what the axioms require as a matter of deduction, it is possible to a large extent to make of Plato whatever one wishes. Ficino came to his task of reading and translating steeped in the Neoplatonic tradition which the Roman Catholic Church had preserved from the Hellenistic period of Philo and Plotinus, and with even this covered over with a goodly measure of sheer mysticism. He found in Plato what these ideas required him to find, and so construed the rest. He wished to construct a system consisting of Church dogma interpreted as natural theology together with a liberalized and ethicized Platonism. But there were also the traditions of magic and superstition, of astrology, witchcraft and the philosopher's stone; and Platonism was made to justify all of these.

Hence it was that the rediscovery of Plato's writings and their availability through translation did little to restore the truth about Plato's own thoughts but instead reinforced the Neoplatonic tradition and indeed gave it a new impetus.

Professor Shorey has translated a passage from Ficino's *De Christiania Religione*, chapter XII, from which two sentences tell the story. 'The primitive theology of the gentiles in which Zoroaster, Mercury, Orpheus, Aglaophemus, and Pythagoras are at one is to be found entire in the books of our Plato. In his letters Plato prophesies that these mysteries can be made plain to mankind only after many centuries. And that was what happened. For it was first in the time of Philo and Numenius that the thought of the primitive theologians, embodied in Plato's writings, began to be understood.'[1]

Orpheus!

And so the Orphic tradition had passed into Christianity, via Plato, the Neoplatonists and the Christian theologians. It had long ceased to be recognizably Orphic. References to Orphism as such degenerated to the level of artistic representations of mythology, to fables and pretty stories. 'The earliest dramatic production on a classical theme in a modern language was *Orpheus*'[2] written for the court of Mantua in 1471 by Ambrogini, called Politian. We find Orpheus in the sixteenth century contributing to the wisdom of the Flemings[3] and listed not only with Zoroaster but also with Hermes Trismegistus,[4] and credited in the Renaissance with being the father of poetry[5] and garbed as a troubadour[6] and even becoming Christ Himself.[7]

There was, it is true, another tradition struggling for acceptance in Italy that was less recognizably Platonic, at least in the tradition of Plato that has grown up as a result of the astonishingly long and widespread success of Neoplatonism posing as Platonism. This was the beginning of the empirical tradition. If one admits the existence in Plato of a second philosophy and a second religion, a philosophy and a religion of metaphysical realism and epistemological naturalism, as we have done from the very outset of the present work, then it is fair to assume what others have indeed insisted in recent times (notably Peirce and Whitehead): that the scientific tradition is also Platonic, basing itself on belief in natural law and on the relevance to nature of mathematics. The immortal Galileo is first in this tradition, with

---

[1] *Platonism*, p. 124.

[2] Gilbert Highet, *The Classical Tradition* (New York 1949, Oxford,) pp. 135–6, 139, 174.

[3] Jean Seznec, *The Survival of the Pagan Gods* (New York 1953, Bollingen), trans. B. F. Sessions, p. 24, n.   [4] *Op. cit.*, p. 29.

[5] *Op. cit.*, p. 31.   [6] *Op. cit.*, p. 197.   [7] *Op. cit.*, p. 213.

his public experiments with falling bodies, his telescope and his mathematical calculations; but the Church had another understanding of Plato, and Galileo was forced to recant.[1] Bruno was in this tradition when he advocated humanism, and sought to establish the unity of the universe; but he was burned at the stake in 1600.[2] Leonardo was in this tradition in his notes where Plato's concept of natural law reappears[3] but Leonardo miraculously escaped. In 1633 Galileo's *Dialogues* and his *New Sciences*, both forbidden, were smuggled out of Italy and printed in Leyden in 1638.[4] From then on the natural philosophy which had begun by Plato, and which had been augmented by Aristotle, but repressed by the Roman Church and only preserved by accident by the Hellenistic Alexandrians, the Byzantines and Moslems, was passed on to the Protestants of northern Europe, where it thrived and gave birth to the experimental sciences.

B. THE CAMBRIDGE NEOPLATONISTS

The Cambridge Neoplatonists of the seventeenth and eighteenth centuries, in particular More and Cudworth, were, as Coleridge observed, 'Plotinists rather than Platonists'. They endeavoured to reintroduce both mysticism and rationalism into Christianity. Plato came to England from Italy—more specifically, Neoplatonism came to Cambridge from della Mirandola and Ficino. The so-called 'Cambridge Platonists' were followers of Plotinus.

Men like Henry More and Ralph Cudworth took philosophy into religion where their concern more properly was, and towards this end, of course, Neoplatonism had prepared the way.[5] More was a believer in the Kabbala, and he was convinced that the Platonic philosophy had been derived from Hebrew revelation. He followed Plotinus in endeavouring to combine the power

---

[1] Olschki, *The Genius of Italy*, p. 384.
[2] *Ibid.*, p. 279.   [3] *Ibid.*, p. 310.   [4] *Ibid.*, p. 391.
[5] John H. Muirhead, *The Platonic Tradition in Anglo-Saxon Philosophy* (London 1931, Allen and Unwin), pp. 27-9, 53.

which he held resides in man to apprehend the divine truth with the Christian doctrine of the super-natural. Cudworth retained, as they all did, the theory of the Ideas as thoughts in the mind of God. Emanation and the Logos were somewhat attenuated into a 'plastic medium' which was the organizing principle of the natural world. There is, too, a scale of being in which goodness is prior. Cudworth is a true Platonist, perhaps, only in his ethical theories, particularly in his supposition that the moral values are independent and can be apprehended by the right reason.

C. PROTESTANT CHRISTIANITY

Any estimate made in the broad terms of the present work must of necessity draw its lines roughly, eliminating and avoiding backwaters which might seem to affect the argument logically when they have failed for the most part to affect events historically. In these terms, then, it is fair to say, Protestantism revolted against Christian theology and returned to the sources of the revelations—in short, to the Bible. The corruption of the Church was associated, chronologically at least, with the theology and so both were to be abandoned. The theology was held to be—correctly enough—part of the institution of the Church, and it was institutionalized Christianity that Protestantism was revolting against. The return to the direct relations between the individual and his God as represented by the Scriptures and by prayer was to be justified by faith and not by reason.

Of course, some kind of Protestant theology could have been worked out from the writings on which Greek Orthodox and Roman Catholic Christianity had drawn. Philo's work had never been institutionally adopted in his religion, nor, for that matter, had any other theology. Philo's writings were borrowed by many an institutional theologian but there has never been an official Jewish theology. As for Plotinus, the case is even sharper. Plotinus was an individual and independent thinker whose religion was that of Greece. His work suffered the same adventures in other hands, although he himself was never an institutional thinker. It would indeed seem as though institutions were, generally speaking, founded on the work of non-institutional men. It would have been possible for the Protestant religions to found a theology of their own, drawing on the same sources. There was even, for instance, a Protestant justification in Plotinus, for whom individual man could attain to an intuitive knowledge of God. And judging by the ideas of the next world in the hands of the standard theologies, Jewish, Christian and Moslem, where the social life of this world was hardly reproduced, Plotinus' flight of the alone to the alone was an attempt to reproduce in this world the unsocial conditions of the next; Protestantism could easily have taken fire from this inspired kind of individualism. Yet it did not.

It retained instead the transfinite and super-natural God and the mundane strivings towards Him on the part of individual man, unmediated by institutions or by their established and very philosophically-supported theologies. And in this effort, which has given rise to tolerance and liberalism, and made possible democracy and science, Protestantism has had need neither of Plato nor of Neoplatonism.

That there was a second religion in Plato's *Dialogues*, and also in Aristotle, which could have been shown to be in accord with Protestant notions, has been passed over. The Protestants in this connection have never properly understood what their positive and affirmative theological position could be. They can claim the realistic philosophy of the Greek religion, with all the tentative and exploratory character that Plato and Aristotle were able to give it. The threat to Protestantism is that it lacks the very deliberate kind of rational justification which has ensured the establishment of other religions. Many attempts have been made in the modern world to supply the deficiency. We shall examine several of these, and then conclude our investigation.

The construction of a proper theology requires speculation and imagination and does not properly belong in this kind of investigation. It will be undertaken in another place.

The rediscovery of Plato did not occur in connection with religion but instead took a secular turn. The philosophical tradition as it occurred within and without the academic walls now included the study of Plato. But it was a secular interest rather than a religious interest. Indeed, for all practical purposes it would be fair to say that religion in the western world went one way and the study of Plato another. Plato was valued for his insights, metaphysical, epistemological, logical, ethical and aesthetic, but not particularly theological. Such interest as there was in Plato's religious ideas was carried on outside of religious institutions. Neither the Jews, the Roman Catholics nor the Protestants as such cultivated religious Platonism. Nor have there been any new attempts at institutional religions which have embraced religious Platonism. In one sense, of course, Plato permeates all of western culture, so that it would be entirely fair to say that there was no western religious institution which had left him out altogether or on which his impress had not made some mark. Such influence is implicit, however, and the explicit exploration of Plato's religious ideas has been a matter for philosophy departments within universities and not for practising institutionalized religions.

CHAPTER XIII

CONTEMPORARY RELIGIOUS PLATONISM

A. INSTITUTIONAL NEOPLATONISM

In the eighteenth century the theology of Thomas Aquinas was declared to be the theology of the Roman Catholic Church. The peculiar combination of Neoplatonism and Aristotle which Maimonides, Averroes and, after them, Aquinas, made in the thirteenth century has survived in any kind of official dress only in the Roman Catholic Church, one of the three broad divisions of Christianity. It is not official in the Greek Orthodox Church. Protestantism has no official theology, but such theology as it does have depends more on faith and works than on theology.

Since the endorsement of Aquinas, much effort has been spent by Jacques Maritain and others to bring Aquinas up to date, or, rather, to interpret more recent developments, both in events and in intellectual realms, as it is supposed Aquinas' theology seems to require. The official philosophy of Aristotle and St. Thomas is still emphatically accepted by the leading theologians of the Roman Catholic Church. To men like Maritain and Gilson, it is the absolute truth, and there can be no departure from it. Despite the rediscovery of Plato, the mediaeval point of view, formed when the writings of Plato were not available, is retained and reaffirmed, and Plato is held to have committed errors which Augustine and Aquinas ably corrected.[1] In the Moslem religion, the tonal effects of

[1] Cf. e.g., Jacques Maritain, *An Introduction to Philosophy* trans. Watkin (New York 1930, Longmans, Green), pp. 7, 75 ff.

Neoplatonism became permanently imbedded, and they are still around today. The Jewish religion has no official theology, but its passage through the long period when Neoplatonism was interpreted to mean Greek philosophy and was tantamount to rationalism has left its mark. No one of the three Western religions has any important place in its theology for the world of nature. In short, in the western world, the super-naturalism of the Orphic religion of idealism won out absolutely over the naturalism of the Greek religion of realism. The religious overtones of naturalism had to await the new institution of experimental science to find a place, and that place has not yet been spelled out. It may not be clear until we have learned somewhat better how to live with science as an institution among other institutions.

B. UNOFFICIAL AND LAY NEOPLATONISM

The evidence of the powerful effect of Neoplatonism is to be found not only within official Catholic Christianity (though there alone of the western religions) but also in the lay world. The confusion between Neoplatonism and Platonism, in which Plato was credited with some of the ideas Plotinus had inherited from Philo but which Plato himself had never believed, continued to exert the same grip upon secular thinkers that it had upon theologians. Leibniz, for instance, who acknowledged himself a Platonist[1], mentioned as one of the 'many most excellent doctrines of Plato' that 'there is in the Divine mind an intelligible world, which I am also wont to call the region of ideas'.[2]

Plotinus' name in modern times has had a separate attraction, an interest quite apart from that of Plato or of Neoplatonism. It was so for Taylor, for Coleridge, and, in our time, for Dean Inge. Plotinian Neoplatonism was, of course, an altered version of Platonism. Plato shone through Plotinus, even though it

---

[1] Leibniz, *The Monadology* trans. Robert Latta (London 1948, Oxford University Press), pp. 154–5.   [2] *Op. cit.*, p. 241, n. 68.

was only some of the rays, and these, as we have seen, greatly distorted.

One development of free religious speculation takes its departure from Descartes. It is difficult to estimate the degree of inadvertence contained in the change of categories from Aristotle's 'form and matter' to the Cartesian 'mind and matter'. For nowhere in Descartes' pair of categories is form to be found; not, that is, unless one makes the nominalistic hypothesis and assumes that whatever is not matter is mind, and so consigns form to matter or to minds. In any case, an emphasis was given to the knowing of forms by minds, and it is not a far flight from human minds with mundane thoughts to the divine mind with divine thoughts—to the Ideas in the mind of God. The latter, as we have noted, has been around a long time, and it had prepared the ground for the Cartesian empirical version, which in turn gave it a new lease. And the notion that the Ideas are resident in the mind of God did not die, then, with the scholastics, though they had adhered to it almost to a man. It was to be found in Berkeley, for instance, and in Malebranche, and furnished a sort of theological subjectivism for both the Continental rationalist and the British empiricist alike.

The Orphic tradition in explicit form split off from speculation and theology and took a purely literary turn. It was sentimentalized and largely confined to the story of Eurydice. Andre Chenier wrote an elegy on Orpheus.[1] In the nineteenth century Gluck wrote an opera on the theme, and much later there were sonnets by Rilke, and, more recently still, a play, *Eurydice*, by the French dramatist, Anouilh. It is safe to say that 'the Orpheus legend has become part of world literature'[2] though many would regard this as a thin fate and a sad end for a belief which had powerfully motivated a Plato and changed the western world's religions.

[1] G. Highet, *The Classical Tradition*, p. 402.
[2] *Op. cit.*, p. 511.

C. PLATONISM

As late as the eighteenth century, Vico could still speak in the approved and by then time-honoured Neoplatonic fashion, of the 'divine Plato, who affirms that providence rules the affairs of men'.[1] Before the eighteenth century was over, however, the truth was out.[2] Neoplatonism was not Platonism; the mysticism and irrationalism of the former was not to be found in the latter. Something of Platonism could be reconciled with the new enterprise of empiricism, through the study of the objective reality of nature. For the fact is becoming increasingly clear that in religious theory, in speculative theology, Platonism is not Neoplatonism. Professor Lovejoy credits Schelling with exposing the incompatibility between the two religious philosophies in Plato only one of which Plotinus followed and in following changed. 'The two Gods of Plato and of Plotinus cannot both be believed in', he correctly insists.[3]

The great generation of the nineteenth-century German scholars was followed by French and English equivalents. All of them lent a valuable hand in recovering the lost Plato. He was translated, annotated and commented on, until something of the clarity of his views emerged from the cloud of Neoplatonism through which they had been seen by everyone from Augustine to Ficino and his successors. One result has been a lively interest in Plato which has prevailed ever since, and the almost continual discussion of his work, both for and against. The revival has not affected institutionalized religion, which long ago was reduced to the memorizing of formulæ, the pursuit of ritual observances, and the conduct of a defence against attack from other quarters, political and scientific. But there has emerged as another result a considerable amount of lay speculation concerning theological matters.

[1] *The New Science of Giambattista Vico*, trans. by Bergin and Fisch (Ithaca 1948, Cornell University Press), p. 382.
[2] See e.g. Edward Gibbon, *Decline and Fall of the Roman Empire*, Ch. XIII.
[3] *Great Chain of Being*, p. 326.

The return to the Plato of the Ideas *apart* from the mind of God, the idealistic Plato stripped of the Plotinian effulgence, was begun by a Protestant theologian, Schleiermacher. He saw Plato's philosophy as a process and an open-ended inquiry rather than as a finished system.

Within the Catholic Church, Rosmini endeavoured to restore the true Plato to Christian eminence, and in this realistic tradition to turn the Church towards liberalism. This is one of the rare appearances within the Catholic Church of Plato's second philosophy and of his second religion. What would have happened had his ideas prevailed? What might not have been the excellence of the result had he succeeded in convincing Pius IX and in instituting liberal reforms within the Roman Catholic Church as well as gaining acceptance for his moderate realism? We shall never know, for he failed.

But where he failed within the Church, another on the outside succeeded. Alfred North Whitehead, the philosopher, endeavoured to construct a theology of a Platonic type on the basis of a process god, a theology which, it appears, accords more with the Plato of the second philosophy and of the second religion, the Greek religion of realism.[1] For Whitehead, the eternal objects, i.e. Plato's Ideas, stood in splendid isolation and hence outside God. They were for Whitehead most emphatically not thoughts in the mind of God. God himself, moreover, sounds more like the demiourgos of the *Timaeus*. He works to bring the Ideas and the actualities together by actualizing the Ideas.

D. CONCLUSIONS AND PROSPECTS

Greek philosophy proved to be a rational phenomenon, perhaps it would be better to say the phenomenon of rationalism, and with it Jew, Christian and Moslem has had to deal. They did so

[1] *Religion in the Making* (New York 1930, Macmillan); *Process and Reality* (New York 1936, Macmillan), esp. Part V.

by reducing metaphysics to theology, or by theologically separating the two, so that metaphysics was in no wise prior. Aristotle, however, considered metaphysics prior, when he made the distinction at all; when he failed to make it, theology was imbedded in metaphysics and not the reverse. Theology we may suppose was in this sense the mythologizing of metaphysics; it was the business of reading metaphysics theologically, that is to say, analogically and allegorically. Metaphysics remains, however, the highest theory, and the feelings it engenders are responses to theological qualities. To render of metaphysics a kind of apologetics, whether of theology, politics or whatever, is to abdicate from its high office and to prescind from its highest function.

If we take metaphysics on its own ground, as an independent inquiry, then Plato has been neglected as a religious source, and the Neoplatonism which stemmed from him cannot be considered to be a responsible representation of what his philosophy would mean when called into the service of theology. There has never been a Platonic Church. The first thousand years of Christianity the Church ruled in Plato's name yet never understood Plato. During the second thousand years, the Church was undermining itself through the misunderstanding of Aristotle. Needless to add, neither Plato nor Aristotle were at fault; neither were Christians, and neither was adequately or accurately represented. For the fact is that to read Plato's realm of Ideas or Forms as revealed or transcendental is to subvert it. Plato had just succeeded in divorcing essence from its crypto-materialistic colouring, when the religions came along and made it into the mind of God. There is no religious Platonism, there is only Neoplatonism. Socrates as a consequence has had to wait for his religion, but the situation is not without precedent. After all, the Christian theology of Aquinas had to wait some thirteen hundred years to be written and another five hundred years to receive official endorsement. If we distinguish between Neoplatonism and Platonism, then there was no Platonist to our knowledge until the eighteenth century, but since then Platonism has continued to flow unabated, until its strength in modern times is powerfully felt in the revival of realism, culminating in Laird, Peirce, Whitehead, Hartmann, Santayana and others. What has been called Platonism from Plotinus onwards was the Neoplatonism which Plotinus learned from Philo, introduced into Christianity chiefly by Augustine. Platonism, then, may be regarded as a long-neglected philosophy, rediscovered within comparatively recent times.

Despite its reputation for brevity, Greek culture permitted some enterprises the longest runs. If for instance we consider the Greek philosophical tradition to be from the birth of Thales about 624 B.C. to the closing of the philosophical schools at Athens by Justinian in A.D. 529, then the period is something like eleven hundred years. Plato's Academy alone lasted only some two hundred years less than that. During this period Greek philosophy was free, with certain notable exceptions. While it is true that Socrates in his old age was legally executed and that Aristotle found it expedient to leave Athens for awhile, still each case was for special reasons and, moreover, both were exceptions. The point is that no rival institutions had perpetrated dogmas that were being challenged by the rationality of the philosophers or by their searching speculations, unless it be that their the opportunism and expediency of the Sophists with its attendant beliefs constituted such a vested interest.

The situation unfortunately was not to continue. We know the subsequent history; how philosophy became the willing handmaid of religion after its own decline, and how it emerged from that bondage only to run into another, which, however willing, is still a bondage, namely, the subservience of philosophy to science. The results in neither instance have been good for philosophy. When the enterprise of philosophy becomes the handmaid of some other institution, it accepts dictation and loses its own power of discovery as a consequence. The benefits bestowed on religion by philosophy did not come from a set of religious dictates, nor did they come from a religious philosophy. They were the work of philosophers who concerned themselves with philosophy rather than religion, from Plato and Aristotle—in short, from just those men who advanced philosophy independently of religion. The moral is that if you wish to develop a philosophy which is the most useful to religion, develop it independently of religion. It is the pagan philosophers: Plato, Aristotle, Plotinus, who have most fully furnished forth the Christian theology. The theologians are in the habit of modelling their systems after the work of lay philosophers: Plato, for instance, who was readied by Plotinus and adopted by Augustine, and Aristotle who was adapted and adopted many centuries later by Aquinas.

The situation which results from allowing religion to dominate philosophy may be good for religion—it is bad for philosophy. For the grounds upon which the philosophy is selected have little to do with philosophy and much more to do with revelation or with some practical expediency.

Again, the situation which results from allowing science to dominate philosophy, or, what is worse (for the scientists do not agree about philosophy enough to issue an official pronunciamento in the name of science), allowing the *philosophers* of science to dominate philosophy, is equally bad for philosophy since it banishes metaphysics so long as it continues under that name. And the fact that it can be approved under other names, such as 'phenomenology' or 'ideology', is not sufficient or to the point, since the change of names also involves a change of emphasis which cannot be neglected in such a subtle subject-matter, because it is after all meaningful. An established inquiry depends more or less upon a stable society, though of course there have been inquiries without this advantage and stable societies without philosophy of any overt kind. Plato's Academy survived all sorts of political and economic vicissitudes, perhaps by putting establishment in the wrong place: namely, on the Platonic philosophy as conceived by Speusippus and Proclus chiefly. The United States has never been very receptive to philosophical inquiry, though of course as a state it has been firmly established. Philosophy in times of social upheaval has often been the only rock. When social organization fails and with it all basis for individual self-respect, the individual is tempted to fall back upon himself, and he will be receptive to any philosophy which pledges him to do so. Hence the success of the Stoics and Epicureans after Athens lost her independence. Hence the success of existentialists after Europe had lost hers. But this is philosophy pulled this way and that for practical reasons.

We shall not have philosophy that is worth anything until we have a field of philosophy in which we are allowed to operate independently for as long as the Greeks. Of course, an established philosophy acts to prohibit the free development of philosophy; for it is never held worth-while to pursue the truth in philosophy when the truth is already known. But it does no harm to oppose a socially powerful philosophy which is in the act of becoming established, except of course possibly to oneself, provided one does so in the name of something affirmative, in the interest of calling attention to some positive element which has been in danger of being overlooked; for in the end either one's philosophical contribution will prevail and itself be socially established, or the contribution one seeks to make will become incorporated in the prevailing philosophy.

Did the western religions lose their force some while ago? The recent revival of religion has all the marks of a synthetic affair. It has no new message of a practical nature and it boasts of no new theoretical insights. Religion always begins as a matter of theoretical purpose, chiefly that of fundamental inquiry, and of practical purpose, chiefly that of agricultural assistance. When it leaves both, it becomes a thing of dead formulae and ritual observances, an empty and dying institution.

In order to be born again, religion will have to be conceived anew. Science has worked successfully on the practical problems of agriculture and also on the theoretical problems of inquiry. Neither task will ever be finished, but science is now the institution to which we look for aid in these matters. What, then, of religion? At the very least, it will have to be reconceived in terms of what we hold to be the truth. A religion is not a true religion unless what it asserts to be the case is not inconsistent with what is held to be true. Now one problem of the contemporary world has been that of getting the finite back into philosophy. Kant did something in this direction by means of the knowledge process itself; he brought the finite back within the limits of knowledge through epistemology: the results of the act of experience are limited by the conditions under which experience must take place. Protestantism went the way of all nominalisms in banishing the Platonic Ideas altogether. We need now a finite metaphysics and a consistent religious ideal. These are not at all beyond the bounds of the possible.

INDEX